WHO OWNS LEARNING?
QUESTIONS OF AUTONOMY, CHOICE, AND CONTROL

Edited by
CURT DUDLEY-MARLING
AND
DENNIS SEARLE

HEINEMANN
Portsmouth, NH

HEINEMANN
A division of Reed Elsevier Inc.
361 Hanover Street
Portsmouth, NH 03801–3912
Offices and agents throughout the world

Editor: Carolyn Coman
Production: J. B. Tranchemontagne
Cover design: Catherine Hawkes

Every effort has been made to contact copyright holders for permission to reprint borrowed material. We regret any oversights that may have occurred and would be happy to rectify them in future printings of this work.

The authors and publisher are grateful to the following for permission to reprint previously published material:

Chapter 3
Reprinted by permission of Lynn K. Rhodes and Nancy Shanklin: *Windows Into Literacy: Assessing Learners K–8* (Heinemann, A division of Reed Elsevier Inc., Portsmouth, NH, 1992).

Chapter 4
Excerpts from *Clifford's Kitten* by N. Bridewell (1984) and *Gingerbread Man* by E. Arno (1967) were originally published by Scholastic, Inc. Reprinted by permission of Scholastic, Inc.

Excerpts from "Ice Cream" in *Frog and Toad All Year Round* by Arnold Lobel. Copyright © 1976. Published by HarperCollins Publishers Inc. Reprinted by permission.

Credit lines continued on page 213.

Library of Congress Cataloging-in-Publication Data
Who owns learinng? : questions of autonomy, choice, and control /
    edited by Curt Dudley-Marling and Dennis Searle.
            p.   cm.
    Includes bibliographical references.
    ISBN 0–435–08827–0
    1. Language arts.   2. Language experience approach in education.
3. Intellectual property.   4. Teacher-student relationships.
I. Dudley-Marling, Curt.   II. Searle, Dennis.
LB1576.W48629   1995
372.3'044—dc20   94-27338
                                                                          CIP

Printed in the United States of America on acid-free paper
99 98 97 96 95 CC 7 6 5 4 3 2 1

Contents

iii

Introduction

Current theory and practice in literacy education emphasize the importance of student independence, autonomy, and choice—what has commonly been referred to as "ownership." Writing theorists have long stressed the benefit of students exercising some measure of control over the topics and audiences for their writing (for example, Atwell 1987; Calkins 1986, 1991; Fox 1988; Graves 1983). Macrorie (1970) blamed the dead, vapid writing he found among college students on teachers—himself included—who prescribed the form and content *of* and the audiences *for,* student writing. In his book Macrorie describes his efforts to encourage students to take more responsibility for their writing without relinquishing his responsibility to support and guide students' development as writers.

In the last decade the works of Donald Graves, Lucy Calkins, and Nancie Atwell, emphasizing student ownership, have had a profound effect on writing instruction in American and Canadian classrooms. Graves observes that good writing is tied to students' personal investment in their writing. Students are more likely to be invested in their writing when, for example, they write on topics of their own choosing. Graves concludes that students who do not have (some) control over their writing are less likely to edit and revise their work and are less likely to discover their "voices" as writers. Commenting on what he learned from the Atkinson study, a longitudinal study of young children's writing development, Graves (1983) concluded: "When people own a place, they look after it. When it belongs to someone else, they couldn't care less" (in Calkins 1986, p. 23).

Whole language educators also stress the importance of students' having some measure of control over *what* they read and write and the *purposes* for which they read and write. Ken Goodman (1986), for example, states:

> Language development is empowering: the learner "owns" the process, makes the decisions about when to use it, what for and with what results. Literacy is empowering too, if the learner is in control with what's done with it. (p.26)

The concept of ownership is not limited to literacy instruction. Discussing the importance of students' taking responsibility for their learning in an integrated language arts program, Pappas, Kiefer, and Levstik (1990) conclude that "by having ownership in what they do, by following their own questions about topics, they are able to create new concepts and make new connections in their schemas" (p. 44).

Influenced by this important work from the whole language and writing process literature, student ownership has become a guiding principle in our work with students and teachers. But, even though we have long been convinced that meaningful learning depends on students' assuming an active role in constructing their own knowledge, we still find ownership to be a slippery concept. What is *ownership*; that is, what does it mean for students to "own" their reading or writing? And how do teachers support students' learning to read and write without forcing students to cede responsibility for their learning to someone else? Is ownership an affirmation of rugged individualism and all the political baggage that comes with it?

Clearly, ownership cannot mean that teachers withdraw their support for students' learning. The laissez-faireism resulting from teachers' withholding their support for students—often because they are concerned with students' ownership rights—is perhaps the worst perversion of progressive, child-centered education. The public's perception that teachers have abdicated their teaching responsibilities may be behind much of the criticism of whole language and the writing process. Conversely, too much teacher support may have the effect of taking control of learning away from students. But how do teachers strike a balance between their responsibility "to teach" and students' responsibility "to learn"? And how do cultural and individual differences factor into this complex equation?

To begin answering these questions, we turned to some of the outstanding teachers and teacher educators we have been lucky enough to know. We asked these distinguished teachers and scholars to think about ownership—both what it means and how teachers can encourage students to take responsibility for their learning. This text is their response to our invitation to share their stories and reflections with other educators.

In the opening chapter, "Complicating Ownership," Curt Dudley-Marling reflects on his efforts to encourage student ownership when he took a year's leave from his university duties to teach third grade. Although Curt began with what he soon realized to be a rather simplistic view of ownership, the process of reading and reflection produced a much more complicated, and uncertain, notion of ownership.

In Chapter 2 we draw on data from our study of language use in three primary classes for students with learning disabilities to illustrate situations in which students were able to exercise control over their oral language use and those in which their teachers severely limited students' use of language. One of the most interesting examples of teachers' encouraging language development, yet honoring students' intentions, came during informal language interactions between students and their teachers, what we came to call "talk-around-the-edges."

Lynn Rhodes draws on her rich experience as a researcher and a teacher educator to illustrate several ways in which children can take more responsibility for their learning: children can share ownership and responsibility in teaching reading, in assessing reading, and in advocating for themselves about literacy issues. Lynn emphasizes the relationship between student ownership and teacher support and guidance. One point we take from her chapter is that students may have difficulty taking responsibility for certain aspects of their learning without teacher support.

Chapters by Odette Bartnicki and by Cheryl Ames and Hilary Sumner Gahagan expand on two themes introduced by Lynn Rhodes. Odette shares what she learned about peer tutoring in her master's thesis research. She found that when fifth graders were put in the role of peer tutors their natural tendency was to support their second-grade partners' efforts at meaning making. This contrasts with the instincts of many of us who, in an attempt to exploit the teachable moment, often succumb to the pressure "to teach," ending up by taking responsibility for making meaning from text.

Most discussions of ownership have focused on language arts instruction. Mary Burke-Hengen provides a wonderful example of how the notion of student ownership can be extended beyond reading, writing, and speaking. In Mary's eighth grade the social studies curriculum stems from, and builds on, students' interests and concerns.

How much teachers are willing to grant students some control over their learning may relate to their perceptions of student ability. Struggling readers and writers, for example, may be receive far fewer opportunities to exercise meaningful control over their learning (see, for example, Allington 1983). But in "Lessons from Little Bear" Susan Stires links the story of a struggling reader's development as a reader and writer to her ability to manage her own literacy learning. Of course, this is also the story of her teacher's creating opportunities for her to exercise control over that learning.

Similarly, Cora Five tells the story of two special needs students who were drawn into reading and writing when they were allowed to exercise some control over its content. In an interesting twist Cora links the struggle of these two boys to take responsibility for their learning with her own frustrations with special education rules and regulations threatening her ownership over her curriculum. Teachers' ability to share responsibility for teaching and learning with their students may well be a function of the control that teachers feel they have themselves. Those who have little control may find it difficult to share control with students.

Issues of control and responsibility are not limited to school-age children. From a constructivist perspective, meaningful learning will always depend on the degree to which learners are able to make learning their own. Teachers are also learners, and attempts to effect meaningful educational change cannot be achieved by forcing change upon teachers. Successful change, whether initiated from the "top-down" or from the "bottom-up" depends on teachers' personal investment in, and responsibility for, change. Margaret Stevenson tells of her efforts and those of her colleagues to change the language arts policy in the Edmonton, Alberta, public schools. This chapter illustrates the delicate balance between ownership and control in the context of educational change. Someone has to initiate change, but without teacher commitment this reform will never go very far.

As a political concept, ownership describes the power relationships between teachers and students. As an epistemological notion, ownership describes the complex ways in which individuals make sense of their experience and of the world around them. As part of the human enterprise of teaching, ownership is complicated by the individual personalities of teachers and students, their respective background knowledge, culture, gender, race, ethnicity, and socioeconomic status. All these complicate the teacher-learner relationship. Linguists sometimes invoke the principle of ''Occam's razor'' which holds that the simplest solution is to be preferred; but the human enterprise resists simple solutions, and, for concepts like ownership, may prefer complex explanations. Chapters by Shannon; by DuCharme, Poplin, and Thomas; and by Lensmire pick up and expand themes hinted at in other chapters on the complications of what it means to own one's learning.

Patrick Shannon's chapter demonstrates how students can take control of their learning in a context where adults also exercise some control. While acknowledging the importance of student ownership, he nevertheless challenges the individualistic notion of ''language as property'' implicit in the ownership metaphor. Patrick points out that each of us knows the world through social and historical voices. Ownership may have more to do with honoring these *voices* than the ''property'' rights of individuals.

Catherine DuCharme, Mary Poplin, and Sally Thomas recall Lisa Delpit's critique of (some) writing process classrooms by arguing that narrow, individualistic interpretations of ownership may disadvantage students from nondominant cultural and linguistic backgrounds. They say:

> We are suggesting that we dampen our enthusiasm for individuality and ownership in the writing process and infuse our writing process with a kind of critical reflection that can be accomplished only in a culturally inclusive and sensitive environment. This environment must explicitly teach and demonstrate multiple points of view. This critical reflection must allow all of us to talk and write about the important things in life.

Timothy Lensmire, by pointing out the pitfalls of ''liberating student intention,'' acknowledges that progressive pedagogy is not without its difficulties. Still, the conflict that emerges in Tim's writing workshop when students are given more control over writing topics is not just a caution but an opportunity. Bringing student politics out into the open, teachers can have students examine their life experiences as a means of helping them live together in and out of their classrooms.

In a brief piece reprinted from *Language Arts*, Dennis Searle examines what ownership means as he explores the tension between teacher support and student control. Dennis cites the work of Graves on writing conferences to acknowledge the need for teacher support but worries that some teacher support may have the effect of taking control away from students.

Most whole language and writing process advocates define ownership in terms of students' choice and students' intentions. In the concluding chapter David Dillon begins by drawing on constructivist learning theory to expand our notion of what it means for students "to own" their learning. From a constructivist perspective, learners make knowledge their own by filtering new knowledge—(re)constructing it—through the unique lens of their culture and experience. David then reviews his own efforts to encourage ownership in one of his graduate classes. True to the theme of this book, he relies on student voices to tell stories of student ownership.

Editing this book has been a tremendous learning experience for us. The contributors have helped us understand what it means for students "to own" their work and how to create opportunities for them to take more responsibility for their learning. At the same time, the contributors to this book have complicated our notion of ownership. Ownership will always be an imprecise, uncertain concept, but a useful one nonetheless. Students who are not able to take responsibility for their learning will always find learning more difficult. What is more important, students who have no opportunities to control their lives in school may find it more difficult to do so outside of school. Ultimately, ownership is not about learning, but about living. Creating a more just and democratic society depends on citizens who are willing and able to examine and, if necessary, to challenge the conditions of their lives and those of their fellow citizens. In this sense ownership is not about individual responsibility, but a collective responsibility in which each of us works to ensure that all Americans and all Canadians are able to share in their countries' cultural and economic riches.

Finally, writing a book about ownership has raised for us questions about who owns this book and, more significantly, who should profit from it. It did not seem appropriate that we, as editors, should profit from this book, nor did sharing the profits among the contributors seem entirely equitable. We therefore decided that all authors' royalties would be donated to UNICEF. We hope that the revenue generated may, in a small way, give a few children the material support necessary for gaining some control over their lives.

References

Allington, R.L. 1983. The reading instruction provided readers of differing abilities. *The Elementary School Journal*, 83:548–59

Atwell, N. 1987. *In the middle: Writing, reading and learning with adolescents.* Portsmouth, N.H.: Heinemann, Boynton/Cook.

Calkins, L.M. 1991. *Living between the lines.* Portsmouth, N.H.: Heinemann.

Calkins, L.M. 1986. *The art of teaching writing.* Portsmouth, N.H.: Heinemann.

Fox, M. 1988. Notes from the battlefield: Towards a theory of why people write. *Language Arts,* 65:112-25.

Goodman, K. 1986. *What's whole in whole language?* Richmond Hill, Ontario: Scholastic-TAB.

Graves, D. 1983. *Writing: Teachers and children at work.* Portsmouth, N.H.: Heinemann.

Macrorie, K. 1970. *Uptaught.* New York: Hayden & Co.

Pappas, C.C., Kiefer, B.Z., Levstik, L.S. 1990. *An integrated language perspective in the elementary school: Theory into action.* White Plains, N.Y.: Longman.

1

Complicating Ownership

Curt Dudley-Marling
York University

It had been thirteen years since I left the classroom for life at the university. I continued to experience schools as a researcher, an occasional supervisor of student teachers, and as a parent, but I began to lose confidence in my work with teachers. It seemed to have been a very long time since I "walked in their shoes." Then, during the 1991–92 academic year, I arranged to free myself from my university duties to work fulltime as a third-grade teacher.

Having been influenced to see the importance of student ownership, by the works of Ken Macrorie (1970), Graves (1983), Calkins (1986), Goodman (1986), and Edelsky (1991), among others, offering students some control over their work was an important goal for me as I prepared to teach third grade. Months before the school year began, I wrote in my notes:

> To fill our classroom with our voices and our lives will be a major goal for me next year.

During those hot days of August when I worked to organize my classroom, finding ways to make the classroom theirs/ours was an important guiding principle.

> I've also tried to do what I can to make sure that it's their classroom. I've placed the Kleenex on the bookcase with the writing materials, for example, because they are for their use. Putting them on the teacher's desk ... suggests that they're mine and I'm sharing with them. .... The placement of books, writing materials, and art supplies is intended to send the same message—this is their classroom. (Aug. 27, 1991)

Once school began, student ownership was almost always on my mind. Early in the year I made this note:

I have to avoid taking responsibility for students' behavior. We need to emphasize the social skills training here to encourage them to take responsibility for their behavior. The key questions I should ask myself each day are these: What did I do today to help students make the classroom (and their learning) theirs? What did I do to make it mine? (Sept. 17, 1991)

Overall, I was able to offer my students some control over decisions affecting their work. For example, my students exercised substantial control over *what* they read and wrote, *with whom* they read and wrote, *why* they read and wrote, *where* they read and wrote, and, by the end of the year, over *when* they read and wrote. Concerns with ownership also restrained my unfortunate tendency to want to be on center stage.

I told them the story of getting locked out of my father's house last weekend. Several of them then shared their own "key" stories. I was poised to tell another key story of my own when it occurred to me that this was their show and that the classroom wasn't my stage; in fact, several more stories followed. (Sept. 18, 1991)

Looking back it's clear that I wasn't always successful in supporting students' intentions and in increasing their control over their work. I also learned that ownership is a much more subtle and complex concept than I had imagined. In this chapter I draw on my daily notes to share what was on my mind as I struggled to offer my third graders some control over their work without abdicating my responsibility to support their learning. I will also discuss how my reflections have complicated my concept of student ownership.

Balancing Student Control and Teacher Support

I understood that offering students control over some of the decisions about their learning did not lessen my duty to "teach." In fact, I saw "laissez-faireism" as the worst perversion of whole language. Before the school year began, I wrote:

Nudging: Even in some of the best whole language classrooms I see, I'm not sure they "nudge" enough. Perhaps too much patience and too much dependence on a language rich environment. Something I can explore next year—the tension between nudging and taking control. Given my daughter Anne's difficulties in grade 1, I would tend to want to try to nudge and challenge as much as I can. (June 11, 1991)

I wasn't afraid to offer my expertise and experience to support students' intentions, as the following examples illustrate.

During reading assessments a couple of the kids got really hung up on proper names . . . so at the conclusion of reading I did a quick lesson on how to deal with proper names in text. I asked the group what they did when they came to a name like this, which they couldn't pronounce [holding up a copy of *Malcolm's Runaway Soap* (Bogart and Hendry, 1988)]. Most volunteered that they sounded the name out but one did say that she just made up another name and went on reading. I picked up on this suggestion and noted that this is what I do. (Sept. 6, 1991)

I gave Crystal a quick spelling lesson. She spelled "never" "nivr," so I asked her what vowel she heard in "never" [exaggerating the "e"]. She first said "a," then "e." I also told her that the "ı" sound at the end of a word is usually going to be spelled "er." (Oct. 29, 1991)

Razika is writing a long story called "The Witch." She used dialogue in this story so I used this story, as an opportunity to teach her about quotation marks. (Oct. 28, 1991)

Similarly, when some of the students started writing letters to their favorite stars from "Beverly Hills 90210," I did a minilesson on a format for personal letters and put an example on the wall. I found that I could also give strong direction. For example:

Today I asked Razika and Benizar and Jennifer and Barbara to move off letter writing. (Oct. 2, 1991)

Nicholas is spending too much time writing silly notes to people ("singing telegrams," he calls them) with nothing much on them. They seem to annoy the other students and they waste a lot of paper, so I told him to stop writing them. (Oct. 8, 1991)

But I worried about how hard I could push students without taking control of their work. This tension is illustrated by my response to Wayne, who wanted to quit the literature sharing group he had (voluntarily) signed up for.

Wayne had signed up to read *The Stolen Horse,* and when I asked him to read it he said he changed his mind. At the time I told him that if he signed up to read the book he had to finish it. Part of me feels that he should follow through but I worry about his choice. Right now I feel justified on insisting that he finish this book since he made the choice. But what I need to do is announce this "rule" to the whole class. (Jan. 8, 1992)

As I look back, I'm disappointed that I made such a big deal out of this. I never made a fuss when students abandoned writing topics or books they were reading individually. I eventually did back off, though, perhaps influenced by the fact that, about this time, my wife quit John Irving's (1985) *Cider House Rules* about two-thirds of the way through because it was making her "too sad." I did not insist that *she* continue.

Perhaps the best example of my struggle to achieve a balance between teacher support and student control is illustrated by my ongoing efforts to encourage students to produce multiple drafts of their writing. There were instances of students' revising their work early in the year, but such efforts were rare. Getting students to revise their writing became a major goal for me.

> Some of the students are ready to be nudged in the direction of more crafting of their writing. (Sept. 20, 1991)
>
> Razika (and now Benizar) continue to crank out stories at the rate of one/day. Need to get a group of these students together to start nudging them a little bit more. (Sept. 25, 1991)
>
> During writing spent a lot of time meeting with kids but still have had little success getting students into more sustained writing efforts. Getting students into multiple drafts is my major goal this month; but, other than modeling it, I'm not sure what else to do, short of requiring it—which I'm not particularly comfortable doing, although this may be something I can do as I respond to individual pieces of students' writing. (Jan. 7, 1992)

I frequently modeled revision, and often I offered students explicit advice to encourage them to revise their work. On September 26, for example, I wrote:

> Did lots of roving conferences in writing today. I talked to Razika about a story she was writing (part of "Four stories by Razika"). I talked to her about the possibility of adding more details. In this instance she had written that the kittens were "naughtily," so I asked her why they were naughty and she gave some thoughts.

Although Razika listened politely when I suggested she add more details to her kitten story, she ignored my advice. In general, neither modeling nor explicit advice did much to encourage students to engage in more than minor editing of their work. Concluding that I wasn't pushing individual children hard enough to revise their work, I resolved to push harder.

> I told Razika that I would insist that she take one piece tomorrow and work with it for a period of several days and then publish it. (Jan. 13, 1992)

But this still wasn't enough.

> Talked again to Benizar and Razika about sticking with a piece. I just don't seem to be able to get them to do this. They also insist that they will "just as soon as they finish this piece" but they never do. (Jan. 28, 1992)

Finally . . .

> Benizar was actually revising her piece about her brother. She erased lots of words, usually because of problems with spelling or grammar or just personal preference, e.g., mom—> mother; hole—> whole. I read some of what she'd written and she made more changes; e.g., I read, "Then had to fix it" and asked her if this was OK and she changed to "Then they . . . "

Most of the changes she made without me and came as a result of her conferencing with Razika.

Within a few weeks Benizar and Razika both took pieces of writing that they had revised and published them. Soon almost everyone in the class was working toward the publication of a book; revision was part of their process. At the time this reinforced my belief that I hadn't been pushing students hard enough.

> These books and the editing/revising that was part of them came about only after I began really pushing. Maybe a nudge isn't a command but it may not be a hint either . . . I think I was going too far in the direction of student control, at least in writing.

I now believe that this conclusion was incorrect. I did push students harder, but I pushed them to publish their writing.

> At the beginning of the (writing) session I warned them that I would be expecting them to take a single piece of writing and work with it over a period of some time with the goal of publishing it. When someone asked if they'd have to I surprised myself by saying yes. (Jan. 15, 1992)

In this context my students did a lot more revision, but publishing their writing gave students reasons to revise their work and gave me an authentic reason to talk about revision. I realized that encouraging kids to publish their work, not pushing them to revise, was what made the difference; but I still ended up pushing harder than I ever expected to.

In this context I also found it easier to respond more directly to students' writing, as, "I don't understand this. I think you need to make some changes." Giving students personal reasons for revising their work also made it easier for me to provide less direct support. When Catherine confessed that she was having trouble with a piece because she didn't know how to start, we did a minilesson the next day on leads, using a piece of writing I'd been sharing with them about my daughter's birth.

Despite these successes I continued to worry about how hard I could push students without taking control over their work. Sometimes I found I pushed too hard. On February 25, for example, I wrote:

> I spent most of my time going over Ali's story with him. I was a bit intrusive and, as happens too often, I was frequently distracted by behavior problems as he read to me. . . . I also started offering advice, or at least confessing confusion, with the first line of the story. What I might have done was to listen to the whole story first and perhaps make a note or two and then receive his work before I comment on it. I gave him an unfortunate message, I'm afraid.

Other times I concluded that I wasn't pushing hard enough.

> When Crystal told me she had written something she wanted to publish I gave her what is now my standard advice that she should read over her piece, perhaps out loud, and then read to a couple of other people and make any necessary changes. . . . I said that we would then meet to talk about her piece, but I warned her that I might suggest some changes. She told me firmly that she really liked her piece and that she didn't want to make any changes. When we met, I did have a couple of suggestions . . . but she told me again that she liked her piece as it was without changes. So I agreed to publish it. It is her piece in the end.

I'm pleased that I recognized that, in the end, Crystal's writing was hers, but now I wonder if I failed to push her hard enough.

Focusing on the Here and Now

I am relatively satisfied with the balance I achieved in my literacy program between student control and teacher support. But, upon reflection, I discovered that I didn't permit students similar degrees of control in all parts of our program. In math and science, for example, students had much less control over the decisions affecting their learning than they did in reading and writing. The following excerpts from my lesson plans are illustrative.

> Science Center: Monday morning: Group activity on trees. With notebooks (and small-group discussion) talk/write about similarities and differences between trees and plants. What is a plant? What are some of the common features of plants? Use plants and pictures of plants. (Sept. 16, 1991)

> **Math**
>
> 1. Do the daily survey
> 2. Do the daily estimation
> 3. Work together to solve the problems at your table
> 4. Use clocks to make the following times and record in your notebooks:
>   1:00; 3:00; 6:00; 9:00; 10:00; 12:00; 11:30; 3:30 (Sept. 9, 1991)

These tasks, which derived from curriculum guides and resource books, were entirely teacher directed. They had little to do with students' interests, although I suppose that I hoped to "get them interested." Arguably, I set the task and offered support to help students to fulfill *my* intentions.

My concerns about math and science, as reflected in my notes, are just as telling. In general, my notes about math and science focus on the need for more explicit directions, better organization, behavior problems, and getting things done. The following examples are typical.

> Centers [math and science] went OK, although I frequently had to ask them to be more quiet. At one point during the last center rotation I had them all

come to the carpet so that I could remind them to keep their voices down. (Oct. 2, 1991)

The last center rotation wasn't very successful, with lots of kids wandering. Some of the kids at the math center were doing "cat's in the cradle" because they "didn't want to do flash cards." Charles kept gravitating to the sand table even though he was supposed to be at the listening center, and the science center people were all over the place because, I'll have to admit, they weren't sure what to do. (Oct. 17, 1991)

The bubble activity was very successful, *at least in terms of keeping them interested and on task.* (Apr. 21, 1992)

Noticeably missing from these entries is any sense of what, if anything, students were learning.

My notes also indicate a search for ways to encourage students to finish their work. For example:

Note is going home tonight. Among other things, this will inform the parents that they can expect their children to bring tracking sheets home each day. (Feb. 24, 1992)

I introduced tracking sheets because I was concerned that students weren't finishing their work in math and science. And, when I introduced a comprehensive point system in January to deal with some serious behavior problems, students were rewarded for, among other things, finishing their work. At various times I also used performance contracts and withheld recess from some students to encourage them to complete their work.

This preoccupation with the here and now, with getting things done in math and science, contrasts with my response to students' reading and writing. When I worried about what students were accomplishing in their literature sharing groups, for example, I responded with more support, not artificial contingencies.

Literature sharing still not great. One problem: Sometimes I'm not keeping on top of this, as in the case of Jennifer and Catherine, who barely remembered *Bridge to Terabithia* (Paterson 1977). Actually, there is a lesson in this. If I talk to students daily or every other day, then I'm going to help them make sense of text by giving them opportunities to talk about what they are reading and giving them a social context within which to understand the text. Frequent literature sharing meetings also will encourage students to keep up with their reading. The trade-off: Fewer literature sharing groups but more meetings with individual groups. (Jan. 14, 1992)

My concern with "getting things done" in math and science gave students few opportunities to exercise much control over decisions affecting their learning. Most important of all, focusing on the "here and now" obscured long-term learning goals (see Jackson 1968). My notes suggest that I recognized this problem early in the school year.

Science continues to be a problem for me. We're doing experiments, but we're not really learning much of anything. Need to supplement with group activities, integrate into the rest of the curriculum. Any way to fit with folk-tale study? One thing I might do is to encourage them to bring in things related to units, like plants. I also need some more support. Maybe I should involve students more in planning experiments . . . (Oct. 6, 1991)

Despite this insight, my preoccupation with getting things done in math and science only intensified as the year progressed. In reading and writing, on the other hand, students seemed to exercise more control over their work as the year went on. This begs the question: Why was I so concerned with getting things done in math and science? Two possible explanations have occurred to me.

One possible reason for my focus on the here and now in math and science, with the concomitant of increased teacher control, is that I have had little experience, direct or indirect, with models of math or science that build on students' interests, experiences, and intentions. Such models of math and science instruction are, of course, relatively rare.

Another explanation for the way I treated math and science differently from reading and writing is related to my background knowledge. Perhaps I focused on the here and now in math and science because I know less about them than I do about reading and writing. This hypothesis occurred to me early in the year.

There is a natural tension between teacher and student control. It is interesting, I think, that I've given students the most control in the areas of the curriculum that I know the most about—oral and written language. Or perhaps these areas are easiest for teachers to give up some control over. (Sept. 15, 1991)

It may be easier for teachers to offer students more control over their reading and writing. I'm not sure. But I am convinced that my focus on the here and now in math and science had everything to do with my own knowledge. Knowing less about math and science, I had less of a sense of my long-term goals for them. My goals were, in large part, limited to doing the curriculum, or getting things done. This is even more apparent when contrasted with the way I approached reading and writing. I know something about what readers and writers do in the process or reading and writing. I have given relatively little thought to the processes used by mathematicians or scientists[1]. Knowing what readers and writers do in the process of reading

---

1. I don't limit the terms *mathematician* or *scientist* to people with advanced graduate degrees. From a holistic perspective anyone who uses math or science to fulfill personal intentions is a mathematician or a scientist in the same way that anyone who uses reading or writing for some purpose is a reader or a writer. That we tend to think otherwise may partially explain the dearth of examples of math and science education that build on students' intentions.

and writing, I never lost sight of my long-term goal: to help students realize the potential of literacy to affect people's lives.

As a result, when students wanted to quit a literature sharing group they had signed up for, I finally remembered that is what readers do. When students didn't have anything to write about or abandoned a topic, I didn't (usually) ask them to stay in for recess or offer them incentives to finish their work. I recognized that this is what happens to writers. And when students demanded more flexibility so that they could read and/or write during other times of the day, I eventually gave in because I know that these are important needs for readers and writers.

Because I knew what readers and writers do, I was able to shift my focus from the here and now to my long-term goals for literacy. I never had the same sense for math and science.

Confusing Ownership with Independence

Getting kids to work independently—which I seemed to have equated with ownership—was a major concern reflected in my notes. For example:

> What did I do today to help kids own the class? Well, twice students read to the group, and I continued to give them lots of freedom at the centers. (Sept. 26, 1991)
>
> This afternoon went a little better. Both center rotations were very nice. They worked more independently than they ever have before. I think that combining clearer directions and making sure that there is always one good reader at the science center seems to be very helpful. (Oct. 7, 1991)

When the year began, I had hoped to encourage independence as part of creating opportunities for students to explore their own interests. From this perspective there may be a relationship between ownership and independence. But, increasingly, working independently came to mean working without teacher direction or support. I reasoned that if students could do their math and science work, for example, without too much direct support I would be free to use my time for assessment interviews, literature sharing groups, or writing conferences.

Ironically, my goal to increase students' independence, which was rooted in my desire to increase their control over their work, may have decreased the amount of control that students had over their learning.

> I'm very, very pleased with how the math center has worked this week. The worksheets we've been using has allowed students to work more independently. (March 27, 1992)

And when students had difficulty with open-ended tasks I concluded that the problem was theirs: they just couldn't work independently.

The activity of sorting geo-blocks didn't work much better this time than last time. The group sorted them only one way and spent most of their time recording this sorting by means of a picture. Open-ended tasks like this seem to consistently befuddle even the most capable students in my class. (Jan. 8, 1991)

I began to see a relationship between what I saw as students' inability to work independently and the failure of some of the themes and projects we attempted throughout the year. I responded to some of the problems we had with a study of the Winter Olympics, for example, by abandoning this unit.

My students just can't handle much freedom or open-ended tasks. They do just fine cutting out articles for their scrapbooks but didn't do well at much else. I'm going to return to our usual routine as quickly as I can . . . (Feb. 11, 1992)

Too late, perhaps, I recognized that the problem wasn't students' ability to work independently. They worked independently all the time and did quite well. The problem was the quality of support they were receiving from me.

We haven't had much success with independent work, and yet reading and writing are entirely independent and they go very well. Perhaps the problem isn't working independently but knowing what's expected of them. I just can't expect them to have entirely open-ended projects. They need to know what they are to do and what kind of product they're going to have. . . . They're not going to learn how to work independently unless I give them opportunities and teach them how. (May 4, 1992)

It is instructive to note that an animal study we did in the fall (emerging from a folk-tale unit) included significant teacher support and was relatively successful.

Chris [my wife] suggested I think about studying some of the animals in the folk-tale units. So I'm going to begin by getting them to list the animals in the unit and maybe do a web to relate. Or maybe do a web more generally to build a conceptual framework from which science may emerge. May also want to start teaching them about webs as part of both science and language arts curricula. This is heartening but will keep being a challenge. I will need to work at it. It won't just happen by itself. (Oct. 6, 1991)

Today need to give them a group lesson to support the more independent study in science, e.g., picking out some animals from our folk-tale study to learn more about (as a group). I'm asking them to pick an animal each (or an animal as a group or several animals) and develop a plan to learn more about them. We need to begin as a group by modeling a plan of study. I'd like to start that today. (Oct. 18, 1991)

Continue with animal study but do several minilessons on the possible products for this theme. (Oct. 28, 1991)

> Last night I went to the library: got 8–10 picture books for my class.
> also got a number of books to help support their animal studies: e.g., a book
> on saber-toothed tigers for Hugh; a book that has some stuff on crocodiles
> for Ali; and, books on foxes and wolves for several students who are study-
> ing these animals. (Nov. 2, 1991).

Two decades ago Macrorie (1970) alerted teachers to the costs of giving students little control over their writing, but he found that nondirection did not substantially improve the situation. Macrorie argued for a "Third Way," in which teachers increased student responsibility for their work but continued to provide strong direction.

Working independently—with limited teacher support and direction—is a perverse notion of ownership. My students were able to read, write, and pursue an animal study fairly independently because, I believe, I provided them with sufficient support. There is a tension between teacher support and student control. Too much teacher support can result in teachers' taking over responsibility for students' learning. But without teacher support and direction students will always find it difficult to exercise much control over their learning.

An Evolving Sense of Ownership

Reflecting on my notes the last several months has transformed my concept of student ownership. Like many educators I believed that students could learn to read and write only if they engaged in "authentic" reading and writing. Reading and writing are authentic only if engaged in for students' purpose. Anything else is, at best, a simulation and, the argument goes, what is learned in a simulation may not transfer to instances of authentic reading and writing. That means if a student writes a book report because she is directed to by the teacher, then this writing is, by definition, inauthentic. Similar arguments could be made for reading. But there are problems with this argument (see Edelsky, Altwerger, and Flores 1991). The reality of schooling is that children are not there voluntarily (Herndon 1971; Jackson 1968), so it is doubtful that anything done at school can ever truly be authentic (Bloome and Bailey 1990). There are also examples of out-of-school writing (people writing for someone else's purposes, such as a report for your principal), and no one would want to say that these people are not really writing (Edelsky, Altwerger, and Flores 1991).

Although school reading and writing may never be truly authentic, it is still important that students exercise some control over the decisions affecting their learning. There is good evidence that students without a personal stake in their writing will not write very well. I imagine that the same is true for reading. What is important to remember is that, if students do not use reading and writing in school to fulfill *their* intentions, they may not discover the power of reading and writing to affect their lives. Without some control over the uses of literacy in school, they are much less likely "to use print for examining and critiquing taken-for-granted conditions in one's own life and within one's own society" (Edelsky 1991, pp. 93–94). Critical literacy is an important part of a more just and democratic society.

Sociolinguistic (Bloome 1987), critical (Shannon 1995), and deconstructive (Crowley 1989) voices have also forced me to revise my notions of what it means for students to "own" their reading and writing. These voices argue that reading and writing are sociolinguistic acts; thus, whenever we make meaning with language—as readers, writers, speakers, or listeners—we are influenced by the voices of our community and culture. These views have helped me discover subtle ways in which my voice affected the meanings that my students made with written language.

I regularly tried to influence the meanings that students made as readers and as writers, including the purposes for which they wrote. For example, I often encouraged them to use their background knowledge, including their knowledge of language, to make sense of texts. "Why don't you just skip that word and come back to it?" "Does that make sense here?" By stressing the role of background knowledge in reading, I encouraged a particular belief about reading: The meaning isn't just in the text.

A major goal for literature-sharing groups and for discussing books that I read to the class was to encourage students to talk in literate ways, to get some sense of literary elements like plot, characters, mood, setting, and so on, and to read texts critically.

> At the end of reading I again asked them if they had come across any interesting characters in their reading and they did volunteer a number of characters. They mostly found them interesting because they were funny and did funny things. May need to model some of these things. Crystal did note that the character "lazy bear" was interesting because he reminded her of her sister, who also never did anything. (Sept. 26, 1991)
>
> When I read on page 47–48 "Clouds of breath exploded from her mouth," I stopped. I read the line again. I noted how I liked the way this sounded and asked the group to tell me what they thought it meant. One of them noted pretty quickly that this told us that it was cold outside. (May 14, 1992)

Similarly, the modeling of writing topics influenced students' writing topics.

> Writing time began with my sharing of a brief story on the chart about getting locked out of my father's house. Usually they listen in silence and we move on, but today they started sharing stories about losing car keys or house keys. At least eight of them shared such stories, and a couple told more than one "key" story. At least three or four of the students I checked with during writing time were writing key stories. (Sept. 18, 1991)

I also influenced the processes that students used as writers.

> Catherine had started a poem about snowfall but hadn't got beyond the title, so I had her come to the window with me and asked her to look out the window and tell me what she saw. Then I asked her to try writing these thoughts down—and that this would make the basis for a poem. (Jan. 14, 1992)

Overhearing the conversation, several students imitated this process.

When I noticed that students who were writing personal pieces were more successful in discovering their voices as writers I pushed several students to try personal narrative.

> Had a wonderful talk with Roya on the playground at morning recess. She told me she had a four-year-old brother and a two-year-old sister. When I asked her if they were both born in Canada, she said that her brother was also born in Iran. We talked a little about Iran, and she told me she didn't want to go back there because "there's always war and everything." She related how they had to sleep by the door at night in case "those things . . . bombs" came. She also told me about having "to cover up," which she hated. She said that her grandfather died recently (in Iran) and that her father was homesick. (Sept. 18, 1991)

At my encouragement Roya wrote about her experience in emigrating from Iran, and she later returned to this theme for her first publication in early March.

I was one of the many voices that my students heard when they tried to make sense of, and with, print. Recognizing the influence of my voice and of the other voices in students' communities and cultures, I was forced to reconsider what it means for students to own their reading or writing. They may be able to exercise control over when, how, why, where, and for whom they use literacy, but the meanings they make as readers and writers will always be socially influenced. That I was one of those social voices is not bad; in fact, we hope that students will hear their teachers' voices as they read and write. This is one way we might define what it means "to teach." But I do wonder what happens when the teacher's voice conflicts with the voices of a student's community or culture. In the following example my transactional view of literacy may have conflicted with a view in Ali's culture that (some) texts can, and should be, interpreted literally.

> Today when I read from *The Haunting of Grade Three* (Maccarone 1984) there was a picture of a gravestone. . . . We had a discussion of gravestones and our visits to graveyards. Among other things we talked about the DOB and date of death on the gravestone and how to determine the person's age when he or she died. Someone said she had seen a gravestone with a DOB of 1750 and date of death of 1950. Then we figured that this person would have been 200 years old when he died, and we had a discussion of how

long you could live. Most of us, including me, argued that few people lived beyond 100 and no one ever lived beyond 130. But some didn't agree, arguing that some people had lived to be over 500 years old.

The following day:

When Ali came into the classroom he walked up to me and said sternly, "My dad said Moses lived to be 950 years old."

I have also begun to wonder about my efforts to push students toward more personal writing. My students came from a range of cultural traditions. When I pushed Razika, my most prolific writer, to draw on personal experience in her writing, she resisted for several weeks but finally wrote a piece about visiting Canada's Wonderland, a large amusement park. Did my advice to write about herself conflict with her cultural values? I don't know. But I think it is at least worth acknowledging the possibility that the voices of our classroom communities have the potential to alienate students from their communities and culture (Edelsky 1991).

Conclusion

Ownership isn't something we can *give* to our students; however, even if we can't give it, we can create conditions that permit (or deny) students opportunities to assume responsibility for (some) decisions affecting their learning. There is no magic prescription or formula for this. From my perspective at the university, ownership seemed to be a fairly straightforward notion. I learned differently from my third-grade students. In practice, ownership is a very tricky concept.

Other teachers may discover, as I did, that encouraging student ownership requires striking a careful balance between student control and teacher support and direction. Too much teacher support risks taking control of the learning away from students. Too little teacher direction denies student access to the voices that support their intellectual growth and development and their ability to take responsibility for their learning. How much is too much support? Or too little? What constitutes too much or too little support can be determined only by reflecting on our daily encounters with students.

But teachers who create conditions that encourage student control over their work are not doing their students a favor. Ownership is not a gift—it is an entitlement (D. Dippo, personal communication, December 14, 1992). Children's language—their "ways with words" (Heath 1983)—and their ways of knowing express who they are and the communities and cultures from which they come. Restricting students' control over their learning limits their right to express their personal and cultural identities. Permitting students to bring themselves and their lives into their classrooms is, I believe, a moral imperative.

References

Bloome, D., and Bailey, F. 1990. *From linguistics and education, a direction for the study of language and literacy: Events, particularity, intertextuality, history, material, and dialectics.* Paper presented at the National Conference on Research in English, Chicago.

Bloome, D. 1987. Reading as a social process in a middle school classroom. Pp. 123–49 in *Literacy and Schooling,* edited by D. Bloome. Norwood, N.J.: Ablex.

Bogart, J.E., and Hendry, L. 1988. *Malcolm's runaway soap.* Richmond Hill, Ontario: North Winds Press.

Calkins, L.M. 1986. *The art of teaching writing.* Portsmouth, N.H.: Heinemann.

Crowley, S. 1989. *A teacher's introduction to deconstruction.* Urbana, Ill.: National Council of Teachers of English.

Edelsky, C. 1991. *With literacy and justice for all.* London: Falmer Press.

Edelsky, C., Altwerger, B., and Flores, B. 1991. *Whole language: What's the difference?* Portsmouth, N.H.: Heinemann.

Goodman, K. 1986. *What's whole in whole language?* Richmond Hill, Ontario: Scholastic-TAB.

Graves, D. 1983. *Writing: Teachers and children at work.* Portsmouth, N.H.: Heinemann.

Heath, S.B. 1983. *Ways with words: Language, life, and work in communities and classrooms.* Cambridge, England: Cambridge University Press.

Herndon, J. 1971. *How to survive in your native land.* New York: Simon and Schuster.

Irving, J. 1985. *Cider house rules.* New York: Bantam Books.

Jackson, P. 1968. *Life in classrooms.* New York: Holt, Rinehart, and Winston.

Maccarone, G. 1984. *The haunting of grade three.* New York: Scholastic.

Macrorie, K. 1970. *Uptaught.* New York: Hayden.

Paterson, K. 1977. *Bridge to Terabithia.* New York: Harper & Row.

Shannon, P. 1995. Dialectics of ownership: Language as property. *Who Owns Learning?* Portsmouth, N.H.: Heinemann.

2

Understanding Ownership in Classroom Interaction

Dennis Searle and
Curt Dudley-Marling
York University

This chapter is based on interactions that we observed in three classrooms, which had been established to teach first- and second-grade children identified as learning disabled by the local board of education. Spending a week in each of these classrooms we focused on the role of oral language in the life of the classroom. The board of education described the teachers as experienced, successful practitioners in these special situations. In these classes, limited to eight students, the teachers had a wide latitude in their planning. Their aim was to prepare pupils to reenter regular classes as they moved to grade 4.

The classrooms included in their organizational structure many approaches associated with giving students ownership of their learning. The students had opportunities for free reading and for talking about their reading interests. Each classroom featured some form of self-initiated writing and student-directed talk on items of personal interest. Two classrooms included opportunities for self-scheduled time so that the students could arrange their daily schedule. Clearly, there were attempts to have the students share responsibility for their learning. We have reported on some of the meaningful talk resulting from these classroom structures, in particular a type that we call ''talk-around-the-edges'' (Dudley-Marling and Searle 1991).

Ms. Price, one of the teachers we observed, used the time when students were coming and going for regular informal chat. Building a bridge between the childrens' world and the world of the classroom, she encouraged the students to take ownership for the talk's content. The following is a brief example of talk-around-the-edges.

Melissa: Today, ah, today's not my day. Today when I . . . before I went out . . . I kissed my Mom before I went out and I . . . my glasses were on the floor and I stepped on them.

Ms. Price: Oh.

Melissa: And the glasses fell out.

Ms. Price: But she said it's okay.

Melissa: At least she didn't . . . at least . . , I didn't get in trouble.

Ms. Price: Oh, I'm glad. Melissa, you're ready quickly.

The talk is not necessarily profound. Its importance is that it sets a tone for children to recognize that their words and meanings are listened to and valued. Ms. Price listens through Melissa's false starts and confused narrative to hear her relief that things worked out all right. This regular, careful listening helps establish a climate for talk. The children see that their experience and feelings have a place in the classroom, that they can share ownership of classroom discourse. One result is that the students then feel encouraged to use their language resources more fully and carefully.

This chapter looks at how ownership is a consideration in the moment-to-moment interactions of the classroom. Before examining this, however, we should acknowledge that ownership of learning is fraught with complexities.

How much ownership does a teacher have to begin with? Curriculum is set outside the school. Selections of textbooks and resource material affect what happens within the classroom. And parents have a sense of commitment and ownership of their children's learning. Any teacher attempting educational change knows that parents must be sold on the change before it can succeed.

The culture of the school also exercises ownership of what happens in classrooms. Teachers live under the official supervision of principals and the informal supervision of peers who have a vested interest in having classrooms share certain characteristics; at the same time, the teacher role calls for leadership within the classroom and for creating a climate for learning. When we talk about teachers sharing ownership, then, we presume that the culture of the school gives teachers some ownership to share.

Finally, we must also understand that the students need to be considered. It is impossible to "give" ownership to someone who will not take it, and students bring to the classroom a host of prior understandings about their role there. At the very least, ownership of learning in the classroom must be seen as multi-dimensional and as constantly subject to negotiation amidst a variety of forces.

With the concept of ownership in mind, we can examine how talk functions in the classroom. On one hand, we can see how ownership is claimed, given, or shared within the classroom; on the other, we can look at how the positioning of ownership affects the language and the learning occurring there.

The interactions presented below demonstrate appropriations of ownership as teachers work with students in learning important processes related to their school learning. They show how teachers respond to students' sharing their own experience and how teachers relate learning to students' experiences.

Finally, we will look at a few successful incidents of ownership that happened in unexpected situations.

Owning the Process

One of the catchphrases in current education is "process over product." In understanding processes, students develop the knowledge necessary to apply learning to new situations. They learn to use a process as the basis for continued growth and learning. Process learning seems to occur best as learners become involved with the process. A teacher's problem is to provide enough information to keep students' process going and to help them understand the process more explicitly.

As we see the students in Ms. Crane's class respond to Jay's story, We notice how Ms. Crane has developed a standard routine that allows the class to focus their response.

Mike: I liked the part where you shoot the ghost and missed him. That's the part I like.

Keith: I like when Lorne flattens him and, Jay, whose wall did . . . what wall did Lorne burst his hand through?

Jay: I didn't mean . . . no, in the living room 'cause there's a couch in it and the couch is in the living room.

Ms. Crane: I wonder whose house we were in?

Keith: Mine.

Ms. Crane: Do you know?

Jay: Keith's.

Keith: Mine.

Ms. Crane: Okay.

Jay: And his and . . .

Ms. Crane: Oh, um. The part of the story that tells us where it happens has a special name. Do you know what that special name is? Do you, Jay?

Jay: I don't know.

Ms. Crane: Oh, it's a big word. The part that tells where is called the setting. That's a word . . . um, the setting of your story tells where it happens. That's a word you might remember. You'll hear it a lot more as you write more stories. Yes, Mike?

Mike: I have something else to say to Jay. Jay, I liked the part where Lorne got so mad he flattened the ghost.

Clearly, Ms. Crane has a different agenda than the boys do. They are enjoying a story in which they feature as the characters. Ms. Crane picks this moment to teach something about the process, the concept of setting. On the surface, at least, there is a link between the reading and the concept of setting, as the story is set in Keith's house. It is also apparent, however, that the setting is not a feature of which Jay is conscious.

"Naming of parts" intervention, as with Jay's story, is deeply engrained in the teaching tradition. Four-year-old Tiina, for example, stands directly in front of her two-year-old neighbor Nathan as he sits on his tricycle for the first time. "Tricycle, can you say 'tricycle'?" she asks, as if the naming must proceed the learning to ride. Ms. Crane's focus on the term *setting* may seem as irrelevant to Jay's writing process as Tiina's vocabulary lesson is to Nathan's learning to ride. Although Ms. Crane probably was not thinking of control, she asserts teacher ownership in this interaction. The teacher reminds the student of his inadequacy in comparison to the teacher's knowledge of this "big word" that Jay must learn as he writes more stories. In this case, the interjection is short-lived; in fact, the ownership of the sharing process that Ms. Crane has given the students reasserts itself. The boys return to the discussion of the story, and Ms. Crane accepts this focus. There is a fine line between inserting knowledge to empower students—giving them a way to talk about a concept—or using the same knowledge to disenfranchise students by reminding them of their limitations. Teacher-led drill, a very common classroom activity, is one in which teachers are very much in control and own the discourse. The familiar "teacher questions, student answers, teacher evaluates pattern" is a cornerstone of classroom discourse. The question of ownership, however, goes deeper than just the discourse pattern to an understanding of what is involved in learning and problem-solving. In the following two excerpts the teachers warn the students to look out for "tricks" that the teachers may try. In the first exchange the student is reading from word cards that the teacher selects and displays.

Ms. Henry: Don't get tricked now!

John: [long pause] Yellow.

Ms. Henry: Two "yellows" in your pile. I tried to trick you.

John: Brown . . . [corrects] green.

Ms. Henry: What does that one start with?

John: Buh.

Ms. Henry: Good, it's a color word. What one is it? Sit up, sweetie. What color word is that? What does this letter say?

John: Yuu.

Ms. Henry: Put them together, buh luh . . .

Together: Blue.

Ms. Henry: Ahm. What's this one?

John: Green.

Ms. Henry: [laughs] I didn't trick you this time, did I?

In the second exchange Marty and Ms. Crane are working matching patterns made with geometric shapes. Ms. Crane makes a pattern and Marty tries to re-create it.

Ms. Crane: I think I might trick you if you're not very careful, Marty.

Marty: You won't trick me. I bet you won't.

Ms. Crane: Fit it on the pattern for me.

Marty: Okay!

Ms. Crane : Um. You've done a pretty good job. There's just one thing that's wrong.

Marty: What?

Ms. Crane: In your pattern . . . are those two the same size?

The notion of "tricking" raises interesting issues. Certainly, on one level it is apparent that the device is used for motivation. As the activity itself has little intrinsic meaning, turning it into a game involves students and allows them to enter into a contest with the teacher. On the other hand, however, framing the activity in this way takes away some of the ownership of learning. It emphasizes, for example, what many students already suspect, that the enterprise is arbitrary and subject to teacher whims. This view intimates that learning is a matter of outguessing the teacher, rather than a matter of using available knowledge and problem-solving abilities to make sense of experience. In other classes Searle (1981) noticed a different version of this same view of knowledge. On two occasions different teachers interrupted similar teacher-led question-and-answer sessions to warn students: "This time you have to use your common sense." By this warning, teachers meant that there was a special twist or trick in the next question and that students should not rely on the specific learned knowledge on which the activity was based. The implication, however, was that common sense is ordinarily not a useful tool for answering teacher questions and emphasized that students depend on their teachers to select and frame experience for learning. This dependence, in the end, works against students' taking ownership of their learning.

The flash-card excerpt also shows Ms. Henry leading John through a sounding-out process. Again, the activity of leading a student step-by-step through a process is very common in classrooms. Teachers regularly guide students through a process, be it problem-solving, reading a graph, spelling a word, or shooting a basketball. In the following example Ms. Price leads Josh through a problem using base-ten blocks.

Josh: Miss, I'm having a little trouble.

Ms. Price: All right.

Josh: Right here. If I, I had, I couldn't take t . . . I can!

Ms. Price: What?

Josh: Take, no I can't . . .

Ms. Price: All right . . .

Josh: I can't do that.

Ms. Price: All right . . .

Josh: So I have to take one from here . . .

Ms. Price: Right . . .

Josh: When I bring it in, I'll, I'll have . . .

Ms. Price: How many will you . . . ?

Josh: Ah . . . three?

Ms. Price: No, let's go back a little bit. You have sixteen ones, and how many tens did that leave you?

Josh: Ahm . . . so that, one?

Ms. Price: All right, you need to have that written down. I think you have erased that.

Josh: Yes.

Ms. Price: Well, write it down again, so we can see it. Now you have one ten and you need to subtract three, and you can't do it, so you're going to get some more tens from the hundreds. How many tens are you going to get?

Josh: Ten?

Ms. Price: And how many do you have?

Josh: One?

Ms. Price: So how many will you have now?

Josh: Eleven.

Ms. Price: Write it down.

Josh: Oh!

Ms. Price: — There you go.

There is no doubt that Josh was terribly confused at the beginning of this exchange and was unable even to articulate the problem. Certainly, by the end, if we look at Josh's book, we will see that the problem has been solved. The question remains, however, whether Josh has any short-term or long-term ownership of the knowledge needed for such problem-solving. As teachers, we often assume that if we lead students through processes often enough, they will take over the process for themselves. Undoubtedly, this works with *some* processes for *some* students *some*times. Too often, however, as in this exchange, the student becomes a scribe for the teacher's skills. In mathematics, for example, one rationale for working with concrete materials is that it allows students to work with the concepts of mathematics in personally meaningful ways. To do this, students need to be able to use their own processes; teachers, who should intervene, must do so in way that helps the students take more explicit control over the implicit knowledge being tested in the activity. If we fail to do that, we disenfranchise students further by leaving the impression that teachers have access to some secret knowledge denied to students and that teachers reveal in small doses as necessary.

We often see this control of process when teachers help children to spell a word. The child asks for the word and the teacher replies with a procedural suggestion. Perhaps the teacher will say, "Sound it out" or "Remember that rule about the *e*," or "Think of another word like it." In almost all cases the suggestion leads to a correct solution. But we know that none of these strategies is infallible; students trying to reapply the advice with another word may be lost. Real learning enables the student to know which strategy works for which word, or to know enough to apply another strategy when the first one is unsatisfactory. Teachers need to work to enable students to become owners of process, not solutions.

Working with Students' Experience

Most teachers aim to relate learning to students' experience. We encourage students to talk about and share their experience, we try to become familiar with their interests. We find that linking our teaching matter with students' lives makes the learning applicable and relevant. We also assume that students will have more ownership of their learning if they see that it connects to their world.

One concern when using students' experience is that teachers may take the experience away from the children and, in a sense, replace it with their own related experience, or with what they think may be the significant aspect of that learning. The students in Ms. Crane's class were sharing family news. Jack talked about his brother's trip to the United States from Canada. It is obvious from the following exchange that Ms. Crane saw this experience as the basis for some teaching.

Carl: When you're going to the United States, you also have this big bridge you could go across.

Ms. Crane: Why?

Carl: That's the border so you could get to the United States.

Ms. Crane: Often you have to go across a bridge.

Jack: You have to bring your driver's license and I forget the other thing.

Ms. Crane: Does anyone know what?

Carl: Credit card!

Ms. Crane: I don't think . . .

Carl: Your ID.

Ms. Crane: Identification, you need something. What do you have to have for identification if you want to go to another country?

Carl: Like on a plane you have to. . .

Jack: Your, your birth . . .

Ms. Crane: That's one thing, your birth certificate, and if you're going farther away than the United States sometimes you have to get what we call a passport then take that with you. It has a picture of you in it, too. All your information. Yes, Lyle?

Lyle: You'll have to get a credit card so you can get United States money.

Ms. Crane: Well, sometimes you can go to the bank and get United States money before you go. Some people take a credit card, but some people do both.

Jack: He drives a car. That's why he has to bring his license.

It is apparent that these boys know a great deal about traveling to the United States. This knowledge was obviously idiosyncratic and related to their personal experience. There are, after all, several places where a Canadian can cross into the United States without going over a bridge, but the experience of crossing on some of those bridges is indeed unforgettable. At the same time, Ms. Crane apparently saw the conversation as an opportunity to teach about passports. It is equally obvious that, although this topic comes out of the children's talk about their experience, it is in no way related to it. The students, however, resist this diversion into teacher knowledge and provide more credible replies to what is essential when traveling to the United States.

In the following example, we again see a teacher taking a child's experience and giving it the teacher's perspective. The children have each brainstormed a list of places, people, and objects that they plan to include in their story. Dave is just reading his list to Ms. Price.

Dave: ... sheet, mountain, Albert, case, Vancouver ...

Ms. Price: Oh!

Dave: Oh! Why did I say Vancouver?

Ms. Price: Well, it must be mentioned in the story, that's what we want to know. What is Vancouver?

Dave: A place.

Ms. Price: It's way out west; it's a big city, and something special is going to happen out there this year. Do you know what it is? A big fair called Expo.

Dave: Expo?

Ms. Price: You might see something about it on television. Vancouver is a beautiful city because it has mountains on one side and sea on the other, so it is a pretty city. Let's see if you can make pictures with those. What do you think you're going to do down here? [points to a space on the page] You know how to do that. You are pretty good at making pictures, so off you go.

Dave's mere mention of Vancouver triggered an immediate lesson on the city from Ms. Price. There is no indication, however, of what Dave's experience of the city is. He may know the name only, or he may have visited there. The teacher is not adding to the experience, only taking it over. Teachers do this with children's language as well. Ms. Henry hears Bert tell Andrew that "it takes one to know one." She immediately responds as follows.

Ms. Henry: Where did you hear that expression? Was that you?

Bert: Yep.

Ms. Henry: What's that mean?

Bert: I don't know.

Ms. Henry: That, that's a good expression, what does it mean?

Bert: I don't know.

Anne: What did he say, anyway?

Ms. Henry: "It takes one to know one." You don't know what that means? It takes one to know one? If I say, "You're crazy," and you say to me, "It takes one to know one," you're actually saying to me that I am also crazy. [children laugh] So if I think you're crazy, then you must, then I must know about crazy, so I must be crazy, too, Okay? That's what it means, "It takes one to know one."

Ms. Henry is trying to help her children develop their language and their awareness of language. Working with what the kids say is useful and, certainly, she explained the saying in a way that the class found amusing. Again, though, by usurping language or experience and giving it our personal, adult, and educated meaning, we risk alienating the children from their own experience and depriving them of confidence in a key part of any real learning.

There are also instances when, assuming that we understand children's experience, we try to give them ownership of learning by letting them use their own experience to discover key ideas or concepts. This can be a powerful way of letting children become owners of their own learning. It can also lead to problems because we may find that we are still assuming that the students draw the same meaning from experience as we do. Two examples demonstrate how assumed experiences and values can clash with the children's real experience. In both cases the teachers are trying to establish an emotional connection between a character in a reading passage and the student.

Lyle: [reading] "... go up when you said, Tom." "Oh, Grandfather, may I go? I want a ride in a helicopter," he said. "Say I may go, please."

Ms. Crane: Um hm ... How would you feel if someone said, "Do you want to go for a ride in a helicopter?"

Lyle: I would say, "No."

Ms. Crane: Would you? Would you be afraid to go? Oh.

Ms. Henry encountered a similar and more poignant surprise when she tried to get Todd to share his experiences with racing.

Todd: Raced to the beat.

Ms. Henry: Raced means to run very fast, doesn't it? Have you ever been in a race?

Todd: Nope.

Ms. Henry: You've NEVER been in a running race? Or a bicycle race?

Todd: Nope.

Ms. Henry: Well I, on Play Day We'll have to get you out there and have a race, won't we? You've never had a race with your daddy?

Todd: No. He's not really there. Just mom.

Personal experience can be a useful tool for allowing children to build bridges between their learning and their lives, and thereby taking ownership of their learning. Learning that is alienated from experience is rarely owned. Even as we teachers try to build these links, we must be especially careful to ensure that it is the students' experience at the heart of the discussion. We must be careful neither to alienate children from their own learning nor to imply that their experience is not a suitable grounding for what really counts as learning.

Ownership in Unusual Places

The examples provided above demonstrate that ownership is not always apparent in places where it might be expected. Certainly, these teachers have provided many opportunities for their students to enjoy control of their school experience and learning. And if they have developed a climate for ownership they find that at times opportunities for ownership happen unexpectedly.

Dave is reading a story to Ms. Price. His task is to answer a fairly standard set of questions, and there is little reason to see him being particularly interested in this story about a family who trick their daughter by pretending to forget her birthday.

Dave: ... they didn't wish her a happy birthday. Jean made her breakfast and still no one said a word. And then her mother said, "You'd better hurry, the school bus is waiting outside." Jean walked sadly out the door. No one had remembered her birthday. [here Dave interjected into the text] I would.

Somehow Dave has been able to put himself into this story. He has also taken over ownership of the questions. When the teacher asks whether the family had really forgotten the birthday, he treats this "teacher question" as a real inquiry and replies, "No, because there was the sign across the bus, remember?" The word *remember* signals a real communication with the teacher in which he is sharing his expertise with her.

Sharing expertise is one way of developing ownership. The following excerpts taken from a longer discussion among Ms. Crane and her class show how a teacher can follow the students in expertise displayed during a class sharing time. Lyle had brought in a transformer toy, and the class was talking about transformer creatures. Slowly, the teacher stops trying to impose learnings and becomes a learner herself.

Ms. Crane: You guys are always bringing in transformers. What does that word mean? Transformer.

Kurt: To transform.

Ms. Crane: Well what does that mean?

Lyle: They could change into stuff.

Kurt: Can you play with it much?

Lyle: Um hm.

Ms. Crane: Did you tell us, does he have a name?

Lyle: Yeah, Beachcomber.

Ms. Crane: I'm sorry, I'd forgotten that.

Lyle: Kurt?

Kurt: Do you, which autobot do you like best?

Lyle: I like all of them.

Ms. Crane: What did you just call that, Kurt? I missed what you said.

Kurt: Autobot. The good guys are called the autobots and the bad guys are called the deceptacons.

Ms. Crane: Okay, that's a big word. Deceptacons. I'd like to know how to spell that. Do you know how to spell those words?

Lyle: I do. I have them in my book.

It was very unusual to hear Ms. Crane asking these students how to spell words and admitting to not knowing something. Clearly, however, as she realized that there was more to the world of transformers than she had assumed, she acknowledged the expertise around her and began to learn from it.

We have tried to show that ownership involves processes and personal responsibility. As a final demonstration of ownership in unusual places, we offer this conversation that followed the oft-heard question, "Can I have your homework, please?"

Will: I forgot it.

Ms. Henry: Is there something you could do at night to, to help you remember it in the morning?

Will: Yeah.

Ms. Henry: What could you do with your homework sheet before you go to bed at night?

Jack: In his shoe . . .

Ms. Henry: In his shoe? That's a good idea. What else could you do with it so you wouldn't forget it? Roy, what do you do with your homework?

Roy: My Mom, my Mom puts it in the lunchbox.

Ms. Henry doesn't berate Will for forgetting his work. Instead, she starts to create the idea that this is a process he must learn to control. Involving other students, she lets each of them share ways in which they meet the challenge. The matter becomes one of personal problem-solving. We don't know what the outcome will be, but in this case, at least, Ms. Henry gives Will ownership of his problem.

We have tried to show that ownership is as much a product of day-to-day interactions as it is the result of a grand plan. Teachers try to develop a learning community that presents certain ideas about what it means to learn and to be a learning person. It is in the day-to-day interactions that these attitudes are formed.

By contrast, curriculum practice and change is often considered in terms of overall activities. A school may boast about emphasizing drill or using whole language approaches. School Boards may conceptualize their approach as outcomes based education or emphasize a close link with technology. These topics often become the focus of theoretical and research initiatives. To focus on these more recognizable aspects of curriculum and instruction, however, may encourage us to forget that the immediate context in which education is provided also affects learning.

Given the complexity of the work, it is clear that no teacher reacts perfectly in every situation. Part of our ownership is to continually review and reflect on our practice. We learn from what we do and from what our students tell us.

References

Dudley-Marling, C., and Searle, D. 1991. *When students have time to talk: Creating contexts for learning language.* Portsmouth, N.H.: Heinemann.

Searle, D. 1981. *Two contexts for adolescent language: Classroom learning and the discussion of extra-school experience.* Unpublished Ph.D., London, England: University of London.

3

Students and Teachers: Sharing Ownership and Responsibility in Reading

Lynn K. Rhodes
University of Colorado at Denver

As teachers, most of us do too much for children. This is how it often plays out in reading: We decide what they will read, we give them words when they can't read them, we set instructional goals for them, we determine the reading lessons they need, we assess their progress as readers, and we rescue them from problems they encounter as readers. In the process of doing too much for children, we delay the development of responsible independence, confidence, and effectiveness that, I'm sure we would agree, are overarching goals for children's education. In fact, it is my belief that children who develop these characteristics of responsible independence, confidence, and effectiveness as readers often do so outside the classroom, in settings like home where they can take ownership and be responsible for themselves as readers. Children who do not read outside of school and, therefore, do not have the opportunity to take ownership of the process for themselves often remain dependent, lack self-confidence, and are ineffective as readers. It is not surprising to find that students who have more than one teacher doing too much for them (such as those who have regular classroom teachers as well as special education or Chapter I teachers) are those who are frequently the most dependent, the least confident, and the least effective readers.

Of course, there is a real tension here. On the one hand, we became teachers to help and to teach children. A major role of teachers is to help children learn to read. In classrooms where we are in charge of twenty-five or more children, helping children learn to read often becomes translated into the teachers making most or all of the decisions because it seems to be too difficult, at least on the surface, to manage children otherwise. On the other hand, our job as teachers is to gradually release responsibility to children to do and learn for themselves. We want children to take ownership of their own learning and responsibility for their own reading.

I have had the pleasure of observing a number of teachers who have dealt effectively with this tension between being in charge and releasing responsibility to children, thus allowing them to take ownership for their literacy in the classroom. These teachers are clearly in charge of the children in their classrooms, yet they also continually work to create responsibly independent, self-confident, and effective readers. They don't do too much for children. Instead, they continually nudge them toward doing for themselves by inviting them to share the responsibility for teaching, assessment, and advocacy that many teachers assume only for themselves. In the remainder of this article, stories about what some teachers have done with their students will reveal the potential in teachers sharing the responsibilities for teaching, assessment, and advocacy with their students.

Learning to Read by Teaching Reading

An old adage suggests that one of the best ways to learn something is to teach it. As teachers, we've all had the experience of knowing something far better after having taught it; teaching makes us ask questions we might not have asked otherwise and involves us in a very active way with information and/or processes. A powerful way that many teachers have found to help children assume ownership and responsibility for their own reading is to engage them in teaching others what it is that they need to know as readers through such techniques as cross-age tutoring and partner reading. However, it is not enough for a teacher simply to set up tutoring or partner reading sessions and then expect learning to take place. The teacher who wants to take advantage of the twenty-five or more pint-sized teachers in her classroom has to assume the role of teacher educator—someone who helps her students become effective teachers of each other . . . and of themselves.

Cross-Age Tutoring

Roxanne Torke, a teacher of first and second grade, arranged to have her second-grade students who were still struggling as readers work as cross-age tutors with some kindergarten children in the school. In advance of their first session together, Torke worked with her students on selecting appropriate books and on learning to read them well. They talked about what kind of books kindergarten children might enjoy and how to select books that the second graders could read fluently with practice. In addition, they discussed how they could work on their own to become fluent readers of the books they chose and how they would know when they were fluent at reading a book.

After the second graders had read with the kindergarten children twice, concerns surfaced during a session Torke conducted about how the teaching was going. One complaint the second graders had was that the younger children were "fooling around." When queried further, the second graders defined "fooling around" as not looking at the words when the second graders read the books. Torke conducted a problem-solving session with the second graders in which they addressed several of their concerns. Here is a portion of the discussion that focused on getting the kindergarten children to look at the print as they were being read to:

Torke: Now, what could you do about this? Have any of you found a way to solve that problem?

Dave: I have. I think you just ask them to look at the words.

Torke: So you ask them to look. Like what do you mean? Let's say I'm your kid, okay? And you want me to read this page along with you. And I'm saying, "Run, frog, run. Jump, frog, jump." Am I looking at the words? [Torke is looking at the ceiling as she says this]

Students: No.

Torke: How could you get me to look at those words?

David: "Please look at those words." [pointing to the words on the page as he talks]

Torke: Good, you could point to the exact words you want me to look at, huh? Great. So that's one thing. What else could you do when they fool around and look around the room when you want them to look at the book?

Jeremia: You could say, "You're not going to get a job if you don't know how to read."

Maurice: It's really important you learn how to read quickly in kindergarten. Because if you get a job and you never read before, and then they send up a thing where you have to read what you're supposed to do, but then he goes, "What's it say, I don't know." And then they go, "I'm sorry, I can't help you." Mostly you can't get a job when you don't know how to read.

Jeremia: In kindergarten you need a running start because in second grade they teach you more how to read, and if you don't even know how to read that, and they give you different hard books and you don't even know how to read the other little books, you might feel sort of embarrassed.

David: If you yell at her, she'll think you're playing with her and she'll just keep fooling around.

Jeremia: Or she'll start crying or something.

Lisa: And she might be afraid of you.

Torke: And then do you think she would be serious and work really hard?

Students: No.

Torke: Then she might not try at all. Now, watch this. Is this better? [turns to Lisa] "Lisa, I really want to help you learn how to read this book. Is this a book you'd *like* to learn to read? I notice that you're looking around the room. And it's really important that you point to the words while we read. Now, if you don't want to read *this* book, we could get a different one." Is that a better way to get her to pay attention?

Students: Yes.

Torke: Why?

This session, as well as the teaching that Torke did earlier about how to choose books and how to learn to read fluently, are invaluable for children who are still struggling themselves to become readers. Through talking about how to help younger children become readers—by looking at the words on the page and by selecting books of interest—they were reminding themselves of what they themselves need to do in order to become readers. Talking about why it was important to learn to read reinforced the need to learn to read for themselves.

When Torke established this teaching opportunity for her students, she clearly considered it as a learning opportunity for them—a chance to learn to read better themselves, and a chance to learn to help others learn to read. When they were given responsibility for reading to younger children, the second graders' motivation for learning to read a book fluently rose markedly. When they bumped into problems in their teaching, the teacher helped them think through their problems in the way a teacher might think through such problems. Torke placed the children in a situation where they were in charge of teaching, and in the process, provided an opportunity to develop their own answers to the questions: why is it important to be a reader, and what actions are helpful in becoming a reader?

Partner Reading

When teachers pair children to partner-read a book, it is not uncommon for them to witness circumstances similar to the following that were captured by Patty Mozena in her anecdotal notes during partner reading:

Brooke & Larry (are) reading a Nate the Great story together—switching off at each paragraph. Brooke jumps in to correct Larry or give him a word at the slightest hesitation.

Aaron & Shawn (are) reading—switching off after every 2 pgs. Shawn loves the story—keeps telling Aaron the next part will be funny & chuckling as he reads aloud. Shawn is the leader in this situation. He interrupts with immediate help when Aaron hesitates with a word.

Especially when the partners are uneven with regard to reading ability, the child with more ability views "teaching" as providing the less able reader with words, as the teacher notes, "at the slightest hesitation." In such cases the more able reader does too much for the less able reader, taking away the child's responsibility for processing text. Over time, especially if the teacher also responds to children's miscues in the same way, the child becomes dependent on others for processing difficult text and does not develop independent strategies that are important for effective reading.

After recording several anecdotal notes similar to the one above, Mozena decided to teach her students how to help each other learn to take personal responsibility for their reading. To do this, she told them about what she had learned in her graduate reading class about how to help someone having difficulty reading words or about how to help someone who had read words differently than the ones on the page. Over the period of several lessons, conducted just before the students did partner reading, she explained and role played the following teaching strategies:

- Don't say anything at all if the word makes sense. The children learned to make judgments about what made sense by listening to the reader with their eyes closed. This helped them think only about whether the reader made sense rather than whether the reader was getting the words right.
- Wait if the partner encounters a word s/he doesn't know. To learn to wait, the children counted to ten silently so that the reader had a chance to figure out the word on his/her own.
- If the partner reads a word that does not make sense, wait until the end of the sentence and ask the partner to read the sentence again, thinking about what might make sense.
- When none of the above works, tell the partner the word or give a hint.

Of course, the children enjoyed finding out what their teacher had learned in her university class and discovering that there were people who studied children and teachers in order to make these recommendations. Once the teacher taught these lessons, she saw marked changes in the way children allowed each other to take ownership when it was their turn to read. After each partner reading session, she read a few anecdotal notes from that day to the students, especially when she saw a student able to figure out a word because the partner waited and gave the student time, or because the partner suggested that the reader think about what made sense. Through the anecdotal notes, she also provided the children with ideas about what hints were most helpful in particular contexts.

In addition to finding that partner reading improved, the teacher also observed steady improvement in the children's independent reading. The children discovered that they could help themselves in their own reading by using the same strategies—giving themselves time to think and considering what might make sense.

In the cross-age tutoring experience and the partner reading experience, the teachers helped children learn how to share the ownership and responsibility for teaching reading—not just by providing the opportunity for children to act as teachers but also by teaching them that teaching meant helping others become responsible for their learning. The skill and disposition to help others become responsible will not only have immediate pay-off in the students' reading with other children but will also have a likely pay-off in their interactions with others around a variety of problems. Helping children learn how to be better teachers in such circumstances may even have long-term pay-off when these same youngsters become parents. In the process of cross-age tutoring and partner reading, children learned not only how to help each other become better readers but also how to help themselves become better readers. They became more responsibly independent, more confident, and more effective as readers.

Assessing Reading and Setting Goals

Assessment is a major responsibility of teachers. Just as with teaching, we can do most of it for the students or we can share the responsibility with them. In many classrooms, teachers "own" assessment and do too much of it for students. The teacher passes judgment, sets standards, gives grades, determines goals, conducts conferences, fills out report cards. Children are the subjects of these assessments. What I'd like to propose is that we help students develop the capability to form well-founded judgments about themselves as readers and then to use those judgments to set goals for themselves as readers. In other words, we need to invite children into the assessment process, to share responsibility with us for assessing their attitudes, behaviors, and progress in reading.

When teachers share ownership and responsibility for assessment with students, they are triangulating their data collection about students. That is, instead of relying only on their own observations, they are also taking into account students' views of themselves as readers. Sometimes children's self-assessments confirm what a teacher has already surmised; sometimes children's self-assessments help the teacher develop a new perspective about what is observed and/or help the teacher understand what children find important in their development as readers.

Just as is the case with teaching, students need guidance in order to learn to assess themselves well and to learn how to participate in the assessment process. Effective assessment, whether done by teacher or child, requires that the assessor knows what to look for. We can help children learn what is important to assess and what standards to use by providing a structure for self-assessment that helps them learn what to look for. For example, if you want students to assess their use of comprehension strategies, you might begin with a structured self-assessment such as the one seen in Figure 3–1.

After students understand each of the strategies and know what comprehension strategies they can call on when reading, the self-assessment can become less structured, like the one in Figure 3–2.

Focused and formative self-assessments like these also aid students to engage in summative types of self-assessment. Kathy Hoerlein, a third-grade teacher who continually involved students in self assessment, asked her students to reflect back on their reading and writing during the previous school quarter and then to set goals for the next quarter. The one who struggled most with literacy responded as shown in Figure 3–3.

Hoerlein's students were able to respond in specific ways about their reading and writing because they engaged frequently in self-assessment. The summative self-assessment (Figure 3–3) and their daily formative assessments told Hoerlein a great deal about what was valuable to her students in their learning experiences, what they had learned, and what they were interested in learning.

Figure 3–1   A structured self-assessment

Name _____ Date _____

Title of reading material _____

Underline the strategies that you used to help yourself understand the book you are reading. Circle the strategy you used the most.

I thought about what I already knew.

I made predictions and read to see if they came out.

I reread what I didn't understand.

I made pictures in my head.

I asked someone to explain what I didn't understand.

Give an example of how you used one of the strategies.

Figure 3–2 A less structured self-assessment

Name _____ Date _____

Title of reading material _____

What strategies did you use today to help yourself understand the book you are reading?

Give an example of how one of the strategies you listed helped you understand something in the book.

Figure 3–3 A summative type of self-assessment

READING

These are some things I do well in reading.

I am good at reading
Beverly cleary books.
_____

This is a problem I have.

my problem is thet I prblums
in choling books

This is what I plan to work on next quarter.

To read choling books.
_____
_____

choling – challenging

Hoerlein also prepared students in her classroom to take even more responsibility for assessment by having them conduct parent conferences. During the child-led conferences, the children sought their parents' and the teacher's reactions to their self-assessments, just as the teacher sought the child's and parents' reactions to the assessment information she had gathered. Hoerlein believes that no one person knows or understands what is important about the child as a reader, but they can all understand and plan for the child's continued growth more effectively, especially with the child's involvement.

In engaging students in ongoing and summative self-assessment and in sharing what they know about themselves with others, teachers provide children with opportunities to share ownership and responsibility for assessment. If children are to learn to look critically at what they can do and what they believe, if they are to learn to set reasonable and data-driven goals for themselves, they need to engage in that process in the classroom under the guidance of a teacher.

Self-advocacy

In whole language classrooms, teachers often find themselves acting as advocates for children's literacy. To ensure that a child can obtain and use a public library card for the summer, a teacher might need to call a recalcitrant parent. Or a teacher might need to write a grant in order to build up her classroom library to the point where there are enough books to serve her children. She might need to work on a committee to change a policy that mandates standardized testing of reading in kindergarten and first grade.

As teachers act as advocates for children, they can think about how to share the ownership and responsibility for advocacy with the children themselves, to involve them in getting what they need so that when they are in situations where no one acts as an advocate, they understand how to be heard about the issues they care about and/or how to solve the problems with which they are faced.

Ann Christensen, a first-grade teacher in a large urban school district, found herself in a new school that did not allow kindergarten and first-grade children to check books out of the school library. As an advocate for children's literacy, Christensen protested the policy to the librarian, who told her that this was a district policy; it was founded on the assumption that kindergarten and first-grade children were too young to be able to read and to be responsible for the books. According to the librarian, it was better to wait until second grade to allow book check-outs. Continuing her advocacy, the teacher took the matter to the school board. She spoke for the allotted three minutes, providing reasons why it was important for emerging readers to be able to check out books and assuring the board that kindergartners and first graders could be taught how to be responsible for returning books. The board conceded the issue immediately, drawing up a new policy for the district.

Christensen then established a regular time for her first graders to visit the school library and to check out books. After the first visit, one little girl was quite upset by the librarian's actions. This time, the teacher decided that it would be helpful if the child would speak for herself and encouraged her to write a letter about the library incident. After writing the letter shown in Figure 3–4, the child submitted it to the principal. (The librarian's name has been removed.)

Figure 3–4   A appeal to the school librarian

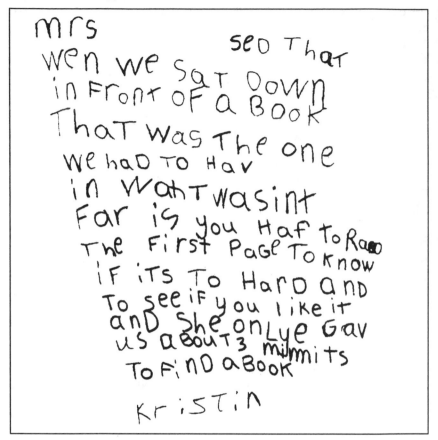

mrs
                              seo Thar
wen we sat Down
in Front oF a Book
ThaT was The one
We haD To Hav
in WahT wasint
Far is you Haf to Raw
The First PaGe To know
iF iTs To HarD and
To see iF you like it
and She onLye Gav
us abouT 3 mimmits
To FinD aBook

        KristiN

In another case of advocacy for children's literacy, a fifth-grade teacher
in an impoverished neighborhood decided to involve her students in creating
libraries in their homes—homes that contained few books, magazines, or
newspapers. The teacher helped the students think of ways that they could earn
money to buy at least one paperback book from a school book club each
month. When the first set of book club order blanks arrived, the students filled
out the forms at school, keeping in mind what they had earned. Since there
were no bookshelves in many of the homes, the students also decided that they
could each create a personal bookshelf by painting and decorating boxes
obtained from the trash of a nearby store. By the end of the year each student
had a personal library at home and exchanged these books with other students.

Besides being active advocates for students' literacy, teachers can show
the children how to become their own literacy advocates by involving them

in helping to solve the literacy-related problems they face. The teachers in the stories above involved their students in such advocacy and, in so doing, taught children a great deal about the politics and economics of literacy and how literacy can become part of their lives outside of school.

Sharing Ownership and Responsibility

Although this article has addressed how students and teachers can share ownership and responsibility in reading, it should be obvious that the teachers in the stories taught their students how to become responsible in their ownership of reading. In fact, they taught their students attitudes, skills, and knowledge that extended beyond reading and that could have been taught in other classroom arenas as well. Students who have learned to teach others to read, who have learned to assess their performance and progress as readers, and who have learned to be advocates for their own literacy have learned much more than reading. They have learned social skills, how to be responsible for themselves and others, how to critically observe themselves and others, how to communicate opinions and beliefs, and probably much more.

In the dictionary, ownership is defined as "having full claim, authority, power, dominion, etc." Because classrooms are typically communities of many children with one adult in charge, student ownership exists only to a degree because space, time, and materials must be shared by all. As a result, ownership must be accompanied by responsibility. A teacher who wants to share a degree of ownership with children must help them learn to do so responsibly—to make intelligent choices and to take actions that help themselves and others in the classroom community increase the potential for learning.

4

Reading with Friends: A Peer-Tutored Reading Program

Odette Bartnicki

Holy Cross School

I work as a resource teacher in a large elementary school near Toronto, Canada. At our school we assume that students learn to read by reading; that means daily reading instruction to achieve good literacy skills. We use a whole language literature-based approach to teaching reading, including the teaching of phonics and basic sight words. But it is hard for us to provide quality reading instruction on an individualized basis for all students every day. The reality is that each child is lucky to read individually with the teacher once a week. Ultimately, teachers refer so many poor readers or non-readers to me, the resource teacher, that I also find it difficult to provide the individualized support that students need. We know that many of our students desperately need more one-on-one attention to become better readers, but we have been unable to provide this support ourselves; even with the help of a few volunteers. Then we hit on the idea of tapping a readily available resource for supporting struggling readers—our students! We implemented a cross-age, peer tutoring that partnered students for the sole purpose of sharing reading experiences on a daily basis under teacher supervision.

My principal had some concerns about the merit of a peer tutoring program, at least at first, so I located and shared with him studies showing that these reading programs benefited both tutors and tutees (DiSibio and Parla 1985; Goodlad and Hirst 1989; Joffin 1988; Topping 1984; Winter 1986). These satisfied my principal, but I was curious about why peer tutoring worked. I decided to investigate our peer tutoring program by studying the fifth-grade tutors and second-grade tutees through direct observation and note-keeping and by audiotaping peer partners during tutorial sessions.[1]

---

1. This study also formed the basis of my masters thesis.

Since research indicates that peer tutoring is most effective when tutor training is part of the program (Hall 1983; Topping 1987; Winter 1986), the grade 5 tutors were given two training sessions consisting of positive reinforcement and encouragement techniques to use with tutees; strategies for supporting reading such as prompting; use of context and picture cues; questioning techniques; choral reading; and fading out.

In this chapter I will use examples from my research to illustrate the various ways that fifth-grade tutors supported the second-grade tutees as they read during pair-reading sessions. In general, I found that the fifth graders supported the second graders' reading while honoring their intentions to read and make sense of texts. In other words, the fifth graders provided the necessary support without unduly interfering with the second graders' ownership of their reading. This chapter will also discuss the positive effects that the tutoring relationship had on both tutors and tutees.

Selecting Reading Materials

Tutorial sessions usually began by carefully examining and selecting reading materials that could be decoded by the second-grade tutees with the help of the fifth-grade tutors. Initially, the second graders chose books they could read easily, perhaps because they wanted to make a good impression on their reading partners. Over time, however, the second graders began to choose more difficult texts even though they recognized that they couldn't decode all the words. This may have reflected a growing awareness of the peer reading situation as a learning situation instead of a demonstration of skill by the reader. I believe that the gentle, nonevaluative encouragement the tutors provided the second graders to "make sense" engendered in them a sense of "self-as-learner" and a willingness to take risks.

The fifth-grade tutors seemed to have their own criteria for choice of reading materials. They often encouraged tutees to choose harder books, sometimes complaining if their young partners repeatedly reread the same text. For example:

Mark: Choose a book you haven't read yet.

Nicholas: No. I want to read this one again.

Mark: But you've read that one before. It's too easy for you.

This pattern may relate to the tutor's perceptions about teaching. Little interaction occurred between reading partners when the second graders were able to read texts fluently. Tutors gave more verbal praise when their partners attempted to read more difficult texts even when the tutee's reading was considerably stilted. The fifth graders may have felt less involved when they merely listened to their partner's reading; they were reinforced in their tutorial role when they cued unknown words or provided other support to help the second graders make sense of texts. Or the fifth-grade tutors may have realized implicity that learning occurs when risks are taken and mistakes are made. But, for whatever reason, the fifth-grade tutors were able to nudge their partners to risk more challenging texts, something that probably would not have happened if the second graders had not viewed the tutor-tutee relationship as uncritical and supportive.

Supplying Unknown Words

The most common strategy used by the fifth-grade tutors to help their second-grade partners during their reading sessions was simply to supply unknown words. Tutors "gave" the word to the second graders when they requested it, after a brief pause by the tutee, or to correct a reading miscue. The following example illustrates the use of this strategy to support fluency. (Tutor-supplied words are shown in italics.)

> I'm Emily Elizabeth. This is my dog, Clifford. He is the only pet I ever had . . . except one time, *last* year. A kitten came to our house. I think he was lost. Mom said we could keep him until we found his *owners*. He was so small that Mom said he could sleep in my room. He slept in the basket Clifford had *used* for a bed *when* he was a puppy.

In another example, fifth-grader Amy supplies words (shown in parentheses) for second-grader Jason when he miscues (shown in italics):

> "What a good idea," said Toad. "*What* (Wait) right here, Frog. I will be back soon." Toad *wait* (went) to the store. He bought two big ice-cream [tutee paused] (cones). Toad *looked* (licked) one of the cones.

One explanation for the predominant use of the strategy of supplying unknown words is that tutors understood, implicitly, that the main goal of reading is to generate a comprehensible text. Equally important, "giving the word" didn't seem to discourage the second graders the way it often does when adults use this strategy. It may be that second graders, who interpret being given the word by adult as a correction, view the same strategy used by other children as encouragement. Of course, this level of trust can develop only if tutors are seen as generally supportive.

Offering Clues to Unknown Words

Another strategy frequently employed by the fifth-grade tutors was to provide clues—including graphemic, sound, picture, and meaning clues—when tutees indicated, either directly or by a pause, that they could not decode a word independently. In the following example Andrew uses questions to help Nicholas decode unknown words.

Nicholas (Tutee)	Andrew (Tutor)
[hesitates] MARTHA got dressed, then read the [hesitates]	What's her name?
	What's in the newspaper with Peanuts and Snoopy?
FUNNIES with daddy	
	[Andrew used his finger to cover "-til."]
UNTIL the bells began to ring. They started at exactly nine- thirty every Sunday_____	When you wake up, what time of day is it?
MORNING, and that meant that it was time to go to church.	

In another example fifth-grader Erica cues Emily by reading bits of text.

Emily (Tutee)	Erica (Tutor)
	THEN SHE MADE
one for Amy . . .	TWO
. . . for Amy . . .	What comes after two?
. . . three for Amy . . .	AND FOUR FOR AMY!

Erica encouraged Emily to begin by reading the first three words while using her finger to indicate the words. She then pointed to the word *one* and held up one finger. Emily recognized the pattern "one for Amy," but then she paused. Erica then supplied the word *two* while holding up two fingers, and Emily chimed in, "for Amy." Then Erica held up three fingers without saying anything, and Emily continued, "three for Amy." In this way Erica taught Emily to make use of both visual clues and pattern cues to make sense of text. Significantly, these cues supported Emily without taking control of the reading from her. By using clues Erica ensured that Emily was actively involved in making sense of the text.

The fifth-grade tutors also cued the second graders through the use of opposites ("What's the opposite of big?") and similes ("It's like _____."). At other times the tutors referred their partners to the same word already decoded on a previous page. Occasionally, they used actions to provide clues to the second graders. Sometimes they pointed to pictures in the text to draw tutees' attention to details that might be clues to unknown words. Like Land (1984) I found that our fifth-grade tutors modeled a variety of cuing systems. In the process tutors heightened their own various cuing systems, accounting for the often-reported finding that peer tutoring benefits both tutor and tutee.

"Chiming In"

Another strategy the fifth-grade tutors used to support the second graders was "chiming in" (also referred to as echo reading and assisted reading). Chiming occurs when experienced readers read a text aloud while less experienced readers join in reading those words or parts of the text that they can handle. The fifth graders varied their support according to the second graders' needs. The tutors lowered their voices, for example, when their less experienced partners were reading fluently and raised their voices when the second graders struggled. The fifth-grade tutors typically chimed in when their reading partners chose materials that were too difficult for independent reading, when they showed some fatigue, or when they had difficulty finding the rhythm in repetitive patterns, as in the following sample:

Rosanna: Then the gingerbread man called out, "Run, run as fast as you can.

Rosanna and Nicole: YOU CAN'T CATCH ME. I'M THE GINGER-BREAD MAN."

Although Rosanna read *The Gingerbread Man* fairly fluently, she had not picked up on the repetitive pattern in the Gingerbread Man's taunt. Nicole chimed in quietly, but with expression, to set the pace, making Rosanna aware of another cuing system, prosodic intonation. The next time that Rosanna encountered this pattern she was able to read it without Nicole's support.

Too often, emerging readers struggling with sections of text resort to a stumbling, choppy, word-by-word reading strategy, what Wardbaugh (1969) calls "barking at print." This slow, dysfluent reading hampers readers from making sense—which is, after all, their primary goal. By chiming in, the fifth-grade tutors offered support that enabled the second graders to keep their reading smooth and fluent and to focus on making sense.

Encouraging the Use of Phonetic Cues

The phonographemic relationship is another cuing system that readers use to make sense of texts. The fifth-grade tutors often pointed out phonographemic cues when their partners had difficulty decoding unfamiliar words, as in the following example:

Melissa (Tutee)	Daniela (Tutor)
He was a . . .	[Daniela used her finger to cover up "ful."] What does this say?
Play.	Yes. Now what does this part

	say? [covering "play" with finger]
Fel. No, fool.	Close. Now try to put them together.
Playfool . . . "playful little kitten."	
"He . . ."	What sound does the "ch" make?
Ch.	That's right. Now let's try this again. What did he do?
"He cha-sed butterflies."	
"He chased butterflies."	Good!

Although there were several examples of the use of phonographemic cues during peer reading sessions, tutors and tutees did not seem to overrely on this cuing system. They used several other reading strategies more frequently, such as tutors' supplying unknown words when the tutees hesitated. Clearly, however, the tutors themselves recognized the value of including both initial consonant cues and syllabification among their word-attack strategies.

Using Context Clues

Tutors also encouraged tutees to guess at unknown words, using the context of the sentence or paragraph preceding the unknown word, or to skip the unknown word and read on, perhaps coming back to the word after constructing more context. In the following example, second-grader Keith hesitated when he came to the word *shut*. His partner, Joe, encouraged him to read the rest of the sentence and then, through questioning, to guess at what the unknown word might be.

Keith (Tutee)	Joe (Tutor)
"Mr. Wong [pause] the drapes and turned off the lights so he could show the kids his new flashlight."	Keep going.
	Now what would he do to drapes to make the room dark?
Close them?	Right. Now what's another way to say close? [pointing to the word *shut* in the

Shut?

"Mr. Wong shut the drapes and turned off the lights so he could show the kids his new flashlight."

text] Right. Now read it again.

Good! Go on.

The need to preserve the meaning of the text seemed to determine whether readers returned to words missed or skipped over for a further attempt at decoding, or if they just continued reading. Tutors' not interrupting the reading process if the meaning was apparent suggests that they, too, were more interested in making sense than in word-perfect reading.

Retelling Stories

The fifth-grade tutors frequently asked their second-grade reading partners to retell part of a story during partner reading or the whole story subsequent to a reading. Apparently, the fifth graders used retellings during the story to check the second graders' comprehension of what they were reading and, if appropriate, to confirm their partner's comprehension of the text up to that point, as in the following example:

Vanessa (Tutee)

Kasia (Tutor)

What's happening so far in this story?

All his cheese is getting took by the other animals.

Why?

'Cause they want it.

Why did he make the cheese?

For the king's birthday.

Okay. Keep reading.

At other times tutors took advantage of these opportunities to correct what they saw as a misunderstanding. For example:

David (Tutee)

Diana (Tutor)

Okay David, what happened in the story so far?

The guy with the yellow hat told George he wanted to go out for pizza.

Yes. Then what happened?

Tony was making pizza, throwing it up in the air too, putting some cheese on it and put it into the

oven, and then Tony's wife called.	No, Tony's wife didn't call. The telephone rang and Tony's wife called Tony. A fellow from the factory wanted a large pizza delivered in a hurry. Right?
Right.	Okay, read on.

This example illustrates how tutors stressed understanding; they supported their partners in making sense, not just in getting the words. The fifth-grade tutors were engaged in a highly complex and multilayered comprehension task when they taught, and this may explain their own gains in reading scores, as mentioned earlier. For the tutees, the retelling provided guided support in story structure; for the tutors, retellings forced them to make explicit their own strategies about reading.

Predicting

The fifth-grade tutors often encouraged their reading partners to stop reading and predict what they thought was going to happen next. For example:

Kaylee (Tutee)	**Mary (Tutor)**
[reading the text] "It [a fish] looked at the worm on the pin. It wiggled its little tail. It looked at the worm again."	What do you think is going to happen now?
The little fish is going to bite the worm.	That's good. Keep going.

Kaylee's response to the tutor's request for her prediction seemed to make sense. Satisfied with the response, Mary praised Kaylee and told her to continue reading.

When the second graders' predictions did not make sense, tutors either discussed the previously read part of the text or encouraged the tutees to reread parts of the text. The prediction strategy also enabled tutors to confirm their partners' understanding of texts and, at the same time, reminded the second graders of the importance of making sense.

Interaction Around Miscues

Reading miscues during oral reading are unexpected responses to print; they may change, disrupt, or preserve the actual meaning of the written text (Goodman, Watson, and Burke 1987). I observed many miscues that significantly changed the meaning of the text. Although the fifth-grade tutors frequently corrected the second graders' miscues, they usually distinguished between miscues that changed the meaning of the text and miscues that did not. In general, if the second graders produced a miscue disrupting the meaning of the text, the fifth-grade tutors corrected it. For example:

Ashley (Tutee)	Francis (Tutor)
"When he took a *lift* turn and went the wrong way . . .	No, left.
Fear and *shook* made both of them holler . . ."	shock

If, however, miscues preserved the meaning of the text, the tutors tended to ignore them. In the following example Franco ignores some miscues and corrects others, but the miscues he chooses to ignore do not affect the meaning of the text.

Kristina (Tutee)	Comment
" 'Yes,' said the big, *bad wolf.*	Text: big, *old* wolf
'No,' said the woodman. 'I *can't* come in now. I have to	Text: I *cannot* . . .
I have to *go see* wood for your grandmother.'	Tutor: I have to get some . . .
He ran far, far away and *never* did see him again."	he ran far, far away, and they . . .

Tutors also modeled this same strategy of ignoring miscues that do not change meaning when they read to their partners, as in the following example:

Jacky (Tutor)	Comment
"He took a *large* blob of mashed potatoes . . . 'No, I	Text: *huge*
guess you can't,' *said* Mom . . . 'No, you *defetly*	Text: *sighed*
can't eat a bridge,' *said* Mom . . ."	Text: definitely
	Text: agreed

Consciously or unconsciously, the fifth-grade tutors used preservation of text meaning as a measure of reading accuracy and proficiency and were most likely to provide support to the second graders when they saw a threat to the making of meaning. It is also likely that the reluctance of the fifth graders to correct their partners' miscues not interfering with meaning contributed to the second graders' sense of accomplishment and self-esteem.

Benefits to Tutors and Tutees

For the students in our school it seems that the peer tutoring relationship is benefiting both the tutors and the tutees, even in those cases where the fifth-grader tutors were struggling readers themselves. For Paul, for example, a legally blind student, the experience of being a tutor helped him begin to see himself as a reader.

I also gained some insight into what there is about the peer tutoring relationship that facilitated students' literacy development. My analysis suggests that here were four general ways the fifth-grade tutors did this for their second-grade partners. First of all, the tutors used a broad range of strategies to support their partner's reading. These included providing unknown words or offering clues, chiming in, encouraging tutees to skip unknown words, demonstrating phonographemic clues, and so on. Significantly, tutors tended to draw tutees' attention to miscues only if they disrupted the meaning of the text. Tutors also used periodic comprehension checks both to assess their partners' comprehension and to keep the second graders' attention focused on making sense. Perhaps most important of all, tutors created a positive relationship and encouraging atmosphere through their support, focusing primarily on what the second graders were trying to do: make sense of texts. The feeling of accomplishment that comes from reading sensible texts may be especially motivating to tutees. That may account for the enhanced self-confidence of tutees observed by Topping (1987).

For their part, tutors engaged in a highly complex task in which they had to (a) maintain an awareness of previously read text on a textual, syntactic, and lexical level; (b) maintain a sense of when to give more or less support to their partners—when help should be supplying words or allowing them to be skipped; reading along; and sketching or emphasizing elements to highlight them; and (c) monitor the comprehensibility of the readers' production as well as the degree to which reader miscues preserved the text.

In the tutorial situation in which texts are generally more easy to read for the tutor, the tutor's awareness of text features may be heightened, since the situation demands this. Furthermore, the tutor must use the metaknowledge of the text to guide the reader. While reading practice occurs for the tutee and the tutor (Gillet and Temple 1986; Harste 1990; Smith 1989), the tutor is actually engaged in a much more complex task than reading because of the demands of metaknowledge of text in teaching.

The power of a whole language approach to literacy instruction is that it recognizes students' intentions, helping them to discover the power *of* reading and to realize power *from* reading. This is, perhaps, what the tutors did best. By supporting the second graders' intentions and not interfering with what they were trying to do—when the tutors ignored, for example, miscues not affecting the meaning of the text—they helped their reading partners discover and realize the power of reading. And the second graders learned what reading could mean to them, apart from pleasing adults.

For the fifth graders the tutoring relationship helped them to discover the power of teaching while affirming their knowledge and reinforcing their confidence as readers. But the power enjoyed by the fifth graders was not at the expense of their reading partners. Both reading partners were empowered by their supportive relationship, demonstrating that ownership does not have to mean giving up power to someone else. Here power is not about control. Reading with friends means getting the support needed to access the power of literacy. Everybody wins, and no one has to lose.

This all began with the willingness of a group of teachers to share their responsibility for teaching with a group of fifth-grade students. It would be tempting to conclude that these teachers gave up some of their control over their reading programs, but this would be misleading. Presumably, their goal is to teach reading, and the peer tutoring program made them more effective, more powerful teachers. Again, everybody wins because the power to teach and learn was not simply shared. Teachers and students working together made each other more powerful because each supported what the other was trying to do—make sense.

References

DiSibio, R.A., and Parla, J. 1985. *Expand children's limits in reading, integrate REAP: Reading experiences associated with reading partners.* New York: New York State Reading Conference. (ERIC Document Reproduction Service No. ED 268 479)

Gillet, J.W., and Temple, C. 1986. *Understanding reading problems.* Toronto: Little, Brown.

Goodlad, S., and Hirst, B. 1989. *Peer tutoring: A guide to learning and teaching.* London: Kogan Page.

Goodman, Y.M., Watson, D.J., and Burke, C.L. 1987. *Reading miscue inventory: Alternative procedures.* New York: Richard C. Owen.

Hall, J.E. 1983. *Cross-peer tutoring for special reading and ESL students.* California Association for Teachers of English to Speakers of Other Languages. (ERIC Document Reproduction Service No. ED 263 766)

Harste, J. 1990. Jerry Harste speaks on reading and writing. *The Reading Teacher* 43: 316–18.

Joffin, B. 1988. A qualitative study of the mutual benefits for tutors and tutees in a cross-age tutoring programme in reading. Unpublished master's thesis, York University, Toronto, Canada.

Land, A., 1984. *Peer tutoring: Student achievement and self-concept as reviewed in selected literature.* New Orleans: Mid-South Educational Research Association.

Smith, C.B. 1989. Reading aloud: An experience of sharing. *The Reading Teacher* 42: 320.

Topping, K., ed. 1984. *National paired reading conference, 1st Bulletin.* Dewbury, England. (ERIC Document Reproduction Service No. ED 284 124)

————. 1987. *National paired reading conference, 4th Bulletin.* Dewbury, England. (ERIC Document Reproduction Service No. ED 298 429)

Wardbaugh, R. 1969. *Reading: A linguistic perspective.* New York: Harcourt.

Winter, S. 1986. Peers as paired reading tutors. *British Journal of Special Education* 13: 103–6.

5

Self-Reflection: Supporting Students in Taking Ownership of Evaluation

Cheryl K. Ames and
Hilary Sumner Gahagan
Beaverton Public Schools

The resource room teacher listened to the tall, dark-haired tenth-grade boy read in a muffled voice that none of his peers could hear. Reading aloud obviously was not his favorite activity, although it was necessary for providing clues about his reading strategies. Even though this boy was labeled learning disabled, his teacher was heartened by the evidence of effective strategies—using the context to figure out unknown words, rereading when there were comprehension breakdowns, phrasing and intonation that made the language sound natural. In addition, the reading was fluent in this sixth-grade level selection; the teacher barely had enough miscues to evaluate. Clearly, this young man could have read an even more difficult story.

The teacher was eager to ask the interview questions: Did he read at home? What did he read? What strategies did he use when he met unknown words or when he didn't understand what he was reading? Was he a good reader? Why? His answers were surprising. Not only did he say that he did not like to read anything, but he also felt that he was not a good reader. He said that he made too many mistakes and that his reading did not "sound good."

Unfortunately, this was not an isolated case. Most of the other students that the teacher evaluated, identified for a high school reading development class, had many strengths as readers, demonstrated by their oral reading and retellings of the content during reading miscue inventories. But, in spite of

52

their strengths, only one of them reported liking to read, and none of them could identify anything positive about themselves as readers.

What shaped these students' beliefs about themselves? Probably a variety of school experiences contributed to their definitions of themselves as readers, including evaluation experiences. Like most students, they had taken yearly achievement tests that spread their performance in a variety of academic areas over the bell-shaped curve; and, as lower achieving students, they had experienced item after item for which they did not know the answer. If they were in classrooms that used traditional evaluation procedures, these students experienced published or teacher-made tests for which they, again, failed on numerous items. After several years of not performing well on a variety of measures selected by the state, district, and teacher, these students began to view themselves as poor learners, weak students, and "bad readers." As Chapter I and special education students, they had experienced a variety of additional evaluations that defined them as having deficits: a student who has a learning disability, a student who needs special reading services, a student with weaknesses to be remediated.

We believe that most evaluation of students in schools is owned by the wrong people—the school, the school district, the state. Obviously, a major purpose of evaluation is to inform the decision-making process of teachers as they plan instructional activities that match the specific needs and interests of their students. Evaluation clearly belongs to teachers, a major stakeholder.

But what about the students? Perhaps if students became owners of evaluation, they might become more aware of their strengths as learners and of their growth over time, producing healthy, positive self-concepts for achieving their maximum potentials.

Reflective evaluation offers teachers a way to support students in taking ownership of evaluation (Paulson, Paulson, and Meyer 1991). This chapter will describe practices that support self-reflection by students as they evaluate themselves as readers and writers.

What Is Reflective Evaluation?

Many educators are turning away from a limited, skills-based view of reading and writing instruction in favor of a view that is holistic and constructivist ist in nature. Students in holistic, constructivist classrooms actively participate in reading and writing by making their own choices about what they read and write. They become authors, they discuss the craft of "real" authors, and they participate in activities that involve the creating of and responding to "whole" texts (Routman 1991). Traditional evaluation procedures do not match these activities. Reflective evaluation offers a way for students to take ownership of the evaluation process actively rather than passively. Through reflective evaluation processes, students develop evaluation criteria, become aware of their present levels of functioning, and learn to establish goals for their development. Learning what constitutes good reading and writing, they evaluate their own efforts as they develop as readers and writers. Just as all children are expected to become proficient talkers when they are young, students who become self-evaluators *expect* that they will grow as readers and writers; and they will understand and value the signs of their development.

Not a static act, self-reflection is a continuous process at both the conscious and unconscious levels. Just as learning occurs at all times, not just when a student is instructed, so reflection occurs. We are constantly making choices, decisions, and judgments in our lives. As we move to more student-centered classrooms, we can best nurture our students' literacy growth and self-concepts by building on their innate capacity for reflection. By our guiding and encouraging their self-analysis, while providing models to strive for, we give them the freedom and incentive to understand, monitor, and set goals for their own growth (Cousin 1990).

Is Self-Reflection Possible for All Students?

Anyone who has worked with children over time knows that even young children have a remarkable capacity for learning and introspection, particularly if they are in environments supportive of critical thinking. The written reflection of Sarah (Figure 5–1) demonstrates the reflective evaluation of an average-achieving fifth grader describing why she believes that she is a good reader: "I'm a good reader because I notice things. I notice foreshadowing

Figure 5–1   An average-achieving fifth grader evaluates herself as a reader

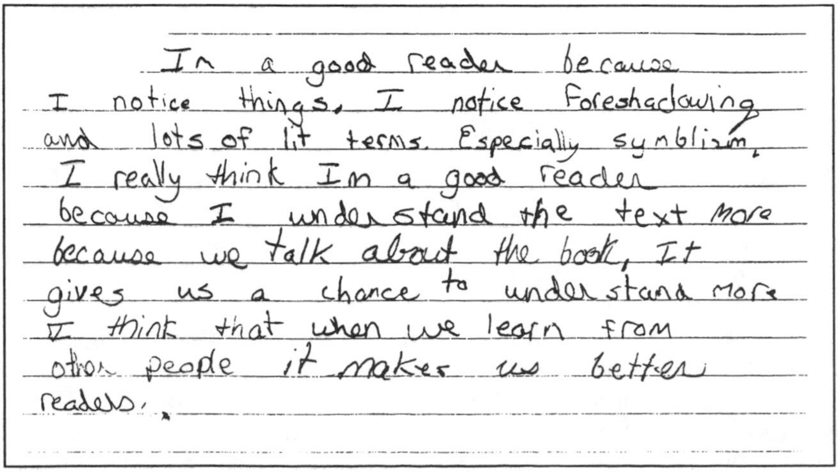

I'm a good reader because I notice things. I notice Foreshadowing and lots of lit terms. Especially symbolism. I really think I'm a good reader because I understand the text more because we talk about the book, It gives us a chance to understand more. I think that when we learn from other people it makes us better readers.

and lots of lit. [literature] terms, especially symbolism. I really think I'm a good reader because I understand the text more because we talk about the book. It gives us a chance to understand more. I think that when we learn from other people it makes us better readers.'' (The writing of this student and most others in this chapter has been edited to assist the reader. The language, however, has not been changed.)

But what about students who have difficulty learning in school? Is self-evaluation possible for them? Our experience with our own students who are labeled learning disabled or who have other mild handicaps indicates that not only can these students effectively learn to self-reflect, but that the experience is beneficial in developing more positive self-concepts as well. A sixth grader identified as mildly mentally retarded demonstrated his ability to write an evaluation of his reading strategies (Figure 5–2): ''I read properly. I think about the book that I read. I read smoothly. I say blank. Then I come back to the word and patch if you make a mistake. I don't sound like a machine gun.''

A second grader identified as learning disabled wrote about her strategies in self-correcting miscues that do not make sense and dealing with unknown words: ''Well, I patch up a word. I skip a word.'' In addition, her writing showed her developing knowledge of authors and how they write books: ''A good reader writes, too, and like Robert Munch. He is a very good drawer and he writes about his kids and probably his kids like his books'' (Figure 5–3).

In response to the question ''How have you grown as a reader this past year?'' a fifth grader in a learning disabilities classroom wrote about his change in attitude toward reading: ''Last year I hated books because I thought they were boring because the teacher picked them out because the books she got for me were boring to me but when I picked out my own stuff,

Figure 5–2 A self-evaluation by a mildly retarded sixth grader

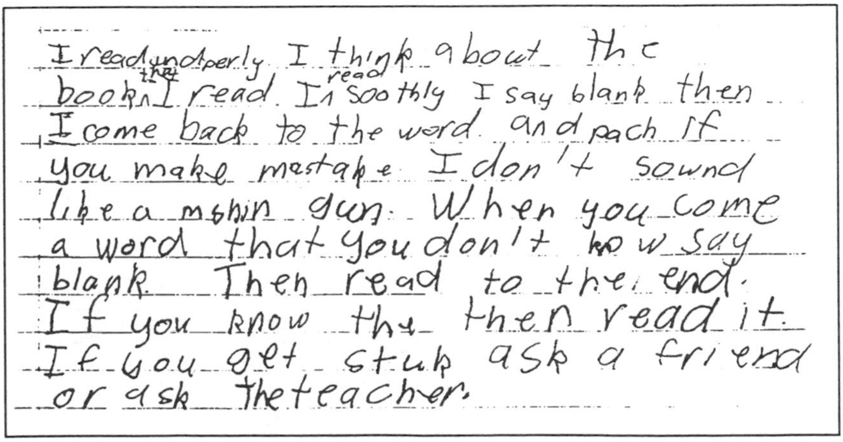
I read undperly. I think about the
book the I read. I read soothly I say blank then
I come back to the word and pach If
you make mestake I don't sownd
like a mshin gun. When you come
a word that you don't kow say
blank Then read to the end.
If you know the then read it
If you get stuk ask a friend
or ask theteacher.

Figure 5–3 A self-evaluation by a learning disabled second grader

> April 15, 1991
> What I do as a good readder
> will I patch up a wrd I scip a
> word and good readder
> rit to and like Rôbert Munsch he
> is a vere good drwer and
> he rits a buwt his
> kids and probble his kids likes his book.

I was a lot happier because you have to find your own pleasure of books, not someone else's'' (Figure 5–4).

Clearly, in our own experience and the experience of other teachers, students with learning difficulties can learn to self-reflect about their reading and writing. Although reflective evaluation is a complex task involving metacognitive skills, teachers can create the environment and instructional activities that support all students to participate in, and benefit from, reflective evaluation.

Figure 5–4 A self-evaluation by a learning disabled fifth grader

> Last year I hated books because
> I thot they where boring becaue
> the teacher picked them out
> becaus the books she got for me
> where boing to me but when
> I picked out my own stuff
> I ease a lot happer becaue
> you have to find your own
> pleaser of booke not some
> ones elees

Teaching Students to Reflect on
Their Reading and Writing

A number of conditions seem to support students' ability, willingness, and confidence in reflective evaluation:

- In classrooms where students have taken ownership of evaluation, reading and writing are treated as processes of constructing meaning, not as an accumulation of long sequences of isolated skills. Students read real books—literature by real authors—not poorly written basals or remedial materials. They respond to their books in holistic, authentic ways: discussion, writing, drama, or occasional projects that they choose themselves and that have an audience besides the teacher. Their reading experiences support the development of efficient strategies for constructing meaning. They participate in writing workshops in which writing is viewed as a process involving prewriting, drafting, revising, editing, and publishing. They become authors and share their writings with others. They write to learn more about the craft of writing, and they write to understand what they are learning in math, science, and social studies.

- Reflective evaluation is a part of each day, not only through the formal process of writing but also through discussions and conferences with the teacher. Students participate in one-to-one and small-group conferences with the teacher and with their peers to respond to, and evaluate, their reading and writing. They are encouraged to think, talk, and write about what they do. Reflective evaluation is an integral part of teaching and learning.

- Reflective evaluation is demonstrated by many people in the classroom—by teachers as they "think out loud" about their own reading and writing experiences, and by other students as they share their self-evaluations. Teachers understand that students need many demonstrations of how they are to think and what they are to do if they are to become effective with reflective evaluation. Participating with students in reflective thinking, teachers share their own written self-evaluations.

- Reflection takes many forms, not just self-reflecting about learning. Readers make predictions about the content of a book, wonder what will happen next in a story, think about the author's message, and examine literacy devices such as foreshadowing and tension. Writers reflect on their own experiences to choose a topic, think about leads that will "grab" their readers, decide if their audience will understand their message, and provide feedback to their peers' writing. Thinking at higher levels is routine.

- The classroom climate encourages students to take risks. Students are supported in extending themselves just beyond what they can comfortably do and know that their teacher will provide the scaffolds they need. Students trust the teacher to view their "mistakes" as signs of learning, as approximations toward a goal. They know that they are all valued as learners and that the teacher believes they will demonstrate growth.

- The teacher understands that self-reflection will take time to develop and that students' attempts will gradually grow richer and more meaningful. The teacher knows that some students may take a long time to learn to reflect in depth but that it will be worth the effort.

Carefully thinking about the above conditions can provide clues for supporting students who have difficulty with reflective evaluation. Chris, a sixth grader, wrote: "I'm an OK reader. I have lots of problems with reading." Although he was in a very supportive classroom, Chris had never before written about himself as a reader. During a reading conference he began to describe himself differently: "If I get stuck, I reread the whole sentence, or the whole paragraph. I pick the hardest book I can actually read. It's not really a challenge to pick the easiest book. I can become a better reader if I pick a harder book." Chris simply needed some dialogue to help him focus on his strengths, and a chance to talk before writing. Later he was able to write about his strengths.

Jennifer was asked if she was a good reader and to justify her opinion. She wrote: "Yes, because I can pronounce words better than most kids. I read loud and not too fast." Her teacher was discouraged because of Jennifer's focus on sounding like a good reader rather than on reading as a process to construct meaning. After some class discussions about what an efficient reader does, Jennifer's responses focused on her developing knowledge of how authors construct stories and what she was understanding about an author's craft. This student was developing an understanding of what was important about the reading process and how she had personally grown as a reader.

Scaffolds for Written Reflections

Open-ended questioning is a powerful tool for reflective evaluation. Appropriate questions help students focus on a single aspect of reading or writing and provide a catalyst to begin reflective thinking. Questions that encourage reflective evaluation of reading abilities include the following:

- What strategies do you use when you read? How do these strategies help you?

- How have you grown as a reader since the beginning of the year?

- What are your goals as a reader? How can you reach them?

- In what kinds of books do you read best? Why?
- What kinds of books are hardest? What do you do when you get stuck in these books?
- What could your teacher do to support your growth as a reader?
- What happens in school that does not help you read well?
- How do you feel about yourself as a reader? Why?

Students can also be engaged in evaluating their responses to reading. Following are several open-ended questions that encourage self-evaluation of personal responses or projects.

- Why did you choose this project?
- What does it show about what you understood (or what you felt was important)?
- Who is the audience for your project (or drama)? Why? What will they learn about the book?
- How does the project show what you have learned?
- Does the project show how the book affected you? Why or why not?

Open-ended questions that support young writers frequently are related to the stage of the writing process that the student is engaged in.

- Where are you at with your writing right now? Where do you need to go?
- Why did you pick this topic for this piece of writing?
- How is it going with this draft?
- If you could work on this further, what would you do?
- What reactions did you get from your partner? What do you think about those comments?

Other questions might encourage students to reflect about a finished piece chosen for their portfolios.

- What makes this writing special?
- Why did you choose it for your portfolio?
- What does this show about you as a writer?
- What do you see as the strengths of this piece?
- What did you wrestle with? How did you solve your problem?

Written reflections can take many forms, depending on the amount of scaffolding, or support, needed by the students to engage in reflective evaluation. Open-ended evaluation forms, like the samples in Figure 5–5, allow

Figure 5–5   Samples of open-ended evaluation forms

BOOK DISCUSSION

Name _____ Date _____

1. Did you participate in the discussion equally to others in the group?

      About the right amount   *Too much*

      Not at all   *Too little*

2. What was the most important contribution that you made to the discussion?

3. Why do you think it is important?

4. What other person expressed a very important idea?

5. What did this person say?

---

both students and teachers to reflect on students' reading experiences (Rhodes 1993). They provide some structure to the evaluation activity but still offer more possibilities for reflection than do checklists or evaluations that ask students only to circle responses. For example, the "Book Choice" form asks students to rate their books (easy, medium, hard), but it also asks students to justify their ratings. The "why" questions are very important. It is this justification that helps students understand what they have learned and how they are developing.

One very important focus for readers, especially for those whose reading has not developed easily, is to become aware of their progress in using the strategies that "good readers" use (for example, predicting the content, inserting substitutions for unknown words or skipping them, rereading when

Figure 5–5 (*cont.*) Samples of open-ended evalution forms

BOOK CHOICE

Name _____ Date _____

Title of book _____   _____

1. Is this a good book for me?

       Yes   *Sort of*   *No*

2. Why?

3. Is this book:

      Easy   *Medium*   *A challenge*

4. Why?

they don't understand, self-correcting miscues that do not make sense, and so on). Many teachers provide meaning-based feedback to their students' oral reading miscues. This helps students to understand their strengths as readers while they also develop new strategies for their repertoires. Students also might keep lists of efficient strategies, and prior to reading a text, they could discuss which ones might support them in constructing meaning. But if frequent self-evaluation of their own reading strategies is added to the students' experiences, their progress is likely to be enhanced. Evaluation forms like the one in Figure 5–6 can provide one way to help students evaluate themselves, particularly if they can discuss the results with a teacher or a small group of peers.

Figure 5–6   Student evaluation form for reading strategies

READING STRATEGIES

Name _____ Date _____ Book _____

1. What strategies did you use today to read words that you did not know?

2. How well did those strategies work?

3. Give one example of how you figured out a word you did not know. Be specific so that someone else could learn how to use your strategy.

Young writers might clip a note card or attach large stick-on notes to their writings and respond to open-ended questions (Figure 5–7). Structured reflection sheets (Figure 5–8) could focus students on different stages of the writing process. For reluctant writers, clip-on starter reflections, such as these, are helpful:

- This is best because. . . .
- This shows that I can. . . .
- I struggled with this because. . . .
- I am getting better at. . . .
- I chose this piece for my portfolio because. . . .

Figure 5–7 One student's response to an open-ended question

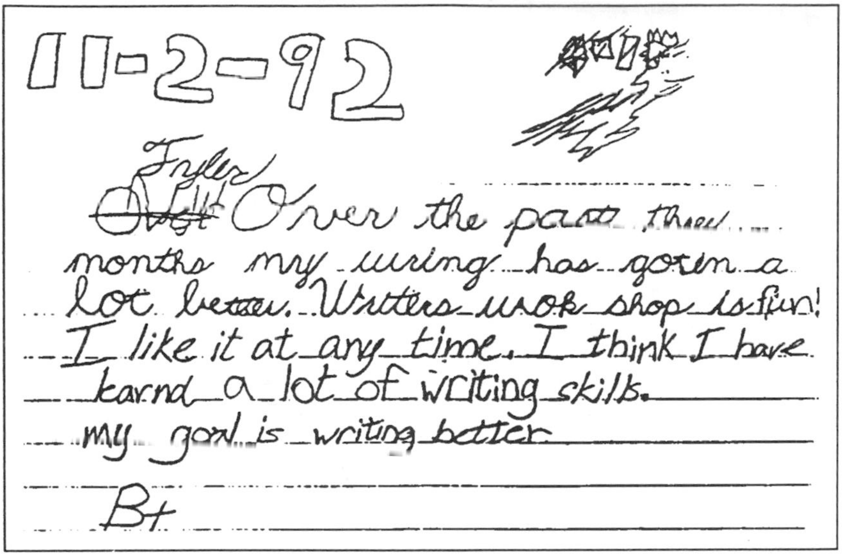
11-2-92

Tyler

~~Ovr~~ Over the past three months my wring has gotin a lot better. Writers wrok shop is fun! I like it at any time. I think I have larnd a lot of writing skills. my gol is writing better

B+

A teacher might want to start the students out with lead-ins like these until they become used to writing reflections. Students for whom writing is not yet a natural mode of expression could dictate their self-evaluations to an adult, but the more freedom and self-direction the students have, the richer their reflections become.

Journals, "reading logs," and written reflections attached to students' writing provide the most open-ended self-evaluation activities. While more structured formats may be necessary at earlier stages of development, open-ended writing provides no constraints and allows students to express ideas in their own words. The nature of writing, a kinesthetic process involving the conscious selection of words, may also be a powerful tool in supporting students as they think about their strengths and redefine themselves as effective readers and writers rather than as school failures.

The physical format of reflective evaluation may not be as important as the timeliness, particularly as students begin to participate in reflective evaluation. The sooner students can reflect, the better. They will be more in touch with their achievements and their needs if they reflect promptly than if they wait. In addition, their passion for a project and the effort they expended can soon be forgotten or at least lose momentum. After frequent opportunities to participate in reflective evaluation soon after their reading and writing, students will be able to try evaluations of their progress over time (for example, "how I have grown as a reader or writer").

Figure 5–8   Reflection sheet with a lead-in starter

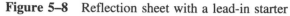

> ## Reflecting on Writing
>
> Name: __J_____ Date: _____
> Title of Writing: __Heroes_____
>
> I chose this piece for my Portfolio
> because_____It shows how
> ____good Igv yot'n in take-
> ____ing Vags out of
> ____books and buting them 'hmy one
> This shows that my writing strengths Sates.
> are__Puting more defa!___
> ____in my sterys hell
>
> _____
>
> If I wanted to revise this piece I
> would work on__Puting more__
> ____bereas
>
> _____
>
> As I wrote this, I worked hard on__my
> ____Calseve

Just as students vary tremendously in other areas of development, we have found that they develop differently in self-evaluation. Students' self-evaluations mature over time, and their comments change in several ways. At first their responses are sometimes primitive or fairly unsophisticated: "I like it." "I read good." As they develop trust, confidence, and skill, the number of their comments increases, and they are less dependent on what they think is the "right answer". In time they focus more specifically on reading and writing growth rather than on the nebulous "I'm getting better" responses. Reflection becomes more focused on personal and classroom standards. As students begin to compare their new learnings to their own previous work, and notice their successes, they more aptly express their progress.

Reflective Evaluation—Worth the Effort

Supporting students in taking ownership of self-evaluation of their own reading and writing is not a simple process. Is it worth the effort? Many students have a difficult time with reflective evaluation; this may be from inexperience, misunderstanding of what is asked of them, a lack of trust, or school experiences that discourage critical thinking. But to those who have observed growth in students encouraged to self-reflect, one thing seems clear: Reflective evaluation *is* a valuable investment. It augments the learning process, supporting students in becoming the most effective, thoughtful, strategic readers and writers they can be. And, above all, when students take ownership of evaluation, they learn to understand their strengths, recognize their growth, and ultimately value themselves and their learning (Goodman, 1986).

One student identified as learning disabled wrote a self-evaluation to advocate that he be totally mainstreamed: "I tried to catch up with my grade [in reading level] but instead I got ahead of my grade. I read fast and slow to get the whole meaning. . . ." (Figure 5–9). It is his first two statements,

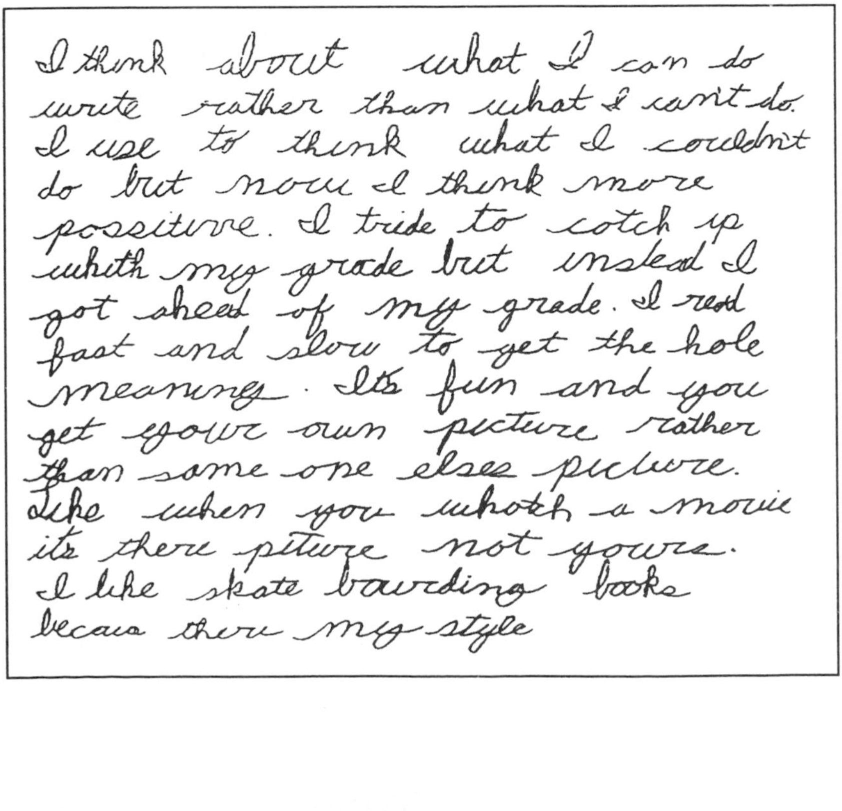

Figure 5–9   A self-evaluation, requesting mainstreaming, by a learning disabled student

however, that simply but eloquently demonstrate how he has redefined himself: "I think about what I can do right rather than what I can't do. I used to think what I couldn't do but now I think more positive."

In order to teach our students to self-reflect, we need to rethink our roles as teachers and the traditional way we have viewed the language arts. We need to become facilitators and "nudgers" who provide models of positive, constructive feedback. We need to provide the environment for exploration, risk-taking, and peer interaction. We need to honor the individual differences of our students, while at the same time creating high standards with them and striving for continuous growth. We need to provide meaningful, relevant, and interesting classrooms founded on authentic, student-centered evaluation. And we need to provide opportunities for our students to take *ownership* of evaluation. Maybe then we will have fewer students who say they are not good readers and writers and instead say: "I think about what I can do right rather than what I can't do. . . . I think more positive."

References

Cousin, P. 1990. The role of reflection and self-evaluation in the learning process: Implications for classroom practice. In *Claremont Reading Conference: Fifty-Fourth Yearbook,* edited by P. Dryer and M. Poplin. Claremont, Calif.: Claremont Graduate School.

Goodman, K. 1986. *What's whole in whole language?* Portsmouth, N.H.: Heinemann.

Paulson, P., Paulson, L., and Meyer, C. 1991. What makes a portfolio a portfolio? *Educational Leadership* 48(5): 60–63.

Rhodes, L. 1993. *Literacy assessment: A handbook of instruments.* Portsmouth, N.H.: Heinemann.

Routman, R. 1991. *Invitations: Changing as teachers and learners K–12.* Portsmouth, N.H.: Heinemann.

6

Integrating Social Studies and Whole Language in a Middle School: Finding a Core in Chore

Mary Burke-Hengen
Beaumont Middle School

When I began to teach at Beaumont Middle School a number of years ago, I was often baffled by the range of abilities and physical, social, emotional, and intellectual development in my classroom. Like many of my colleagues, I was, and am, committed to the concept of random grouping, sort of a pot-luck theory of educational nutrition. I remain committed to the following ideas: (1) we all need and want to be active, fully involved, and respected—in short, successful; and (2) the primary task of education is to produce a literate population who can think, read, speak, and write with intelligence and feeling on a variety of common concerns. No small tasks I have set for myself, but I do not feel alone in them nor more than occasionally discouraged.

The work of Sylvia Ashton-Warner described in *Teacher* (1971) has been and remains a powerful influence for me even though I have never met her or worked with her. She is a symbol of the need to teach children rather than curriculum. In her work with Maori children in New Zealand, she developed what she called the "organic" technique in which she used the words of the children to teach them how to read.

Shared goals are important, yes. A sense of what a literate person in any field should know and be able to do is also important. How teachers apply these ideas is the essence of the art of teaching: they must match, must find common points where the class intersects with the goals of the larger learning community and the society. To be successful, they must reason long and hard, and must, I think, be willing to take some risks and to present themselves as fallible.

Ken Macrorie's *20 Teachers* (1984) was another work marking great change for me. The teachers that Macrorie interviewed and wrote about were enablers; they shared an idea of themselves as fellow learners. They are people who do not view themselves as authorities either on a subject or over other people. They felt that they owed their successes in education to providing their students with models of good learning and encouragement. This was a new concept of educational leadership for me but one I gradually sought to apply to my classroom. I spent many years trying to be an expert teacher in language arts and social studies but was able to teach those subjects effectively only when I acknowledged some of my own ignorance and started working with students toward shared understandings of mutual concerns.

Donald Graves (1983, 1984, 1991), Lucy Calkins (1983, 1986), Nancie Atwell (1987, 1989), and Ruth Hubbard (1989) have also been major influences on my work, as they have been with so many practitioners across the U.S. and Canada. With Lucy I learned the value of taking intense interest in the work of one child as a way to understanding many children. A day with Donald Graves in which he participated fully in every assignment given to us—his students—challenged and changed my concept of the teacher-student relationship. Nancie Atwell taught me "The Dining Room Table" concept of reading discussion; I adapted her "Writing Skills Checklist" and use of student files, a process I continue to modify continually. From Ruth I have learned to appreciate the visual inner life of a child. She has also been for me a mentor who "nudges" me to set new writing and teaching challenges for myself and encourages and supports me to take continual risks in my teaching and professional life.

Besides teaching language arts, I teach social studies. As I have made changes in my language arts teaching, I have wondered: Could we apply our seemingly simple and hard-won language arts wisdom to the social studies? Is it possible that we can learn to be historians, geographers, sociologists, cultural anthropologists, and political scientists by practicing the tools of these professions? If we take the idea of a research focus from these disciplines and, like their practitioners, utilize primary source materials, data banks, collaboration, and interviewing as scholars do, I believe we can.

Recently, there has been a heightened interest in the curricular time arrangements of the middle school. Fueled by the ideas of those who study the development of young adolescents, many schools are moving toward creating an integrated curriculum in some kind of homeroom arrangement for middle schoolers. Teachers now conduct classes that combine social studies and language arts in these schools into a common block of time. Meanwhile, other schools are experimenting with a variety of combinations of subjects.

These blocks of time and subjects are often called "core," but what the word means in middle school has so far not been defined as a set of common learnings, experiences, or readings. In many schools it means simply having the same students for two or three periods and being free to do a long social studies project one day and then a long language arts project on a successive day. Or it may mean using the social studies lesson as that day's reading or writing lesson. To one of my students, the class was identified as "chore" on his papers through Halloween. He did not call the class "core" until he, along with myself and the other members of his class and their parents, had identified and begun to develop the core themes and concerns that would serve as our guide during the year.

Once we had a shared center, a core vision for our work together, we read, wrote, thought, talked, viewed, listened, and experienced with real purpose. Not only exercising skills, we were also embarking together on a quest for understanding of the things that concerned us. One of the ways I have come to know the shared center or core is the worry list.

The Worry List

In mid- to late-September here in Oregon, the rooms are often very, very warm. Students abandon their new corduroy pants and sweaters and resume the jeans, shorts, and T-shirts of summer. They come in reluctantly from the playground after lunch, and a few stragglers mumble an explanation as they take their seats during roll call. If I wish to activate angry feelings of injustice that will prolong the start of class for another short while, I can ask one of my students why he is late. Being "on show," the singled-out eighth grader will often do verbal protestations of "Why are you asking me? *They* were late! Why don't you ask them? Talk to Phillip and Susan." But I decide to bypass today's no-win situation and save it for later reference as to who's used up their one "free" tardy before being assigned after-school time. Funny, how eager they were to come in and be seated just two and three weeks ago; now they are challenging me to enforce the rules that say they must be here and on time. We are ready to begin our real work together.

After silent reading, I initiate a conversation. Sometimes I use ourselves as a point of reference to begin this discussion. Sometimes I use a book we have in common or a movie we've all seen, and sometimes I use pieces of the news about which we daily report and comment. I mention one or two of the concerns I have about the world around me, and I ask for their ideas. By this time we have a list of a few items, and the students have the idea. I begin to withdraw from their thoughts. If anyone still appears to have confusion about the idea, I ask them to think about what comes into their minds when they cannot sleep at night or when they are awakened during the night or early in the morning. Then I work on my own annual list while they make theirs. The room is very quiet for a while.

The first time I compiled a worry list with my students, it was an outgrowth of a project that was not working. I was trying to lead students into writing poems about the sounds around us, thinking they would comment on the calls of birds, the sound of the wind in a storm, the bark of a dog, and so forth. I had written such a poem while doing research and writing in a small community on the Olympic peninsula after being inspired by William Stafford's "The Animal That Drank Up Sound" (1964) and I read my poem and Stafford's to them. I hoped that the students would experience a similar feeling of inspiration and joy in their expression of familiar realities. Finally, after I had given several prompts about cicadas, grasshoppers, bees, and so forth, I suggested to the students that they think of times when they were lying in their beds at night before sleep or when they were awakened by sounds in the night. Responses were slow and needed several invitations. Finally, one student looked at me with understanding in his eyes. "Burglar alarms, that's what I hear in the night." He imitated the sounds of a few he had heard and discussed the finer points of length, double alarming (after would-be burglars think they have found the alarm and disengaged it, another separate alarm waits in a different locale of the vehicle or house), how long it usually takes for the alarm to be disengaged by its owner, and what ways alarms can be set off that have nothing to do with burglars. As an "Ode to the Burglar Alarm," he had the makings of a poem. I had an education on the realities of the lives of many of my students.

A few weeks later, after further discussions and writing starts, I took the students to the park to experience some of the natural sounds I'd hoped we could write about. Meanwhile, I had had a chance to look over the worry lists my students had compiled. I was surprised at many of the things they had to say. Death of parents and grandparents was a bigger worry for many of them than their own health and well-being. Social relationships at school and in the community were not rated as high or mentioned by as many students as were concerns over the environment, gangs, drugs, and racism. Lack of money was hardly mentioned. Physical size and beauty were low-frequency items. Few of the assumptions I'd held about the mental preoccupations of young adolescents proved to be true.

Here's a composite listing that contains most of the items listed that first "worry list" year:

- Depletion of natural resources
- Air and water pollution
- Gangs
- Grades
- Grandparents' health
- Destruction of rain forests
- Having enough money

- Crime
- Greenhouse effect
- War and lesser conflicts
- Too much homework
- Speaking in front of the class
- My (cat, dog, sister, brother, parents) dying

Teaching as a Meaningful Activity

Beginning to learn how to utilize those first student lists was a time of great change for me. It was a similar experience to moving from a skills orientation in reading and writing to a meaning-based program. I began to question still more of my assumptions about student learning. The existing social studies curriculum without modification was often removed from what my students thought about, worried about, cared about. I began to wonder about something I'd taken for granted: that adult perspective is wiser, more informed. We adults teaching now face different problems than today's students do. And, for the most part, the schools are designed around the concerns of the older age group. To whatever degree possible within my scope of choice in curriculum, I decided to respond meaningfully to students' perceptions of the problems we need to face. *Why not talk more about what's important to students?* I thought. *Why not discuss, debate, and engage in roleplays and mock trials some of the issues relating to gang membership, crime, and drugs? Why not read and write poetry and essays that are environmentally based, since this is an area of concern? Why not simulate problem-solving as often as possible instead of spending most of school time acquiring knowledge that has no context for change or for understanding what matters most to students?*

Other questions arose for me to try to answer: *What and who drives the curriculum? And why? If we think of schools as partnerships between students, parents, teachers, and communities, then why not involve students and their parents more actively in what is studied?* I decided to ask for parents' worry lists on Open House night. I wanted to find out if parents would echo some of the students or be supportive of more traditional concerns. It was also the first time I hadn't felt nervous about being on display while trying to rattle off a ten-minute compression of a nine-month curriculum. Parents became a vital source of information to me. We had some real work to do together that would serve their child's education and, I hoped, be interesting to them as well. Here's a composite of the results from the parents' lists that first year as I printed them in a quarterly letters to parents:

- *Drugs:* mentioned by almost everyone and listed as one of the first items on many lists

- *Gangs:* second most frequently mentioned and a high on the lists
- *Crime:* high on the lists, along with the erosion of moral values
- *Poverty:* frequently mentioned, along with the homeless, the national debt, and the growing disparity between rich and poor
- *The environment, depletion of natural resources, and overpopulation:* mentioned by many, though not as highly rated
- *War and world conflicts:* mentioned by many, sometimes with specific references as to place occurring

Also mentioned, though not with as high frequency: *Abortion, productivity, child care, literacy, drop-out rate, instant gratification, poor family life, irresponsible behavior, effect of TV, lack of national health program, divorce rate, noncaring people, terrorism, ethics of government officials, lack of moral values, materialism, apathy, noncaring teachers and parents, college costs, and, not to be neglected, backyard landscaping.*

The lists were not dissimilar to students', though the adult lists were longer, a little more detailed, and contained a few items more typical of their age group. The big categories, however, were much the same: crime, drug usage, racism, environmental issues, natural resource issues, health, national politics and direction, war, and conflict.

This year's lists differed somewhat in content focus, but a similar match between students and their parents is noted. Here's the composite picture of the concerns of both generations:

Crime

Gang violence

Loss of wildlife in the world

Destruction of the environment

Loss of ozone

Abandonment of our nation's cities

Racism, random violence, violence that is related to hate

Kids who are poor and hungry and have a hard time learning

Young people's lives/opportunities and risks facing them

How many kids will turn out well?

My own family's ability to take care of each other

Job performance, advancement, stresses, not enough time

Family finances, college tuition

Whether or not my son is actually learning to spell

Homeless people

More people starving

The plight of those who can't and won't fulfill themselves

Social injustice

What will the world be like when I retire?

Interest rates

Taxes

AIDS

People without health insurance

Illness

Drugs

Being out of control

Death

My parents

America at war

Political unrest

George Bush dying

Extremists: radical and conservative

Aphids eating my flowers

Kellie was especially thoughtful about her list. She took it home to think about and gave her items a numerical order. Here's her list of worries:

1. That a lot of people will die from hunger and that it will spread around the world
2. My grades
3. George Bush will die
4. How I look
5. How much time I have to do things
6. My cat
7. My friends
8. School
9. Speaking in front of the class
10. Money
11. Another war
12. More animals being hurt because of oil spills
13. Racism

Other students wrote quickly and directly. This is what Hasan had to say:

1. I worry about dying.
2. I worry about my mom.
3. I worry about making it in life.
4. I worry about having enough money.
5. I worry about Skinheads.

Although Hasan, at six feet, three inches, is one of the biggest middle schoolers I've ever taught, I think I understand his reasons for worrying about Skinheads. Even though there are just thirty registered Skinheads (a neo-Nazi racist group, something like junior White Supremacists, who in their milder forms, disseminate hate literature and, at their most active, go to any length to establish white dominance) in Portland, Hasan is African American; and this is the city where less than two years ago a young Ethiopian was beaten to death by members of a local Skinhead group. One of the young men tried and convicted of the murder sat in the classroom where Hasan now sits. His teacher, my predecessor, is an African American who, interestingly, reports no experiences of racial hatred or even dislike from the later-convicted racist murderer.

Hasan and Kellie both list many of the expected, ordinary (if you aren't the one experiencing them) life challenges that we all have to face. But, in addition, they have concerns typical to the place they live in and to the times they live in. *I no longer doubt that the world my students live in is as complex and puzzling as the world I inhabit.* And I don't doubt that young people are often confused by it and sorely in need of opportunites to try to make sense out of what seems nonsensical. Beyond listening and listing, what can we do to address their concerns and the curriculum?

Teachers as Learners

Teachers are learners with their students. No matter how many years we've gone to school, how many books we've read, or how much traveling we've done, as we face many of today's problems, we are in the position of being learners and problem solvers with our students. Sometimes students may even have a certain edge of openness to solutions that we might reject out of our past experiences. I reflect on this issue when I think of how long it has taken me to master basic computer technology. The differences between my approach to computers and that of many of my students is that they don't know the limitations of a typewriter. I limit the technology through the expectations I bring from my past experiences. Students do not. They want faster, more, and better technology. And so I decide: I want my teaching to be collaborative. I want to join with students in finding ways to understand, and have impact on, the things that matter most in our society. As shared learners we need to build many parts of the curriculum together.

A teacher's power to influence students has in the past relied on the natural authority of greater knowledge, but in today's world with its rapid changes in knowledge, we all learn many things together. In doing so, we have many natural opportunties to model the behaviors of a learner and to retain and expand our own enthusiasm for learning, The classroom can become a place where all are active learners who sense the importance of understanding themselves in the world. As teachers, if we help to activate student motivations, we stand a better chance of creating a society we all want to live in. Knowledge is power. If we act on our belief that students have a knowledge contribution to make, we share power, yes, and few attitudes are as inviting to calling forth a desire to learn more. As we use our shared powers to design solutions for real problems, we build a sense of belonging and community, further accentuating and encouraging the best that is in all of us.

The traditional curriculum—spelling, reading, writing, speaking, viewing, listening, and dramatizing in the language arts; critical thinking, history, cultural anthropology, political science (civics), and geography—is what we are using and doing on our way to understanding today's world. Whatever the students and teachers are thinking about, reading about, writing about, and speaking about is language practice and language skill development. Some of the curriculum presently prescribed at various grade levels is related to the difficulties that we find ourselves in as a society, but it is organized in ways that are seemingly for adult convenience: native study in the fifth grade, world cultures in the seventh, and so forth. I have wondered many times at this convenience aspect on warm, restless, or even resistive afternoons. *If it is necessary to apply manipulation or threats of poor grades, or worse, might it be wiser to teach a curriculum that can be shaped by those it serves and is timely and responsive to changes in the world and in our society?*

I believe that we can find the ways to dispel educational apathy. I believe that we can have an educational system geared to success both now and in a responsibly lived future. And I believe that to accomplish those goals we must be very active and responsible teachers. First, we must listen to the educational voices of those who went before us and those who are around us, as well as to the voices of change. We must continue basic teaching functions: to structure experiences in a way that enables students to acquire knowledge of the conventions of literacy and the understanding of our history and government. These things matter in the "real world" of which we are a part even as we are preparing for it. To do less, to abdicate our own intense involvement in student learning will limit the lives of those we hope to serve and will not end in our being more than temporarily popular with our students. Success as a teacher is measured by the achievement of long-term goals; and a great deal of tenacity, patience, a willingness to work hard, and an educational vision must match deep caring about the outcomes of our efforts.

As regards the structured following of a preset curriculum, however, I observe that when there is war in the Persian Gulf or government change in Eastern Europe or elsewhere, we respond to changed conditions: we try hard to provide accurate and up-to-date data. As teachers we are happy to put the regular studies aside and to learn more about what is immediately compelling and interesting; we are happy to change textbook information that is becoming inaccurate; we are happy to work with our students toward understanding changes in governments and escalations of conflicts. We may even arrive at improved definitions for conflict. What we seem to find hard to do is to study peace when it is a concern of the students. Or to explore the reasons for adolescent suicide, drug use, and gang membership. Or to look at the racism and sexism in our schools and communities. Or to think about ozone holes and depleting resources and rain forests and endangered species. *Why do we not prefer to study and learn about these things that affect us and to use the literatures and history of past times as guides to wisdom for today?*

Surely, it is not because we don't care or because we are unaware of the futures that may await us all if we don't solve some of the most glaring of the problems in our society. No, I don't think that many teachers are heartless or thoughtless about the seriousness of our options. Rather, I think that our smugness about our own learning may dictate a need for us to be in control of student information, and, therefore, student learning. In so doing, we may lose many possibilities for solving problems and for practicing problem-solving skills. Certainly, we miss opportunites for a relevant curriculum.

A Truly Integrated Curriculum

The single best choice we could make as teachers and curricular leaders is to mesh what we learn from students about their concerns and what we know about communication strategies and the research tools of the subject-matter scholar and forge them together. Would this ignore existing curriculum mandates? It need not. It simply uses student concerns in a problem-solving approach to define a core focus. Although thematic learning is a close description, it is important to note that the themes are student-chosen as well as adult-chosen. In the unity of child/parent/teacher/school/community lies the center we need to define our work.

As whole language teachers we encourage our students in finding books that they will want to read and in exploring topics of interest to them. *The idea of learning by doing while choosing topics of personal meaning is the same in the social studies.* Perhaps the fact that we have for so long divided the two subjects into separate disciplines has blinded some of us to this fact. Separating subject areas may be convenient, may even be desirable on occasion; but if we use them constantly, we lose compelling and intrinsic motivation for learning. That is costly and counterproductive. Why not divide the language arts and social studies curriculum in the way most of us think about it? I worry about the environment. Why not let me study it and teach it in that way? If we truly want to eliminate racism, why not learn about it both in a direct manner and as a reference point to history, geography, and cultural studies?

Here's an example of how racism as a topic of concern could be developed:

Individuals: Thinkers / Feelers
Journal: Write on Personal Experiences
Questions We Have Now / I Search Research
Survey / Interviews / Oral Histories: Family, School & Community
Class Readings of Short Stories / Novels / Poems / Plays / Essays / Documents
Films / Videotapes — **Readers Theater / Roleplays**
Debate / Staff or Gavel — **Literature Study Groups**
Art: Viewing / Making (**RACISM**) **Teacher Read Aloud**
Mock Trial / Convention — **Anti-bias Organization Speakers**
Field Trips — **Semantic Mapping / Brainstorming**
Writing Essays / Children's Books / Letters / Poems / Plays
Designing Our Utopias / Inventing Solutions
What We Think Now / What We Still Want to Know
Individuals: Doers / Agents of Change

Middle school is more than a hybrid between high school and elementary school. By integrating language arts and social studies, we do more than increase the possible connections to be made between past and present learnings. We open our minds to using and further developing literacy skills within a content base in the hope of finding solutions to societal and personal issues. We aim toward a goal of being educated people in a broad sense—education as change in our thinking and education as change in our behaviors. Literacy with a purpose is an apt description of this new curriculum. I would say that a whole language–social studies curriculum that has found its core is another way of saying that literacy is integrated with life.

In finding the core of our chore, we do not ignore the "content base" of social studies curriculum: the American history scope and sequence, the study of other cultures, the awareness of landforms and place and size, the understanding of government processes. Compared to developing a topic of interest in relative isolation, might it be easier to understand where the topic meshes with history, geography, government, and the study of other cultures if we use the curriculum as a reference point? How could one weave a new curriculum born of student/teacher interests and concerns and the scope and sequence? One way is to integrate prescribed content, strategy, and teacher/student focus:

RACISM IN AMERICAN HISTORY
Causes, Milestones, Solutions

Time	Topic	Techniques	Focus
Constitutional Era	3/5 compromise	Mock convention/ debate/writing questions/responses/ visual interpretation/ reading of documents and history books	Why 3/5? Who argued? Arguments? How country was divided Possible results
Jacksonian Era	Indian Removal Act of 1821	Reading documents/ role play/writing interior monologue	Point of View Use of language to slant meaning
Westward Migration	Who went west?	Reading biographies, textbooks, journals, documents, novels/ oral histories/constructing charts, maps, pictures/ writing poems, children's books	Diversity Who is remembered? Journal study Authoring

In looking at this chart neatly laid out, and remembering the confusion of days when we are on our assembly schedule with shortened class periods (sort of a Charlie Chaplin movie day speeding by like the silent films except that my classroom movie could hardly be called silent), I am reminded of one of my primary functions as a teacher: to remember the whole of our classwork, the reference points that explain and carry us from day to day and establish the why's of what we do together. Although I do not dictate the outcomes (the conclusions and understandings that may point to changed thinking and action), I do structure the time we will spend and some of the content we will use on a variety of experiences about our topic of study. I make choices where the outer curriculum (the mandated content) comes together with our inner definition of curriculum (the worry lists or personal concerns).

Another of my teacher functions is to remember which types of reading we have done and which types of writings we have concentrated on in the past, always aiming to extend our repertoire. Shared or whole-group activities offer a way for me to lead students in learning how to study primary source documents. Text rendering of a poem expands understanding of the poetic form, and so on. In much the same way, when I assign, or we come to a class agreement about, evaluation instruments, I can, for example, use that opportunity to teach the writing of an interior monologue. When we wrote children's books last year, I used Linda Christensen's (1991) idea about students charting stereotypes to design an activity to use as a culmination to our study of racism.

I started by bringing in a box of children's books. We enjoyed reading the books to each other and listening. We then discussed the books and examined them for bias. After that, students drew some illustrations to match a story I supplied in order to help build confidence in their drawing abilities, a confidence most of them sadly lacked. Then we began to talk about what they wanted to say in books of our own—whether we wanted to work alone, in pairs, or in a small group and whether we wanted to write a story or nonfiction. It wasn't until near the end of the unit that we knew what size we thought individual books should be, whether the book should be in color or black and white, how long the book should be, whether it was going to be typed or hand-lettered, and so forth. Early in our process I invited a local author of children's books to the class. What she did with the students was to lead them in self-discovery through "I remember" writings (free association or "dwelling for a while," describing a time or incident). The result of these activities were books with depth and real personal investment, in short: they were worth the efforts. On a long-term basis, most of these students on another occasion would have the skills and understanding necessary to determine whether they wanted to choose making a children's book as a way of expressing learning versus using another style or genre.

When we use another technique, small literature-study groups, as my class did last year in reading novels and histories about the westward movement, I trust students' abilities to make connections with prior learning and personal interests/concerns. I also sometimes choose to use these occasions as opportunities to move students along in their connection making: I "jump start" the process by formulating questions that focus our discussions and journal writings and that aid students in their understandings as critical thinkers, readers, and writers. By carefully choosing assignments and evaluation instruments, I influence particular outcomes. For example, I might ask students to choose one ethnic group or to describe the life of the women or children or teachers who went west, then to design a book for younger children explaining what they learned. It is going to become evident that a diverse population is responsible for the movement west. If I suggest further that we work in small groups or together to construct charts, maps, graphs, or other visual portrayals of the information on diversity, what is known becomes highly specific. If I bring in to the class diaries, biographies, and other personal accounts, we have a sense of what the lifestyles of people who migrated were like. Finally, if I have copies of documents from that time and place and a knowledge of their laws, we might narrow our focus to the legal racism of that time.

Literary Connections

One of the happiest links for me between language arts and social studies is the use of literary resources. It is hard to find, and to stay informed about, good literature for young adults; thus, if we hope to reach deeper understandings of life at other times or in other places, we need to think of text as any printed material. And we also need to see films made around books; their impact in the classroom goes beyond our words. The difficulties in making connections between social studies and what we have in the past thought of as literary sources can be easily solved if one has time to research them—and a strong desire to do so. The media specialist can help, and teachers can network information with each other. We can ask speakers and workshop presenters to address these issues. We can develop units in our teaching that are flexible and ever-changing. We can make friends with bookstore owners who carry children's and young adults' books. In a quite natural way, my reading patterns have been shaped by the kids I teach. They bring me books to read, tell me about books, and lead me to other books. We can thumb through old reading texts and anthologies for short reading pieces with an eye to the social studies curriculum instead of reading-skill development. We can divide up the work; we can get together with other teachers and media specialists and ask people to share what they learn.

There are literary pieces of singular power and eloquence that come to mind. The prologue to Julius Lester's *To Be a Slave* (1968) can help students understand slavery in ways that textbooks of facts are not designed to do. Knowing that Lester wrote a collective history of his people when he couldn't find the connections to his own personal history not only adds interest to the readings but also serves as a discussion focus for motivation and for helping to develop voice in writing. Sometimes, when I've used this piece in my social studies/language arts core class, the students and I haven't used assigned parts; whoever is moved to read, reads. The words tend to come out stronger, truer.

Another powerful piece is Frederick Douglass's *Narrative of the Life of Frederick Douglass* (1971). My favorite part to use in class is the chapter when young Douglass decides that he won't be beaten again. Sometimes I read it to students as a prelude to discussing with them the internalization of prejudice and oppression. Most students can well understand from this piece what it means to decide not to be oppressed—not to believe in your own inferiority, but to take a hold on the one life you have. *The Autobiography of Jane Pittman* by Ernest Gaines (1985) spans the Civil War to the 1960s in America; Katherine Paterson's *Lyddie* (1991) tells of work in the mills of Lowell, Massachusetts, and beginning unionization while telling an engaging story. How can we maximize that engagement?

Weaving the Connections

One of the most valuable things about writing is the opportunity it provides to tell the truth to oneself. Since our thoughts become written records rather than transitory images, we can go back to look at accumulated honesties. We are on record, and if we lie, we do so at personal cost. I will not lie here, for my journal is full of the frustrations I've felt in attempting to lead middle school students to "respond reflectively" to literature. It seems to come easier for most of them to reflect their thoughts about a film or about the ideas that come from small- and large-group class discussions. But on the occasions when I use my own writing, asking them for responses, or when I ask them to evaluate aspects of our shared classwork, I am reminded of how capable they are of reflections of deep insight and clarity. The following excerpt from Fred's journal comes after some months of responding to literature and to connecting it with our lives. As a prompt, he was asked to select lines that he thought were particularly significant and to tell how they relate to his own life. Here's Fred's entry on O'Dell's *Streams to the River, River to the Sea* (1986).

> "The travel was very cold and hard." "This journey is far too dangerous." The whole book was about Sacagawea's travel to the "Great Salt Lake." They all told her that it was too hard.
>
> Well, people are always telling me that things are too hard just because they don't want to do them. I just try to shrug them off, just like Sacagawea did. She just kept on pushing, even with a baby on her back.
>
> I think that I would have named the book *River Journey*. It better describes the plot of the book and what it is about. It also has a better ring to it.
>
> Overall, I liked this book. It was very descriptive and used actual language. The plot was real good, and I liked how Sacagawea at the end just left and went on with her life like nothing ever happened even when she loved Captain Clark.

Fred and five other classmates read *Streams to the River, River to the Sea* as part of our class study of westward expansion. They met with each other several times to discuss the book. Students could choose between this story, *Snowbird* by Patricia Calvert (1980), *Comstock Lode* by Louis L'Amour (1981), *Bury My Heart at Wounded Knee* by Dee Brown (1981), *When the Legends Die* by Hal Borland (1963), or *Creek Mary's Blood*, also by Dee Brown (1981). These books were suggested by students, myself, and somewhat limited by resources. Although I tried to meet with each group at least once, mostly they read on their own and set their own expectations of "what page to be on by when." One member in each group served as recorder and would write a report on the discussion. In this way I stayed involved with each group's progress and problems. We all decided on the completion date, and most students finished on time.

Fred is not an atypical pupil. He has his own reading preferences: fantasy involving the future and the past, mainly the Middle Ages, preferably written by Susan Cooper or Lloyd Alexander. He has loyalty. Once started, he reads a whole series of books. Yet, he participated actively in reading, discussing, and writing about *Streams to the River, River to the Sea*. His understanding of the part of history covered by his book choice has been deepened, as has his understanding of himself.

At the beginning of the year Aaron was slow to acquire a journal. When he did, he often wrote no more than a short paragraph. He prefers Civil War materials to any others and reads nonfiction more eagerly than fiction. When he chose *Bury My Heart at Wounded Knee* to read, I was glad to see him branch out from his usual interests. I didn't know how the book would work with my students, as I had a hard time myself sustaining the reading. But they had suggested it, and I was committed to giving it a chance. Here's Aaron's response to a prompt asking whether the events of the text could be rearranged and still tell the same story:

> *Bury My Heart at Wounded Knee* is about the Indian's point of view on the westward movement. It has no real order so it can be switched around in any way.
>
> It tells about Indians that fought the westward movement, helped the movement and even some that became workers.
>
> The white men were brutal at the time and I don't see how they got away with it so often. There was one time where a group of Indians went to a fort and became hired workers that hunted and sold the meat. They cut hay for the horses, and they did whatever people wanted them to. And in a town 50 miles away a man's horses were stolen. The whites believed that the peaceful Indians 50 miles away did it so they formed a party to go and kill them.
>
> Word got to the fort too late and only a few of the Indians survived. The case went all the way to the Supreme Court and the whites lied very badly. One went all the way and said that he followed the thieves to the civilized Indian's camp.

Nathan, a student who also read *Bury My Heart at Wounded Knee*, chose to write his summary without reference to a prompt that expanded his reactions and allowed him to set his own questions. Nathan says:

> The result of my reading *Bury My Heart at Wounded Knee* was that I began to question if any of us really deserves to be here, and if Portland should exist here at all. Then I tell myself that throughout history this has been happening, the conquerors taking over the land of the conquered. I shall feel sorry for those people who were here before us, for they were surely mistreated. I am almost ashamed of the way the greedy people of my heritage lied, cheated, and killed to fulfill the white dream of Manifest Destiny. We tricked these people into giving us their valuable land for next to nothing. When they wouldn't leave, we massacred them. To justify this, we called them "savages" in our papers. Since they didn't know our language, they had no means to defend themselves against these written attacks. We got what we wanted, but not honorably.

Dee Brown's book reads like fiction, and I wish it was. The Indians probably should have just killed the Pilgrims instead of inviting them to Thanksgiving dinner.

These responses, as well as those of their classmates, both delight and puzzle me. Often, I'm not confident about how I should respond. At one level, as a teacher, my assessment is that these students learned and demonstrated their understandings much more than satisfactorily. On another level, as a person trying to make meaning for myself and trying to enable others to do so as well, I want to ask questions that may expand thinking. I often end up underlining what we once called "main points" but that now I think of as "golden" or "memorable" lines. They are nubbins of understanding born of both thought and feeling. I am often affected by the beauty and clarity of student lines and remember them much later. Although they belong to the one who wrote them, in another sense they are part of our community. Put together artfully, they can make a poem or a summary statement of intense power.

Student responses sometimes dovetail in a way that helps me in developing thoughtful responses to their journal entries and summaries. In the two pieces on *Bury My Heart at Wounded Knee*, we can experience with both students the discomfort of the oppressor, but we can also see the different approaches in thought that they took and the somewhat different conclusions they came to. Aaron points out both the brutality of the whites and the complicity of some of the Indians. He expresses shock at the toleration of injustice and cites a memorable example. We can be with him at the fort and experience his outrage at greed and injustice. Nathan uses "we" rather than "the white men" and looks directly (and courageously) at the morality of what he has learned.

There are several avenues I could take in responding to these two. I could try to nudge Aaron to think more about who the "white men" are; I could encourage Nathan to examine more closely the role of Indian against Indian. I could try to send both of them back to the text for more specifics of who, when, and what as well as why. But in this case I did neither. Instead, I chose to respond with my own thoughts and feelings on the events themselves, on the book, and on the students' writings and, in both cases, ended with questions yet to be answered by any of us.

A Variation of the Worry List

The *worry list* is just one way to bring focus and meaning to an integrated core curriculum, whether it is used as an inner core to the circle or as a weft to the warp weaving outer curriculum and inner concerns. In using it as a strategy, I try to remember to emphasize random thoughts rather than the world as a fearful or evil place. "What do you think about when you sit still for a while, or when you can't go to sleep, or when you awake in the middle of night?" "How would you describe the worst thing(s) which could happen?" "If you were in charge of the world's resources of time and money, how would you like to see the time and money spent?" are some of the questions I use to jog their thinking.

Inviting the students to ask the questions they have is a variation of this strategy. Keeping some file cards or a small note pad handy all during the year helps us continually refine our questions. After a film, reading, or reporting of news, at the end of a grading period or phase of study, or at the beginning of a new course are all times to find out what students most want to know. Here are some samples of student questions at the beginning of the last school year.

Is school important?

Why do teachers give so much homework?

Are teachers important?

Does my teacher like me?

Why can't we check out more than one library book at a time?

Why can't we have pop in the a la carte line?

Will I make it through the eighth grade?

Is there a dance this Friday?

How do teachers decide on a grading system?

At first look, it seems that a duplicated letter from teacher to students could address most of the student concerns; however, with the questions up on the board or overhead and with discussion, the locus changes from teacher as information giver to teacher and students as information providers. And if other students have no information answers or opinions on the questions, you can table the discussion for another day and share responsibilities to find out some of the answers. Students may want to do a comparison study of grading systems and homework and a series of interviews. The worry about making it through the eighth grade suggests several possibilities: a short journal or learning log at some near future date on student expectations, a recounting of the skills and knowledge gained in the sixth and seventh grades, or an interview with an older sibling or neighbor who has graduated successfully. This last activity was much favored by one of my classes. After some gang violence in our area, students were very worried about the high schools they would be attending. In hearing firsthand from students attending those schools, they developed attitudes in which they could see themselves as comfortable and able to handle the situation.

Questions can be used as assessment tools and as aids to teacher planning. They inform the teacher as to what students want and need to know on a given topic. Waiting until after students have some information on a topic often helps them ask more specific questions. Here is an example of student questions on the War of 1812 after viewing an introductory film:

Did France declare war on us?

What started the war?

How did Tecumseh help with the war?

Why wouldn't Britain let the U.S. trade?

How did the war stuff all end?

Was the British population opposed to war?

Why were the British so cruel to us?

Who wrote the peace treaty?

How long did it last?

What did Napoleon do good for his country?

Did blacks fight in the War of 1812?

Who was the president at the time?

Why do countries always fight for land?

Although these questions are fairly specific, there is an underlying sense of larger issues evident. Why fight wars? What minorities were involved and how? Who was the aggressor? Who has responsibility?

A way to share information and develop questions while developing speaking skills is to set up a system in which only one person talks but potentially anyone else in the room could do so in turn. *Two vehicles for this strategy are the* speaker's staff *and the* gavel. The speaker's staff is used by a number of Native American groups to indicate leadership. In some groups all the leaders have a staff, and in still others, a sort of New England type town meeting is held to discuss issues of common concern, with the discussion being directed at the person with the staff. In a variation of both ideas, a student or I start a topic that we wish to discuss while holding a painted and carved stick. (We used to use the high-window opener until a student overheard me describing the speaker's staff. He said he thought he could make something like that. After I brought a book of designs and a pole, Brian and his grandfather made a beautiful painted and carved speaker's stick for the class.) Only the person with the stick can talk and only about the designated topic. And that includes the teacher. In the early stages some reminders of the "talk only with the stick" rule may need to be given. If students are familiar with the term *bailiff* from a mock trial, one can be appointed. Or a "sergeant-at-arms" can be named. Any penalties for breaking the "no talking without the stick or gavel" rule need to be mild and probably student-imposed in order to keep the focus on the topic and to encourage a desire for more discussion times. Reminders are almost always enough as students respond to the seriousness of interest in their thoughts on topics of some urgency to them. Topics range from school issues to national ones. Abortion, homosexuality, gangs, and the Los Angeles riots share talk space with school policies about dress codes and gum chewing.

If the class is initially reluctant to get up and take center stage, we stay seated and employ a pass-the-gavel method. The optimum room arrangement to support this method is to have the desks arranged in a *U* shape; one student stands and moves the gavel from person to person as each indicates a wish to speak. As with the talking stick, the topics are of broad range, involving historical and constitutional issues, current events, and personal concerns. These are special times for a class. Using listening and thinking skills, they express emotional and intellectual concerns in ways sometimes eloquent but always meaningful. When I am asked to judge and to evaluate student learning, I often think back to classroom discussions, to these times when, for many students, their oral expression outstrips their writing skills or motivations. To say that it is an opportunity to wed language arts and social studies does not do justice to the intensity of those occasions, but needs to be noted.

A more formal structure for thinking and discussing is the debate. An item of concern can be turned into a resolution, affirmative and negative sides chosen, and an amount of time for each person on the separate sides agreed to. Three minutes, two minutes, and one minute work well with my eighth graders. The resolution wording seems the hardest part. If an argument comes up (as it did recently in my class when one of the boys commented that he didn't think a woman could be president), a debatable resolution can be formulated, with a period of time given for formulating the arguments on each side. One to three days works well because the argument can be deferred that long and allows time for some clear thinking and research on the topic.

I found the most helpful background for teaching the concept of debate in the Colliers' book *My Brother Sam Is Dead* (1974). In this short novel about the Revolutionary War, two brothers are discussing the older brother's work in college on the debate team. The brothers discuss the scoring of debate and the need to establish "telling points." Using this explanation as a starting point, I tell the class about how to convince people through reason and fact versus emotion. Citing known examples, creating "what if" scenarios, and building a case through logic and evidence, I explain ways to make points. Then, when we have our debate, I model the awarding of points to each side until students internalize the process. Asking students to stand and place themselves on different sides of the room or to write briefly about the resolution before the debate with an accompanying follow-up experience enhances learnings from the experience. Further discussion about whether some changed their minds because of the debate—how they changed it, why they did, or why they didn't—aids in self-appraisal and self-understanding of how opinions are formed.

As the year goes on, "telling points" and the gavel come together in another activity involving the language arts and social studies. They are both used in a mock trial. For several years Judge Thomas Moultrie, who taught eighth grade himself a number of years ago, has come to our school to judge our cases. (Interestingly, in the early days of doing these cases, I told the students that I hoped we could have a "real" judge. Jason, a student in the class, said, "No problem. I'll find us one." Thinking he perhaps had a contact through one of his parents, I was surprised one day when he reported that a local judge who stars in a televison program about the law would be coming for the trial. Having seen Judge Moultrie on television, Jason had decided that he was the one we should have; he looked up the number and contacted him. The point of this story is, of course, that Jason was enabled to do this. Truthfully, I would have been shy to ask, but Jason was not; thus, we were all enriched.)

Starting with a scripted case we read in class together, we look at a variety of possible cases for which we will develop our own script. We sketch outlines of characters and situations, which we fill in as we prepare for the trial. A teacher or a group of students can write their own case from newspaper headlines or a historical situation. Parts must be sketched for those who will participate. Terms and concepts about trials need to reviewed and time and space provided for student legal teams to meet for preparation. Having a lawyer come in and talk about the rules of evidence is helpful, as is asking for a law student to come and to review the cases with each team a few days before the trial. Lastly, videotaping the event produces images that we can study and appreciate when the trial is over.

Roleplays, case studies, viewing and producing visuals, readers theater, primary source document study, journal/learning log writings, and responses are still other active strategies that core teachers can and do frequently use to implement an integrated curriculum. Planning, visualizing, producing, experiencing, doing, and evaluating are added to the traditional listening, viewing, reading, and writing as modes of learning. About writing, I will not say much here because it is so vast in scope. Writing as a character in history is a favorite of my students, and researching background for historical fiction writing is another. Reaction/response is vital to an integrated curriculum. "What do you know?" "What do you want to know?" "What did you learn? What questions do you still have?" These questions are addressed over and over in a seemingly endless variety of ways as the students and I plan, analyze, evaluate, and set new goals.

In an integrated curriculum, reading is much the same as writing. The ways of using it as strategy seem to increase geometrically as one idea for its use turns into several variations on the idea and so on. One of my favorite reading tools for novels and short stories is readers theatre, a technique expanded by Fran Tanner (1987) that omits "he said" and "she said," thus providing a more direct access to the feelings of the characters.

Where Are the Themes of Youth?

Sometimes, especially when student responses are not so beautiful, uplifting, eloquent, affirming, or even pleasant, I abruptly remember their ages. I think about their confusions, their angers, and their resentments, their occasional refusals to partake of any dialogue that might threaten self-image or the security of the status quo. I reflect on the strong needs for group approval that they bring to the classroom. I reflect on conflict, and that it is not just in the books we read together. It exists in ourselves and in our lives. So, too, does the simultaneous beauty and awkwardness of physical growth and the need to experience mastery of adolescent life tasks: finding one's place in society while developing a strong sense of self.

Humor does exist—and love and feelings of personal power and control. None of these can be neglected in a meaningful curriculum for young adolescents. Personal growth and society's growth must be considered together in an educationally effective, as well as a meaningfully integrated, curriculum. If students experience personal growth and mastery as they study and learn about their societal concerns, if they, at least occasionally, are part of solving these problems, then a curriculum organized around a worry list or around questions makes sense.

Curricular Critics: The Voices

There are voices I listen to that, I believe, I need to answer. These voices, though heard only in my head, are my critics—guiding forces for me. Each voice consists of many actual voices, but all are in constant revision, always being shaped by the realities of those present to witness and influence. One of the current voices says:

> My life centers around my family: mom, dad, brother, or sister, and I plan to have the same kind of center in my future life. I'm willing to work in an occupation that pays me well and allows me to live in a neighborhood that is attractive, secure, and comfortable. It's your job to teach me skills that will help me prepare for the life I and my family plan for me to live. I enjoy some parts of school: advanced band, in which I play a string instrument; drama, in which I excel; math, which I love; and student council, where my leadership skills are being exercised. Mostly, though, I like seeing my friends every day. I don't know what I'd do without _____ . He's the only person I like to sit with in the lunchroom. She's the only one who understands. I don't really have much spare time. When I do have some, I like to listen to soft rock music, to go to movies, to talk with my friends, or to curl up with a book, especially if we're at the beach (or mountain) cabin. Sometimes I think about God. I wonder if there is one. Reverend Jones is a lot of fun at teen outings, but I can't relate to what he's saying when he preaches. Life is just not as hard or as serious as he says it is. I don't see

what it matters, anyway, I'm doing fine without all of it. My folks expect me to go to church, so I guess I will.

Another voice says:

It doesn't matter what I think about or what I want for this society. What I'll get is what I'll get. It won't be justice. The only justice is what justice I make for myself. I hope to get a job that pays steady, but it won't be a job other people would much like to have. I plan to have my own house, but it won't be in a neighborhood that lots of other people would want to live in. If I'm lucky, I'll get a job that pays a decent wage and allows me a vacation and a little spending money. This is just how things are. My girl (boy) friend talk about maybe we'll get married someday, but I don't want to be burdened down too soon. If you think you can change any of these things I know to be true because of the experiences of those around me and like me, then maybe I'll listen to you and dream I can have what you call a good life. I dare you to try to teach me what you think I need to know. I try sometimes, but you don't even notice. You give your time to the smart kids. You're probably afraid of their parents. My mother knows a lot more than you ever will. She says I have only to believe in God and I will be raised up. He'll decide what will happen to my life. I go to church sometimes. I believe what those church songs tell you, but I don't really like that music. I like rap and I like hard rock. Those people know where it's at. My friend and I get tapes and we listen to them over and over until somebody makes us turn them off. We ought to go on stage, get our own band up, and go on the road. Folks would love us. But I don't expect you to understand those kind of dreams. I'm the best basketball player on my block, but I don't hardly ever get to play at school. I'll surprise everybody someday. They'll turn on their televisions, and there I'll be, passing the ball to _____ .

And still another voice says:

I plan to fulfill my dreams, and my dreams involve meeting and working with many kinds of people. I want to travel, to experience other cultures. I am going to be able to share my talents and the wealth of my country even though it may mean there's less for me. I believe I can make life better for all of us. I have enough of what I need. My parents are good people but divorced. They have high ideals, and even though we don't go to church, our family has strong moral character. They have faith in me, and more important, I have faith in myself. I'm good at soccer and tennis, and I like how my body feels after I play. My friend and I practice a lot, but it's really just fun to be together. We don't really care who wins, just that we have fun, get a chance to talk about, you know, boys and girls and who likes us and who's having a party. Sometimes I get competitive. I won that writing contest, got my name in the paper, and can look at the plaque they sent me with pride. So I guess I do like to win, don't want to be left out. I expect people to notice me and find me special. My grandmother says I am, says I was born at just the right time to really become someone in life. I don't know. Maybe I'll run for office someday. Maybe I'll find a cure for a disease, or write a book that will help everyone see the truth. It's there somewhere and sometimes I feel it in me. I read a book, _____ by _____ . I've never forgotten it. I've read all of that series. Made me think, helped me understand how other forms of life are intelligent, too, not just us humans.

I am teacher to all of these voices. Like a gifted choir director, I am to know how and when to try to bring harmony to them or to call one or another forward for a solo. I find joy as well as some pain as I listen. What I hear is a defining, striving-for-understanding process. None of the voices bear much relationship to American life as portrayed in popular movies or songs. What is clear about the voices is the desire to make sense out of experience: to understand where one fits into the larger pictures of friendship and family groups, into neighborhood and community groups, and into our society, indeed, into the world. Having the support of significant others—friends, parents and grandparents, teachers, and coaches—is of utmost importance. Feelings of significance and belonging are also vitally necessary. Belonging is defined by music, by clothing, by attitudes, and by the groups in which one is accepted. Significance appears to be an earned quality, a feeling one earns by making the effort to distinguish oneself through superior ability or by making contributions to the lives of others.

These voices are diverse; they offer no clear path to planning for my classes. They do, however, help me to understand that as I strive to define what needs to be taught, I am striving to make meaning myself: to mesh the curriculum guide with the lives and aspirations of the particular students who are assigned to me. How are we to make meaning together? What should we read, write, watch, and experience that will help us understand the world we live in? How can we use learning to help us find our places: to understand the complex relationships of cause and effect that will determine whether we experience mostly joys or mostly sorrows in life? Is there a pattern to the past that can be used to affect the future? What do we value most? How does one make and keep friends? How is one to be with others generally? Is war ever justified? It matters very much what a composite teacher/administrator/ curriculum expert voice has decided is important to learn, to concentrate on, but curriculum needs also to be shaped by those it serves; otherwise, no meaning will be made from the effort.

I believe that if we are to extract meaning from experience, we must observe, talk, think, remember, foresee, and hypothesize. We must study and write together. In such a setting emotional honesty is as necessary as the ability to reason. And emotional honesty must start with teachers who work to create a climate of trust and rapport, teachers who try to be honest about their own biases but who are keenly aware of the subtle and not-so-subtle power of the authority of their position. Teachers who establish a climate of being learners and meaning makers together are teaching the curriculum.

For me, the classroom I occupy, the position I hold with my students, has many similarities to the writing of this piece. There is much I had to leave out in order to meet an internal demand for meaning and an external demand for space and time. Yet, what I am doing in the writing is making meaning of my experiences. What I offer to you are selected solutions I applied or developed to solve the problems I saw: apathy, lack of faith in knowledge to help bring change, lack of interest in an externally based curriculum, and concern with life and societal issues.

The voices I hear now tell me what they think and feel. They tell me of changing lives. They speak of new music and new language but with the old instruments and books of human needs: to make meaning of our lives and our experiences. When I began to teach, our society was just coming to the end of a stable period. What I knew about teaching then was to do my best to impart a stable curriculum, a course of study that outlined specific content for specific grade levels. Any voices of students I heard were soon stifled. For over a decade, I worked at developing my skills at teaching the mandated curriculum effectively. I gave pretests and posttests. If the students didn't improve substantially during our time together, I believed that it was my fault. I needed to learn how to be a better teacher.

It was in studying learning theory and motivation that I began to doubt my prior acceptance of an external curriculum in the classroom and to begin to listen to what the voices of my students were trying to say about what meaning they were making. Whereas before I had listened as a way of determining how I could manipulate accepting of the prescribed curriculum, I began to value, to respect, the viewpoints of adolescent experience and reasoning as valid in themselves. It was when I began to use writing as a tool rather than as a curricular goal that I began truly to learn what those voices might have to say to me. When I wrote with the students, I began to understand that we made meaning individually and together; my role was shifting to contributor rather than determiner. It was in asking students to comment on how the class was run as it related to what they had learned that I began to understand the guidance that those voices could offer in developing meaningful curriculum. It was in working harder at my own writing that I began to process some of the information regarding the lives of my students and not to discount their words because of their young ages.

So, here I am now, tentative and experimental. Thirty years ago I knew how and what to teach. Now, I'm changing rather constantly. By working to create a meaning-making, creative classroom, I have become as empowered as I hoped my students would be to view the world as evolving, as changeable, and as needing of efforts for understanding trying to change in it what needs being changed. Knowledge is power, and education is change.

References

Ashton-Warner, S. 1971. *Teacher.* New York: Bantam.

Atwell, N. 1987. *In the middle: Writing, reading, and learning with adolescents.* Portsmouth, N.H.:Boynton/Cook.

———. *Workshop 1.* 1989. Portsmouth, N.H.: Heinemann.

Borland, H. 1963. *When the legends die.* Philadelphia: Lippincott.

Brown, D. 1970. *Bury my heart at wounded knee.* New York: Bantam Books.

———. 1981. *Creek Mary's blood.* New York: Pocket Books.

Calvert, P. 1980. *Snowbird.* New American Library: Signet Vista Books.

Calkins, L. 1983. *Lessons from a child.* Portsmouth, N.H.: Heinemann.

———. 1986. *The art of teaching writing.* Portsmouth, N.H.: Heinemann.

Christensen, L. 1991. "Unlearning the myths that bind us." *Rethinking Schools* 5:1,15–17.

Collier, J.L., and Collier, C. 1974. *My brother Sam is dead.* Four Winds.

Douglass, F. 1971. *Narrative of the life of Frederick Douglass: An American slave.* Cambridge, Mass.: Harvard University Press.

Gaines, E. 1985. *The autobiography of Miss Jane Pittman.* New York: Bantam.

Graves, D. 1983. *Build a literate classroom.* Portsmouth, N.H.: Heinemann.

———. 1983. *Writing: Teachers and children at work.* Portsmouth, N.H.: Heinemann.

———. 1984. *A researcher learns to write.* Portsmouth, N.H.: Heinemann.

Hubbard, R. 1989. *Authors of pictures, draughtsmen of words.* Portsmouth, N.H.: Heinemann.

L'Amour, L. 1981. *Comstock Lode.* New York: Bantam.

Lester, J. 1968. *To be a slave.* New York: Scholastic.

Macrorie, K. 1984. *20 Teachers.* New York: Oxford University Press.

———. 1984. *Writing to be read.* Portsmouth, N.H.: Boynton/Cook.

O'Dell, S. 1986. *Streams to the river, river to the sea.* Boston, Mass.: Houghton-Mifflin

Paterson, K. 1991. *Lyddie.* New York: Penguin.

Power, B.M., and Hubbard, R. 1991. *Literacy in process.* Portsmouth, N.H.: Heinemann.

Stafford, W. 1964. "The Animal That Drank Up Sound." *Stories That Could Be True.* Harper and Row.

Tanner, F. A. 1987. *Readers theatre.* Caldwell, Ida.: Clark Publishing.

7

Lessons from Little Bear

Susan Stires
The Center for Teaching and Learning

Several years ago I heard language arts authority Judith Lindfors answer the question, "What one message needs to be promoted by the profession about young children's reading and writing?" by replying, "The wonderment of it all." She went on to clarify and specify what she termed "a seemingly naïve response" during a panel discussion on language acquisition. Her remark caused me to step back and think hard about the young children with whom I had recently begun to work. I had been a teacher-researcher working with intermediate resource students, and later I taught primary learning disabled students. Most of the time I provided support for them and their teachers in their classrooms during writing or reading time.

Upon hearing Lindfors's remark, I thought about how most parents celebrate the wonderment of their children's oral language development. They find support from their social communities as well as from language experts who study and do research in the field. As teachers of young children we privately celebrate the wonderment of their language and literacy, but it often stops here. Unless a child experiences difficulty learning to read or write, we rarely mention it, let alone celebrate the minor miracles of literacy development. I wondered why it is this way. Is it because as teachers we typically have had no voices as experts? Or is it because of set expectations? Children go to school to learn to read and write, and it is the teacher's job to teach them.

During the past decade, with its emphasis on process teaching of reading and writing, we have begun to marvel publicly. Researchers and teacher educators like Donald Graves (1989), Jane Hansen (1987), and Jerome Harste (1988) and primary teachers like Mary Ellen Giacobbe (1989), Carol Avery (1985), and Bobbi Fisher (1991) relate the stories and their meanings that we need to hear. These stories of literacy learning enable us to see and to talk about what we experience as teachers. I feel fortunate to have been a part of this movement, for it has given me a new language as well as renewed energy to teach better and to discover more. As I reflect upon the years I have taught young children, I recall many stories attesting to "the wonderment of it all." Several are etched in my teacher's memory; one is the story of Marcy.

Introducing Marcy: At Home and at School

Marcy was a first grader whom I knew at the time I was teaching primary special education students. I went into her classroom daily during writing time to support three boys identified with learning disabilities. Once I had fulfilled my responsibilities with these students and they were busy with their writing, I assisted the classroom teacher by moving around the room to confer with the other students. All chose their own topics and worked on individual pieces of writing. Whenever I approached Marcy, her dark-brown head was bent over a page of drawing with its corresponding text. Her pixie-shaped face brightened when I spoke to her, and she eagerly shared her writing. Her large, nearly black eyes reminded me of her brother, who had been my student in the resource room for several years. He had struggled and was still struggling to learn to read and write. Although a shy little girl, Marcy was quite open with me because I knew her family.

Marcy and her brother lived with their parents in relative isolation on a rural island. Aside from seeing their grandparents and some of their parents' friends, the children had few social contacts outside of school. The family lived in a tiny, two-room cabin on the edge of a small clearing in the woods. A shop, the shell of a new, larger house, an outhouse, junked cars, car parts, lobster traps, and chickens were also in or around the clearing.

The parents loved their children and took good care of them, but teaching them to read and write had not been a priority for them. The mother had a medical handicap, and coping with her handicap and the constraints of their environment took most of her energy. School had been difficult for the father, and the experience left him with some negative feelings. He worked hard on his own father's fishing boat and supplemented his income by repairing cars. Both parents passively supported the school and the teachers. They wanted their children to learn, but they could not and did not provide a literacy environment at home.

Like their parents, neither Marcy nor her brother had many of their own books. When an RIF (Reading Is Fundamental) day was held at school in mid-April of her first-grade year, Marcy selected *Little Bear's Visit* by Else Holmelund Minarik (1961). She chose it because there were Little Bear books in her classroom. She had not read the books and said that she could not read her new book. Not considering herself a reader as yet, Marcy had been refusing her teacher's attempts to get her to try.

Marcy had two teachers during her first-grade year. Both were new to the writing process and to using children's literature as the basis for a reading program. The first teacher had organized the class into reading groups. Marcy was in a group of emergent readers who did shared reading of Big Books, nursery rhymes and poems, and fairy tales and other familiar stories. Although successful with predictable literature as a group reader, Marcy would not attempt to read on her own, as the other children did. In the beginning of April her second teacher moved her to a higher reading group. Even though Marcy had not demonstrated ability to be in this group, her teacher acted on a teaching instinct. And Marcy started to read on her own. Her teacher said that, by the end of April, Marcy seemed to have fallen in love with her reading voice.

Even so, up to this point Marcy had not been making even average strides as a first-grade reader or writer. She did not exhibit the problems that had inhibited to her brother's development, but she had made little progress and appeared to be at risk academically.

Marcy liked writing time because she liked to draw. Throughout the year she drew and labeled her drawings. She readily chose her own topics according to her interests, but they were static and repetitious. She always chose to use the same materials: crayons, pencil, and a six-page booklet of lined paper with a space at the top for drawing. Marcy did not heed her teachers', classmates', or even my few attempts to get her to expand her writing. From September until March, when she began to use expanded labels ("This is a pretty rainbow" or "This is a swan"), Marcy had used one- and two-word labels in a static way. The only notable aspects of her writing were her spelling and the volume of books she produced.

The Story of Marcy's Stories

The day before vacation in April I was in Marcy's first-grade classroom to work with one of my special education students. Marcy brought over a piece of writing that she had titled, "Little Bear's Visit." I was immediately struck with the title and the format. Marcy had drawn an open book on a single sheet of paper with the story written inside its boundaries (Figure 7–1). There were no illustrations; she had obviously used a new approach to this writing. I asked Marcy where she had gotten the idea for this piece, and she told me about the RIF book that she had obtained a couple of days before. I then asked her if she had read the book and had then decided to write about it. Marcy patiently explained that she could not read the book but that she wanted to. She had taken it home. Naturally, my next question was, "Did your mother read it to you?" "Not yet. She hasn't had time." I asked Marcy if I could make a copy of her story and she agreed, but she wanted me to bring the original back before school was over because she wanted to take it home.

I later found out that neither Marcy's teacher nor one of her classmates had read *Little Bear's Visit* to her. Marcy had taken her book home on RIF Day and had not brought it back to school at any time. Based on the writing, I theorized that Marcy had "read" the beginning and ending of the book on her own from the illustrations and from what she knew about how stories begin and end.

During April vacation Marcy's mother did read *Little Bear's Visit*; Marcy "read" it over and over again. She was probably able to get most of the words from her memory of the story, from the illustrations, and from the story context. I believe that she developed what I have called an "in-head text" (Stires 1988). While doing research on the commentary that young children make about their reading, I discovered that they used various forms of in-head texts to support their reading. In-head texts are derived from the child's sense of story and literary language, response to illustrations and print, expressive language skills, and sense of play.

On the first day back from April vacation Marcy went back to her conventional writing materials and topics. Her book "Cats" began with a sentence containing an action verb, "A cat is playing with a dog." (Her most advanced sentence so far had been an expanded label, "This is a red balloon and a green.") Marcy had not sustained this sentence from throughout her book called "Balloons," which she had written before April vacation. She had finished it with the labels: "a balloon, a yellow balloon, three balloon, for black balloons and a balloon.") She completed her cat book with expanded labels: "This is a cat and a dog. . . . This is a cat. . . . This is a big cat. . . . This is a little cat. . . . This is a puppy." That day, however, was the last time that Marcy used the six-page booklets, chose familiar interest topics, or labeled her drawings. She had a new interest: reading.

Since I didn't regularly confer with Marcy, I wasn't aware of what she was working on after the cat book. Knowing that I would be interested, though, she brought over her second version of "Little Bear's Visit" to share with me. This time she had stapled together strips of paper in a booklet form. The text was slightly expanded, and Marcy had drawn tiny crayon illustrations to go with the text after she wrote it. Again, I asked her about reading the book, and she told me about what had happened over vacation. When I asked Marcy if I could make a copy of her booklet, she agreed.

By mid-May Marcy finished her third version of "Little Bear's Visit," and the expanded text was very close to the original story line (Figure 7–2). She now read *Little Bear's Visit* easily and independently at home and wrote the story, not from the book but from the text "inside her head." About this same time Marcy began wanting to share her reading with the other children in her group. (I discovered this later on.) Although I was intrigued with what

Marcy had done in writing and had made copies of her Little Bear stories, I was not aware that she had adopted Little Bear as a character for two subsequent stories and had written her own version of *The Magic Fish* (Gagliardi 1969). Since I wasn't Marcy's teacher and didn't think of my observations as research, I hadn't documented in the beginning. As soon as I was aware that I was missing Marcy's writing, I realized how valuable it was as data for me to learn from.

I conferred with Marcy's teacher about what had been happening in reading and writing, and she filled me in. She had saved a few samples in Marcy's cumulative folder, but not all because it was close to the end of the year. Also, Marcy had been insistent on taking her most recent booklets home to share with her mother and father. Since her teacher knew how proud Marcy was of her writing and how closely linked it was to the book at home, she agreed. She observed, "Marcy is writing all during the day; any extra moments she has, she fills up with writing." Marcy also loved to read the stories of Little Bear, Frog and Toad, and other early reader books. When she was not writing, she was reading, readily sharing her reading with anyone who could listen. Marcy was making up for lost time.

After reading Else Holmelund Minarik's *Little Bear* (1957), Marcy wrote her own version of her favorite chapter, "Birthday Soup" (Figure 7–3). Like her final version of "Little Bear's Visit," her text followed the original story line closely, but she no longer illustrated. This was significant evidence that Marcy had put her energy into her text. She wrote only one version of "Birthday Soup" but maintained the character for her next story, titled, "Little Bear Went Hunting." She also attempted to introduce another character, a deer with whom Little Bear became very good friends. She did not illustrate this story or any that followed.

Marcy again borrowed the character Little Bear and used a structure similar to that of "Little Bear Goes Hunting" to write "Little Bear and the Magic Pebble" (Figure 7–4). It was further inspired by William Steig's *Sylvester and the Magic Pebble* (Steig 1969), which Marcy's teacher had read to the class the day before. Except for the magic pebble, Marcy's story did not resemble the text of *Sylvester and the Magic Pebble*, however, this fusing of elements from Steig's *Magic Pebble*, Minarik's *Little Bear*, and her own developing sense of narrative was the most complex connection that Marcy had made as a reader/writer thus far.

Marcy wrote one last Little Bear story in the beginning of June before completing her final piece of writing for the year, "Sylvester and the Magic Pebble" (Figure 7–5). Although it lacked some of the events, the basic story structure was there. During the week between the time that Marcy's teacher read *Sylvester and the Magic Pebble* and the time Marcy wrote this final piece, she had incorporated the magic pebble into one of her Little Bear stories and had read Steig's book herself. If writing time had not been usurped by end-of-the-year activities—picnics, puppet shows, and field day—she may have written more about Sylvester, returned to Little Bear, or developed her own characters.

Reflections

What Marcy did as a reader and writer and how she did it are exciting for her, her parents, her teachers, and other interested teachers. Primary teachers are familiar with growth spurts in their students but are not always familiar with the causes. In *Breaking Ground: Teachers Relate Reading and Writing in the Elementary School* (1985), Carol Avery tells how one of her students, Lori, significantly changed over time. Carol also describes in her chapter "Lori 'Figures It Out': A Young Reader Learns to Read" the context in which that growth took place. For Marcy, too, there are identifiable elements that enabled her to take her leap into literacy. These elements provide the clues as to *why* this convergency of reading and writing occurred for Marcy and caused change.

Marcy had both time to read and write and choice about what she read and wrote. Marcy's teachers set aside large chunks of time each day for real reading and writing. Besides that, both of her teachers encouraged their students to use other "bits" of time within the structure of the day to read and write independently for their own purposes. During writing time the students were free to choose their own topics, which resulted in a range of genres from Marcy's fictional narrative to poetry, personal narrative, information, and persuasion. The teachers provided a variety of materials for writing: pencils, colored pens, crayons, booklets, and paper of various sizes. For reading, there was a wide range of books displayed and available at all times. During reading instruction the teachers helped to develop students' sense of story, an understanding of how print works, and strategies to determine unknown words. They provided shared reading experiences (big books, charts of songs and stories, etc., read together) with their young readers and read to them frequently, showing their love of literature and information, along with their desire to share it. Marcy's teachers further encouraged sharing by allowing students a choice about what they shared—their own writing or published works—with groups or the whole class.

Besides creating a literary environment with time and choice built in, Marcy's teachers provided her and her classmates with their natural, instinctive responses as teachers. They showed their interest in the content and processes of their students' reading and writing in the form of questions about intentions and meaning, suggestions for change, and comments about effect. They offered genuine human reactions by saying what a text, either by a student or from literature, reminded them of and encouraged their students to do the same. They promoted talk among the children; the classroom was always lively with talk about writing when I made my daily visit. Furthermore, the teachers published the students' work on a regular basis. Most of the publications were schoolmade books, which were also distributed to the class. Other publications were in the school paper, on dittoed booklets, or on the bulletin board.

If these conditions, circumstances, and persons that made up Marcy's literary environment had not been present, this story may have a different ending. Marcy could have been placed in an ability-level group in a basal reader series. There she would have begun in a preprimer text and would have had to complete a number of them, as well as many skills lessons, before moving to a primer text. Marcy was a willing participant of shared reading, but it is unlikely that she would have performed—read orally alone—before a group. The lock-step, sequential skill approach of basals does not take into account how children like Marcy learn. It does not take into account the time needed to observe and make sense out of literacy that Marcy needed from September until April. Although she might have eventually come to read the preprimer texts set before her, Marcy would probably have not taken her giant step under such a system. At best, she might have reached the primer level in reading by the end of the year. Low achievement and an economically disadvantaged home would have qualified Marcy for Chapter I remedial reading for the following year.

With traditional language arts instruction only in the subskills of writing, such as handwriting and spelling, Marcy would not have had the opportunity to support her reading through writing. Furthermore, this type of instruction would have prevented her from risking the spelling of many of the words she used in her narratives. Sentence formation is usually taught as transcription and punctuation exercises. Marcy probably would have done well because of her good spelling and handwriting, but her conceptual understanding of sentences came from writing whole texts. She likely would not have understood the function of sentences or punctuation. Even if some occasional writing were part of a skills-oriented language arts curriculum, the topics would have been teacher-selected and confining. No matter how creatively a teacher selects them, topics may not meet most of the students' needs. Marcy needed to write on Little Bear; her classmates had their own individual needs.

Marcy's reading and writing abilities mutually supported one another at an appropriate level for a child completing the first grade. What is more important is that Marcy became a reader of children's literature and a writer of her own texts. At the end of first grade she had developed a flair for fictional narratives, distinguishing herself as a writer in her classroom. In second grade she diverted from this course to explore new territory. She wrote information books and letters, and she crafted her pieces, using the many writing skills that she learned (Figure 7–6). With Marcy, there were new changes for her teachers to contemplate through the grades. With other young children whom we teach each day, there are stories of equal value to tell and celebrate, as we turn to look closely and focus on "the wonderment of it all."

Figure 7–1 "Little Bear's Visit" by Marcy in April

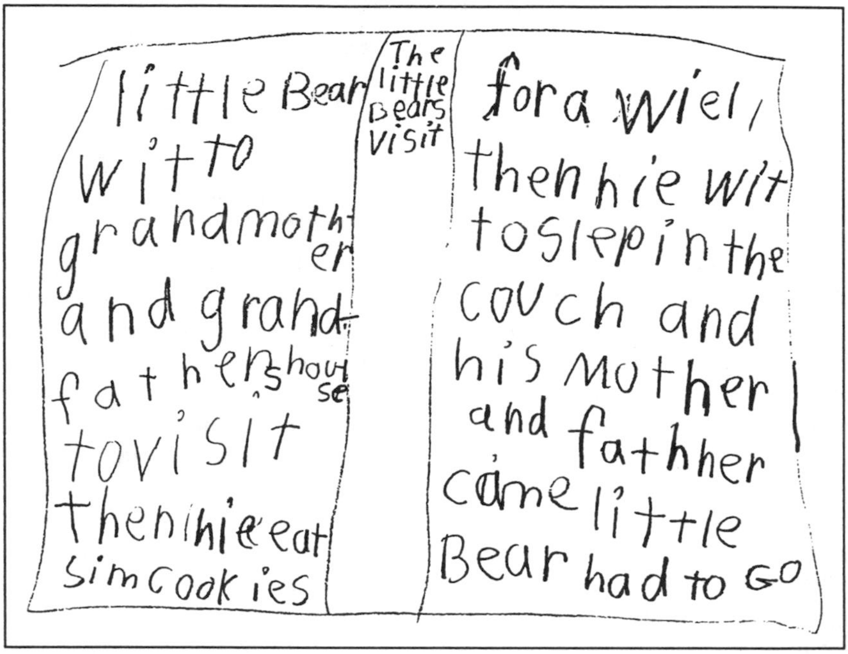

little Bear witto grandmother and grandfathershouse tovisit thenhieeat Sim Cookies
The little Bears visit
fora wiel, thenhie wit toslepin the couch and his Mother and fathher came little Bear had to Go

Little Bear went to Grandmother and Grandfather's house to visit. Then he ate some cookies for a while. Then he went to sleep on the couch and his mother and father came. Little Bear had to go.

Figure 7–2 "Little Bear's Visit" by Marcy in mid-May

the little Bears visit

BY

Thurs,May 15,

The Little Bear's visit by Marcy. Thurs., May 15, 19--

Figure 7–2 "Little Bear's Visit" by Marcy in mid-May (*cont.*)

littleBear went to grand
mother and grandfather's
house to visis that wis
sopthihg little Bear like
to do

Little Bear went to Grandmother and Grandfather's house to visit. That was something Little Bear liked to do.

little Bear went in he liked
to look at grandfather
goBlin joping up and doun
in a jir grandmother like
ve very mech cooking

Little Bear went in. He liked to look at Grandfather's goblin jumping up and down in a jar. He liked Grandmother's cooking very very much.

littleBear went to slep
on the couch wenh
woce up he wen t
for a woke with grand
father Bear grand father

Little Bear went to sleep on the couch. When he woke up, he went for a walk with Grandfather Bear. Grandfather

Figure 7–2 "Little Bear's Visit" by Marcy in mid-May (*cont.*)

Sat down he wentto slep
little Bear went and
got grandmother wih
thia woct down the ro degran
mother tolde little Bedr a
sory wihmother Bearwis

sat down. He went to sleep. Little
Bear went and got Grandmother.
When they walked down the road,
Grandmother told Little Bear a story.
When Mother Bear was

little She foud a Robin
it wis to, little to flie so
She brot it in the house and
med a house for the Robin
She Pet the house By the widoe
wen The Robin got dig

little, she found a robin. It was too
little to fly so she brought it in the
house and made a house for the
robin. She put the house by the window. When the robin got big

anef to flie mother
lit the Robin go that is
the end of the sory

enough to fly, Mother let the robin
go. That is the end of the story.

Figure 7-2   "Little Bear's Visit" by Marcy in mid-May (*cont.*)

grandfather Bear to thi
m a sory therewes
a little green go blin
he wen t for a woc he
hrd Somthing he go
so serd he Jompt out of

Grandfather told him a story. There was a little green goblin. He went for a walk. He heard something. He got so scared, he jumped out of

his sious and run doun
the rode and Jomt in a
tree he likt out of
the tree he Sio his siou
helomt out of the tree and
Jomt in his sious and woc there

his shoes and ran down the road and jumped in a tree. He looked out of the tree. He saw his shoes. He jumped in his shoes and walked down the road.

at the end of the
sory little Bear's mother
and father come little
Bear is going hom
The end.

(At) the end of the story Little Bear's mother and father came. Little Bear is going home. The end.

Figure 7–3 ''Birthday Soup,'' Marcy's retelling of a favorite chapter

By ^{Brithday soup}

made in Tues.
may 27,19

Birthday Soup by Marcy. Made in
Tues., May 27, 19--.

Mother Bear
mother mother
mother is not
home now iT is
my brithday
side little Bear
wer is my cake

''Mother Bear, Mother, Mother.
Mother is not home. Now it is my
birthday,'' said Little Bear. ''Where
is my cake?

the pot is on
the sov the
blak pot is
empte I cen
make brithday
soup I wel in
? vite my frens

The pot is on the stove. The black
pot is empty. I can make birthday
soup. I will invite my friends.''

Figure 7-3 "Birthday Soup" (*cont.*)

so little Bear
sortid to make
the soup one of
his frens came
he brot som th
ing the han
side I sel somp
thing is it in

So Little Bear started to make the soup. One of his friends came. He brought something. The hen said, "I smell something. Is it in

the big blak
pot yes side
little Bear I
em makeing
birth day soup
all of little
Bears frens
came the soup

the big black pot?" "Yes," said Little Bear, "I am making birthday soup." All of Little Bear's friends came. The soup

wes din avre
one wes eating
the soup little
Bears mother
came she had
som cake
little Bear
gav his

was done. Everyone was eating the soup. Little Bear's mother came. She had some cake. Little Bear gave his

Figure 7–3 "Birthday Soup" (*cont.*)

```
mother
a
 big

hug
the end.
```

mother a big hug. The end.

Figure 7–4 "Little Bear and the Magic Pebble" by Marcy

Little Bear and the Magic Pebble by Marcy. Thurs., May 29, 19--

One day Little Bear went for a walk. He found a magic pebble. He brought it home.

Figure 7–4   "Little Bear and the Magic Pebble" by Marcy (*cont.*)

weth·the
shinye red
pebl in
his hend
wen he
got home
he told his
Mother and

with the shiny red pebble in his hand . . . When he got home, he told his mother and

father
wet he
found his
mother
an d father
wer sprisde
very
sprisde

father what he found. His mother and father were surprised, very surprised.

little
Bear side
I found
it wen
I went
for a
walk bet
little Bear's

Little Bear said, "I found it when I went for a walk." But Little Bear's

Figure 7-4 "Little Bear and the Magic Pebble" by Marcy (*cont.*)

father side non sens his mother side non sens to tha did not blv him Theend.

father said, "Nonsense." His mother said, "Nonsense." They did not believe him. The end.

Figure 7-5 "Sylvester and the Magic Pebble" by Marcy in June

selvester and the majic pebel BY made in wed June 4, 19

Sylvester and the Magic Pebble by Marcy. Made in Wed., June 4, 19--

One day selvesteh went for a walk he found a sheny red pebel he

One day Sylvester went for a walk. He found a shiny red pebble. He

Figure 7–5   "Sylvester and the Magic Pebble" by Marcy in June (*cont.*)

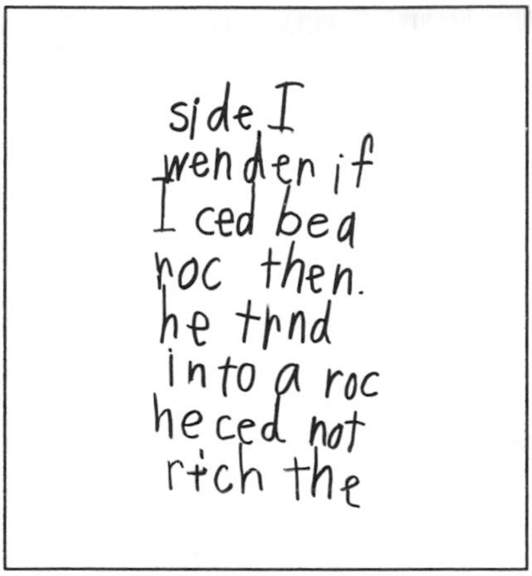

side I
wen den if
I ced be a
roc then.
he trnd
in to a roc
he ced not
rtch the

said, "I wonder if I could be a rock." Then he turned into a rock. He could not reach the

pebel to
tern his
sef ba c
he said
ther all
hite he
wes sad
wen it wes

pebble to turn himself back. He stayed there all night. He was sad. When it was

monning
his Mother
and father
had a pic
nic his
father sa
the pebel
he petiton

morning, his mother and father had a picnic. His father saw the pebble. He put it on

Figure 7–5 "Sylvester and the Magic Pebble" by Marcy in June (*cont.*)

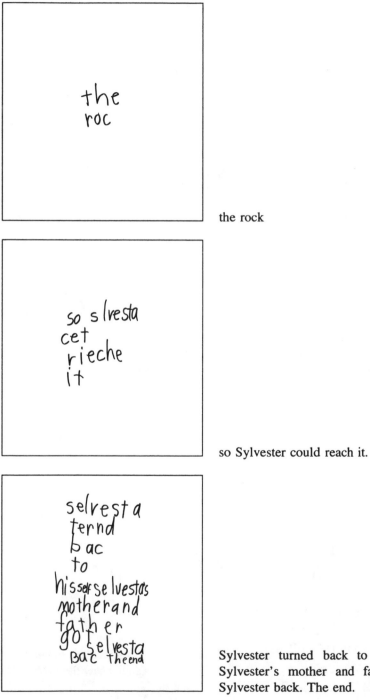

the rock

so Sylvester could reach it.

Sylvester turned back to himself. Sylvester's mother and father got Sylvester back. The end.

Figure 7–6 Marcy's writing in second grade

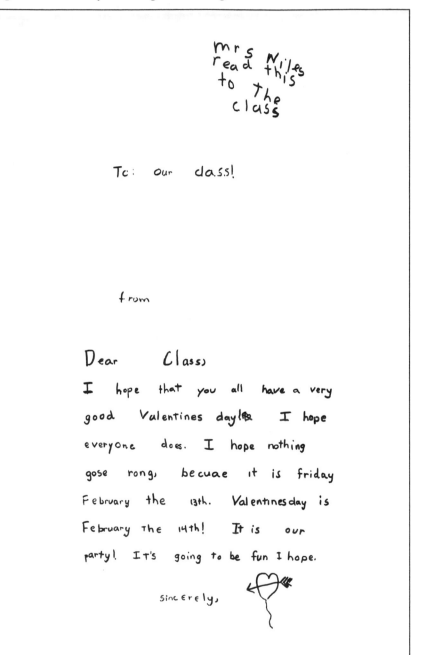

References

Avery, C. 1985. "Lori figures it out": A young writer learns to read. In *Breaking ground: Teachers relate reading and writing in the elementary school*. Edited by Jane Hansen, Thomas Newkirk, and Donald Graves. Portsmouth, N.H.: Heinemann.

Fisher, B. 1991. *Joyful learning: A whole language kindergarten*. Portsmouth, N.H.: Heinemann.

Gagliardi, M.F. 1969. *The magic fish*. New York: Putnam.

Giacobbe, M.E. 1984. Helping children become more responsible for their own writing. *LiveWire*, 1:7–9.

Graves, D. 1989. *Experiment with fiction*. Portsmouth, N.H.: Heinemann.

Hansen, J. 1987. *When writers read*. Portsmouth, N.H.: Heinemann.

Harste, J.C., Short, K.G., and Burke, C. 1988. *Creating classsrooms for authors: The reading-writing connection*. Portsmouth, N.H.: Heinemann.

Minarik, E.H. 1961. *Little bear's visit*. New York: Harper & Row.

———. 1957. *Little bear*. New York: Harper & Row.

Steig, W. 1969. *Sylvester and the magic pebble*. New York: Windmill.

Stires, S. 1988. Reading and talking: "Special" readers show they know. In *Understanding writing: Ways of observing, learning, and teaching*. Edited by Thomas Newkirk and Nancie Atwell. Portsmouth, N.H.: Heinemann.

8

Ownership for the Special Needs Child: Individual and Educational Dilemmas

Cora Lee Five

Edgewood School

I didn't really understand the importance of ownership until I started observing children with special learning needs. I had heard the term *ownership* many times as I learned how to teach writing through the process approach. I knew that for the process approach to be truly effective in my classroom, I would need to create an environment that ensured Mary Ellen Giacobbe's (1986) three basics; time, ownership, and response.

In the writing process environment, students are encouraged to "own" their ideas. Respected as individuals, they have choices; they select their own topics for writing, topics that are meaningful to them. The establishment of a community of writers allows students to respond to each others' ideas. As students write and share their work, they begin to realize that they are vulnerable and that response to writers should be supportive and constructive. Response also means that I listen to students to understand their special ways of learning. Teaching becomes a response to learners.

As I evolved as a teacher of writing, I changed my reading program. Time, ownership, and response were again essential ingredients. Each day I made time for reading workshop and for reading aloud to the class. Students selected the books they wanted to read and responded to their books in a variety of ways. Along with choosing meaningful texts to read, they wrote on topics important to them. I tried to ensure that my students could confer and collaborate and still maintain ownership.

Time and response are oriented toward supporting ownership. Time gives room and respect for the student's own pace, while response derives from an attitude that there cannot be a violation of any child's mind. While criticism and disagreement stay an active part of the learning process, no one's ideas are demeaned or negated. Criticism is something that the child is encouraged to think about: the child maintains the option to accept or reject the input of others.

I again extended time, ownership, and response to my teaching of math, history, science, and other areas. Gradually, I realized that ownership could not exist in isolation. Time, ownership, and response could not be separated. Ownership develops over time through response.

As I grew as a teacher, I began to recognize the importance of ownership for all of my students, but particularly for those with special learning needs. My studies of these children made me see what ownership meant for them. Ownership came to mean that learners were able to follow their own interests, to take some control over their learning, and consequently to accept and feel greater respnsibility for it. In the process of studying two particular children recently, Alex and Mike, (Weaver 1994a, 1994b) I discovered the importance of ownership for me as well. I will discuss Alex and Mike, both of whom were habitually used to renunciation of ownership of their own mental capacities. My focus will be the way in which they were helped to reclaim ownership and the way in which the system colluded against this goal. I will also share how I, too, struggled with ownership within the school system.

Alex's Background

Alex, who had been placed in my fifth-grade classroom, had been classified by the Committee on Special Education as learning disabled. With a history of learning problems he had received skills help since first grade. His Individual Educational Programs (IEP) stated that he had difficulty with reading and was tested at a beginning third-grade level at the end of fourth grade. He could not decode well, and his written and oral language were limited. He had problems with spelling and seemed unable to express his ideas. It was noted that Alex needed much time to process information, often asking for directions and for questions to be repeated.

The recommendation was that Alex be taught in one-to-one situations in the classroom. In previous grades he apparently did not participate in class discussions and was "lost" in a whole class or group setting. He was also to receive help initiating and completing assignments. He was placed in my classroom because an aide would be there for Mike, and it was felt that Alex, too, could receive the benefit of the aide.

Alex's IEP contained a list of isolated skills under each curriculum area. These were the goals and objectives for the year. His IEP also specified that he was scheduled to leave the classroom to work with skills teachers four times a week.

Mike's Background

In kindergarten Mike had been classified as learning disabled because of his speech and language problems. He had gone to a special school for children with language disabilities from kindergarten through second grade in classes of six or seven children. When he returned to my school, he was tested and classified as ADHD and given an aide for twenty-five hours a week.

Mike's IEP noted his reading problems. He was reading well below grade level and had difficulty with phonic skills. He also had problems with written and oral language. Though he had many ideas, he was afraid to write because of his spelling mistakes. Handwriting was a problem for him as well. Mike barely knew how to write in cursive and printed most of his written work. His impulsivity and focusing problems interfered with his oral language, and his distractibility caused problems in learning.

Mike's IEP recommended that he, like Alex, be taught in a one-to-one setting. He had difficulty in the past participating in class discussions and could not function well in a large group. He needed help in beginning and completing assignments and was assigned an aide. His IEP also listed specific skills which became the goals and objectives for fifth grade. Mike was scheduled to leave the class five times a week to work with skills and speech teachers.

With both these boys I saw difficulties in ownership, as expressed in their inability to have interest or direction, to express ideas, and to make decisions.

Fifth Grade: The Beginning

Looking forward to having Alex and Mike in my class, I was interested to see how a workshop approach, one that ensured ownership, would affect their reading and writing. I had realized through my readings and my previous case studies of students with special learning needs that they learn best when they are actively involved in their own learning, when they are immersed in a subject, when they are reading, writing, speaking, and listening for a variety of meaningful purposes. I also wondered how Alex and Mike would respond to a supportive classroom environment, one that valued ideas and treated students with respect. I knew the importance of creating an environment that gives children ownership—chances to make decisions, to take risks, to follow their interests, and to take responsibility for their learning. Within this environment students come together as communities of learners to work together collaboratively and to learn from one another as they develop hypotheses and as they discuss and share ideas. Would Alex and Mike be able to become part of this community of learners? Would they be able to take risks with me, their peers, their own minds? Would they find the freedom to experiment?

My initial problem occurred during the first week of school when I received skills schedules for Alex and Mike. They were scheduled to leave the room during reading workshop to work in a one-to-one setting on isolated skills. How could they become part of my reading/writing community? When I looked at my special class schedule and added in chorus, band, and instrumental music lessons, I realized that there was no way I could find enough time to reschedule reading. I went to speak to the skills teachers, but their own schedule restrictions made them unable to reschedule the boys. I felt the importance of having the boys be in my room each day when reading workshop began. I wanted them to be part of the minilessons; I wanted them to be settled with a book and be surrounded by readers; I wanted them to participate in group shares.

When I suggested that the boys work in small groups in skills instead of in an isolated setting or that the skills teachers work with the boys in the classroom, I ran into the issue of ownership. The skills teachers had *their* programs in *their* special rooms. As the principal tried to help in this matter, I realized that the pressure of state requirements interfered with his ability to grant ownership to other people. The decision was, after examination of the IEP, that Mike would leave the room for skills each day but that Alex would have a skills teacher come into the room to help him in writing and reading for forty minutes one afternoon a week. When I asked about the programs and approaches that the skills teachers would use with these boys, I received little information. It appeared that the three of us would work with the boys in our own way with little communication or connection.

Even though I was glad to have Alex in the room and to have the skills teacher work with him there, I was not happy about Mike's leaving every day, and I was sorry that there was little communication between the specialists and me. We seemed to value our own individual philosophies, approaches, and programs; perhaps we were afraid that communication might expose us, increase our vulnerability, and make us feel inadequate. Perhaps in our busy days there was little time to share our thoughts and observations.

I wondered about the IEP and its list of isolated skills. It seemed to conflict with the philosophy of teaching the whole child in whole contexts. Was the IEP determining what and how the child should be taught? Were the skills teachers required to teach these skills? Was I? Who was responsible for the special needs child's learning? My principal told me that the skills teacher was in charge of the IEP, and I felt confused. The child was in my class, my aide and I worked with him most of the day, I wrote and signed the report cards, yet someone else was in charge of his learning program. Later, the skills teacher told me that Alex, too, had to be removed from the class; he could not be taught skills in the classroom. "It's illegal," she told me. "The state says you have to take them out of the room." Thus began a year of conflict and frustration that made me reflect and take another look at ownership. I considered not only the importance of ownership for the child but also ownership from a different perspective—the ownership of the educational philosophy of the classroom teacher.

Alex's Story

At the beginning of the year Alex displayed behavior problems. He shouted out, usually comments that seemed to be irrelevant. Doing little work, he spent much time crawling around on the floor, under desks, and in the coat closet. He spoke in a babyish voice and walked like a toddler. All the children laughed at Alex's antics; they liked him because he pretended to be (or perhaps he thought he was) dumb. His behavior always got him in trouble in every class. Knowing at the beginning of the year that other students thought that he was funny, Alex seemed to enjoy being the class clown. Easily distracted by his peers and the events in the classroom, he had learned to substitute indiscriminate attention for what he really desired—affirmation of himself as a person with ideas.

I knew from past experience that establishing a positive, supportive environment—one that valued ideas—was the basis for developing a community of writers. I spend much time at the beginning of each year modeling conferences and responses that are positive and constructive. Usually, students learn to respond in a similar way through conferences at my round conference table. I was glad that Alex was in my classroom during writing workshop.

During the first month of school Alex was not involved in writing. I was not surprised because I knew that he had done little writing in fourth grade. Whatever he had written had been with the help of skills teachers. At the beginning of fifth grade, when Alex was not writing, I tried to brainstorm topics with him. He remained silent. Sometimes he answered, "I don't know" in a high-pitched voice and rolled his eyes, causing the other children to laugh. He seemed to enjoy acting dumb and immature; often, he crawled on the floor, examining something he found on the carpet.

At the beginning Alex would not come to the conference table by himself. I encouraged him, but he seemed to have little interest, a sign of renunciation of ownership. I noticed, however, that Alex listened to the conversations as children shared drafts and explained problems that they were having in writing. Eventually, I coaxed him to come to the table to listen to the other children's topics. Wanting him to become part of our writing community, I hoped that the experience might inspire him. He sat and said little; sometimes he made faces. When he returned to his desk and I looked at him, he told me, "I'm thinking." This was a response that I heard throughout the year as he sat for long periods of time doing what I assumed to be nothing. I was never sure what his words meant, but I respected his response and let him think. This is how ownership works at the beginning.

After a month of sitting at his desk without writing but presumably listening to writing conferences, Alex finally decided to write about his trip to the Grand Canyon. He wrote slowly but did not stop, as he had a lot to tell. Finishing his three-page draft at the end of the week, he read it to me. He decided that he liked it and did not want to change it. The skills teacher was coming in the next day, and I suggested that he read it to her and then proof-read it with her. "I know how to put in periods and capital letters," he informed me, attempting to assert himself.

On arrival next day the skills teacher immediately started helping Alex copy his homework. She began to look for his writing piece even though Alex knew where it was. She searched through his desk until I showed her where the writing folders were kept. When I told her that Alex could get his folder himself, she explained that she wasn't sure he'd be able to find it. I told her that Alex's piece was finished and that I hoped they could proofread it together. As Alex read his Grand Canyon piece, she corrected it, having him change and add words and sentences. Unfortunately a well-intentioned adult, eager to pursue her assigned task of skills teaching, had intervened and taken a first story away from a child. In the process she had taken the child away from my writing community. When she left, Alex looked at me and said, "I thought my story was finished." I cringed. Was he really saying, "I thought it was my story, I thought I had ownership?" In the pressure to learn skills this became a repeated experience for Alex and his skills teacher.

When Alex completed his story, he didn't know if he wanted to share it with the class. Although I encouraged him, I let him make the decision. Finally, days later, he decided to read it. Seeming very embarrassed, he rolled his eyes, behaved in a silly way, and waved his cover around for the class to see. At first he read in his babyish voice; then he switched to what I described to him as his "fifth-grade" voice and read very fast. Despite his behavior, the class did not laugh at him (thanks to rules we had established) but responded with many positive comments. He seemed surprised and con-fused at first. He was used to their laughter, not to their positive response. Shame began to be transformed into pride.

Alex's next writing piece was somewhat easier for him to write. After thinking about topics for a week, he decided to write about his birthday party. He was well into his draft when it was time for the skills teacher's weekly forty-minute visit. She came a few minutes late, in the middle of my minilesson on dialogue and how it can add to a story. Before the class and I had finished sharing our ideas on the use of dialogue, the skills teacher told Alex to take out his draft. "We're going to add dialogue to your story," she announced. Alex looked confused. "You heard what Ms. Five said about dialogue," the skills teacher responded. "We're going to add it."

"But nobody said anything," Alex told her.

"I'm sure they did. And if they didn't we'll put it in, anyway," she said.

Alex sat at his desk with a blank face. While I tried to continue work-ing with other children, I was aware of the battle going on at Alex's desk and inside me as well. He was not responding. The skills teacher was doing everything she could to force him to write, especially to learn the mechanics of writing dialogue. Since part of his writing problem, according to his IEP, was how to use correct punctuation, she planned to teach it. Alex remained silent except to tell her over and over again that nobody said anything. I decided to explain my writing program to her after school. I felt that she must understand the importance of ownership for a child like Alex, who was just beginning to express his ideas. But her orientation and goals were different. My explanation was not received well. She was responsible to her job description and told me that Alex needed help in writing. Her job was to help him with writing skills.

Slowly, Alex became a more active learner. During the next few months he began to write on the days when the skills teacher was not there. He came to the conference table to read parts of his draft; and, when he was not distracted by other children, he seemed to listen to the comments of the group at the table. Sometimes he made minor revisions based on the feedback he received, but he did not respond to classmates' writing. Sometimes he came to the table to listen for a short time and then would wander back to his desk. I felt that Alex was gradually becoming part of the writing community. Perhaps, as he listened to other children responding to one another's writing, he began to realize that writing was not easy for everyone, that all writers were vulnerable, and that their ideas were respected.

Later in the fall Alex was showing progress. He was better able to select a topic and to write a draft. Without any help from the skills teacher he wrote a piece and decided that he wanted conversation in it. He came to me to learn where to put quotation marks and when to indent. Alex had realized the need to use the correct skills for his own writing. I was pleased that he took a risk with dialogue, and as a result, wanted to learn. It happened when he was ready, at his own timing. I noticed his changed attitude when he wanted to learn for a meaningful purpose. He was interested, he talked, and he asked questions. After we worked on the beginning of his piece, he experimented with his draft to see if he could put quotation marks around conversation at the end. He was beginning to take charge of his writing.

I also began to notice that Alex adopted a different pattern of behavior when the skills teacher arrived. Becoming stubborn, he would not do as she asked. He sat in silence or answered with "I don't know." The more frustrated she became, the more he refused to do, as if he had experienced some ownership in his writing and did not want to give it up. After she left, he reverted to his babyish behavior and crawled on the floor or disrupted the class with his "class clown" antics. He seemed to find some comfort in acting dumb, or perhaps the fact that she worked with him on his writing made him feel inadequate and humiliated. Perhaps he became angry when he felt that she took away his authority or control over his writing. Defiance can be an early expression of ownership.

The situation was very different when it came to reading. Alex was present without the skills teacher for all of reading workshop and for the stories I read aloud to the class. Although he was free to select the books he wanted to read—books that had meaning for him—at first he had difficulty selecting them. He was not a reader. In the past the skills teacher had given him paragraphs to read, and sometimes aides or his teachers had selected books for him. In my room Alex could choose his own books; but, since he had little experience with making choices, he didn't know how.

In the beginning I suggested a few books I knew from past years to be favorites: short, high-interest trade books. I gave him book talks and encouraged him to choose one. Eventually, he read one of the books and wrote a letter to me about it in his reading journal. He mentioned a particular part that he liked and included a sentence about a favorite character. After Alex finished his book, he came to me for another. This time he selected two, looked at both of them carefully, and made a choice. He read slowly, continuing to read short books for many weeks. Listening to his classmates' ideas during group shares, he drew mazes on pieces of paper but said very little about his reading.

During my first reading and writing evaluation conference with Alex, he had difficulty evaluating his progress. We looked through his reading folder and reread his journal letters. We also looked through his writing folder and tried to determine his best piece. I gave him lots of time to think about, and respond to, my questions. I wanted to hear his ideas. Alex told me that he had trouble thinking of topics in writing. He was concerned about his spelling and set a goal for himself to improve in this area. His second goal was to write more pieces. He was able to select as his best story the one about the Grand Canyon. This was the first piece he had written after selecting a topic that was meaningful to him. Alex felt that he had improved in reading because, as he wrote in his journal, "I anderstand books moor. and I read moor books."

Alex became involved in the stories I read to the class. Even though he drew as I read, I knew that he was listening because he began to enter into discussions about the book with a word or two, sometimes in his babyish voice, sometimes in his fifth-grade voice.

At the end of December Alex selected on his own a book with longer chapters. He loved this book and became hooked on reading, going through all the sequels. From that time on, he had no trouble selecting books. The letters in his reading journal became longer, and he began to connect what he read in books to his own experiences. He often ended his letters with questions or predictions, and he enjoyed reading my responses. When Alex had finished all the books in the series, he found *Tales of a Fourth Grade Nothing* (Blume 1972) and the other books that described Fudge and his adventures. He continued to read slowly but was totally involved in his books.

By February Alex was reading books on colonial America. The class was immersed in this topic through reading, writing, simulations, films, discussions, music, and class trips. Alex was particularly interested in colonial schools and school punishments. He read many trade books on this topic and expressed more of his ideas in his journals and in discussions. During conversations about colonial schools, the other children listened to him, questioned him, and learned from his brief answers. He seemed surprised by their interest and by the fact that he knew so much about the topic.

I began to notice that Alex now used his fifth-grade voice more often and that he had stopped crawling on the floor. Also doing well in math, he discovered that he could help other children and that solving problems with his peers was enjoyable. It seemed as though he was becoming part of the greater community of learners.

Just when I saw Alex's confidence in his abilities increase, the skills teacher decided that Alex needed help in reading. Certain reading skills were prescribed by the IEP, and she wanted to take him out of the room to help him read. I explained that he seemed to have developed greater self-confidence in reading and writing; I thought that removing him from the room for skills in reading might destroy his growing positive image of himself as a reader and learner. Still, because she felt that it was important to follow the IEP, she removed him to help him with reading. I wondered what went on in these sessions. When he returned after forty minutes, he reverted to his baby voice and ran around the room out of control. The skills teacher felt that Alex still had many of his old problems, that he could not decode, that he was slow to process information and slow to respond, that it was difficult for him to write, and that he could not express his ideas. I wondered if she saw any of his strengths. I suspected that he continued to be his stubborn, nonresponding self with her. This was not the same Alex I saw in the classroom.

At this time Alex made another decision. He wanted to pursue his interest in colonial schools by writing a report. He divided his long draft into two chapters based on the response he received in conferences. When his chapters were finished, he drew a colonial school for his cover with detailed illustrations. He even made a replica of a hornbook. Again, I realized that art was an important means of expression for him. When Alex was interested and involved, when the work was meaningful for him, when he felt that he could make choices and decisions, and when he had some control, he stopped his babyish voice and silly behavior and put forth greater effort. He was able to write on his own and even took risks writing in another genre. Reading his report to the class in his normal voice, Alex seemed proud of his final product. He listened carefully as the students told him what they liked and what they had learned. Again, he seemed surprised at their response.

Alex was becoming more involved in the stories I read to the class. He seemed to be thinking about the stories all the time. Once, after I read a chapter from *Tuck Everlasting* (Babbitt 1975) where the spring in the Fosters' wood was explained, he blurted out later in the day while he was copying his homework, "Oh, that's why they call it *Tuck Everlasting*." "Why?" I asked. "Because they can't change, they're everlasting," he explained. He was the first one in the class to express his ideas about the meaning of the title. Respecting his opinion and his comment, the class launched into a discussion of that particular title and of titles in general. And Alex was involved in the discussion.

When I had my second reading/writing evaluation conference with Alex at the end of March, I was interested in the changes he expressed. He described his progress in reading by telling me, "I like books much, much more." I was surprised when he told me that he felt writing letters to me in his reading journal helped him as a reader. He explained, "You hear more words. The letters help you understand the book more." Perhaps, even though he wrote brief letters, he was able to reflect in his own way on the books he read. Alex set goals for himself: to read more books, to read different kinds of books, and to read faster. When he talked to me about his writing, he told me that he liked his colonial report the best because he learned a lot about colonial schools; he liked his illustrations, too. He set goals for himself for the remainder of the year. A child who did not take himself seriously as a learner now wanted to improve by adding details to his pieces and by working faster in drafting and copying. It was interesting that spelling had ceased to be a major concern for him. It seemed that meaning had become more important to him than skills.

Continuing to grow as a writer, Alex experimented with similes and began to express his feelings. In his favorite piece about his part in a team sport, he wrote;

> The ball hit me and I went flying across the field like an arrow hitting the target. . . . I kicked the ball. It went into the goal and we won by 1 point. I felt great about winning the game.

At the end of the year Alex was able to evaluate his writing and reading with greater confidence. He knew that he liked his piece describing how he scored the winning point. "I put a simile in it and I told more about how I felt." He knew that he had improved in reading. He had read more books during the year than he could ever remember reading. Moreover, he planned to read over the summer and to write about some of his trips.

Mike's Story

At the beginning of the year Mike, like Alex, was a behavior problem. He ran around the room, shouted out, did little classwork and homework, and constantly played with tape. Disorganized and unable to find school materials, Mike relied on his aide, Marie, to help him with everything.

During the first month of school Mike did not write on his own. He continued to rush around the room, talking back and forth to his friend. Frequently, he came to me and to Marie to tell us about his various topics. As with Alex, I encouraged him to begin a draft by himself and then to come back to the conference table to share it with me and some classmates.

Instead, he brought his paper and pencil to Marie, and I listened in frustration as he tried to write his draft while she, in her eagerness to teach skills, changed it around, adding words and phrases. It seemed that it was no longer his draft, but hers.·

Mike was not interested in coming to the conference table. Accustomed to a one-to-one setting, he was content to work with Marie; however, he often circled the conference area on his trips to the pencil sharpener and to Marie's desk. He heard the constructive response that classmates gave one another and in October he began coming to the conference table at my invitation. He played with tape while listening to a draft; then he decided that he had an idea for a new story. I encouraged him to write his draft by himself. "I can't spell the words," he told me. I reassured him that his ideas were most important and that we would work on the spelling together after he finished his draft. Looking doubtful, Mike went back to his seat, wrote for a short time, and then started toward Marie. As soon as I saw him heading for Marie's desk, I asked him to join the conferences at the table instead. After that, he returned to the conference table often to read his draft. As a result of the response he received, he gradually began to add to his story to clarify some parts. I helped him proofread his piece, which he was now eager to read to the class. His excitement about the response he received from his peers motivated him to begin another piece. Still, this second story, although much shorter than the first, remained his favorite for many weeks. I suspect that was because he wrote it himself and expressed his own ideas.

Eventually, Mike began to write without the help of his aide but with the support of his peers. He began to enjoy moving parts of his piece around and changing words as he revised. He made these decisions by himself, ensuring his control over his writing. I felt that he was becoming part of my community of writers as he realized that the writing environment was safe for taking risks with his ideas.

During the next few months Mike began to come to the conference table on his own. He did not seek out Marie unless he needed help in spelling. When I was reading poetry to the class, he decided to write a poem. He needed many conferences to follow through on his poem because he was concerned about rhyme; but, when he was finished, he was glad that he had tried because "I've never written a poem." I was glad that he felt secure enough to try a new genre.

Unfortunately, Mike did not have the same success in reading. Since he was not in the room at the beginning of reading workshop, he was unable to get settled. He returned from his skills sessions distracted and confused. He relied on his aide to select the book that he read with her each day. When I suggested that he choose a book that he could read when he went to skills and to continue reading it when he returned to the classroom, he was quite agreeable. We found a book that he enjoyed after we read the first few pages together, and he seemed motivated to read it because it was funny. When I discussed this plan with the skills teacher, she told me that the book I had recommended was too difficult for Mike, that the vocabulary was too hard. Mike never came back with the book to read in reading workshop. When he returned to class, he read the book that Marie had selected for him. His journal letters to me were short and written with the help of Marie. Often, he could not remember much about the books he read and therefore could not express his ideas. With specialized help in skills, he repeatedly seemed to lose track of himself.

Mike's first reading/writing evaluation conference revealed that he continued to be concerned about spelling. He set a goal for himself to improve in spelling. He had little to say about reading except that he thought he was reading more books.

Continuing to grow as a writer, Mike was able to select topics and to make decisions about revision. He was not as successful with reading; in that setting he was still unable to choose books or to read them by himself. When he returned from skills, he continued to be disorganized and unable to sustain interest in a book on his own. When I questioned him about the book he was reading in skills, he told me that he could read the book only with the skills teacher. When I asked him if he could read it with Marie, he told me that he could not because he was reading another book with Marie. I asked him if he would like to select a book to read on his own, but he expressed ambivalence about his abilities and his expectations. He felt that the skills teacher and Marie were there to help him with reading and that he had to read with them.

During his second evaluation conference, Mike was still concerned with spelling, although this time in connection with his reading. He felt that if he read more, he would become a better speller. Writing letters in his journal helped him because "you learn to spell better." He thought that he had improved in reading and mentioned that he could recognize similes, which I had taught in minilessons on some of the days that he was in reading workshop for the whole period. He thought that he might try some similes in his own writing. Setting goals for himself in writing, Mike said that he would write a story about a trip he had taken to New York. Another goal was to improve in proofreading. Spelling, although of concern to him in reading, was not specifically mentioned when it came to his own writing. Perhaps it was not as important to him as it once was. Expressing his own ideas in his writing seemed to be more meaningful to him than spelling correctly.

Fortunately, Mike became involved in colonial times, too. He followed his interest in colonial farming that had developed as a result of our visit to a colonial manor. Suddenly, I noticed, he began in reading workshop, without Marie, to read books about the farm. I was amazed. He was very excited and wrote to me in his journal about the information he had gathered on colonial farms. His interest increased his desire for more information on farming tools.

Going to the library himself, he found a book, which he shared with another boy also interested in this topic; in fact, Mike was able to tell Mark a great deal about farming. Because of his involvement in farming, Mike became a more active participant in history. He wanted to read to the class from the history book and was able to do so with few mistakes. His personal investment in learning about history allowed him to take a risk with reading a more difficult book. His IEP program, though, did not support such choice and control. Its insistence on mandated skills continued to interfere with Mike's claiming ownership. He was not sufficiently independent to enjoy learning skills without feeling that he was being deprived of his own ideas.

In the spring Mike, like Alex, was taking more risks in writing, too. Besides using words in his pieces that he did not know how to spell, he experimented with words from his speaking and listening vocabulary. It was at this time that Mike switched to writing in script. I had not forced him. Perhaps he wanted to write in cursive because all his classmates did, or perhaps his personal investment and pride in his own writing prompted his desire to copy his finished pieces in script. I imagine that he was ready and thus made the decision.

At the end of the year Mike was excited about his writing. He liked the similes that he used and told me, "I use better words and I don't worry about spelling." He felt that he had improved in reading because he was reading longer books. And he was—but most of his reading was done with his aide. It was only when he was personally involved in a topic, when he wanted to pursue his own interests, that he could read on his own.

Both boys left fifth grade feeling successful. They were pleased with their achievement. I was especially interested that they had progressed in writing and that over time they were able to take control of it. Ownership gave them choices. They selected topics, and they made decisions about revision, about sharing their work, and about collaboration. They took risks by writing in different genres and by using similes, dialogue, and vocabulary that they couldn't spell. And they evaluated their work and set their own goals for themselves. Mike was able to leave his aide and to become a writer. He developed ownership in writing because, perhaps, he was in the classroom and became part of the writing community. Alex, too, became a writer and was able to express his ideas despite his "limited language" prognosis at the beginning of the year. He also sensed ownership, which he attempted to preserve when the skills teacher arrived. Alex became not just a reader but an independent reader who chose his own books and responded to them with his own ideas. How would Mike have changed as a reader if he had had greater control over his reading, if he had become part of the community of readers, if he had made choices, if he had believed that he could read on his own, and if his reading had not been composed of the isolated skills established by the IEP?

My Story—Reflections

My story was one of frustration. In the past I felt that I could follow my own interests and philosophy, establishing an environment that I sensed was best suited to my students and to me. By the middle of the year I realized the skills teachers' need for ownership—to teach the boys in their own way with little collaboration with me. I had discussed the situation and the issue of ownership—mine and the boys'—many times with my principal and with other administrators. I explained my philosophy and wondered why there could not be greater communication between skills teachers and classroom teachers. Couldn't we work together for the benefit of the boys? Couldn't there be some congruency? How can personal ownership and collaboration be integrated so that cooperation occurs? It seemed the same issue with which Alex and Mike struggled. I had found a solution in the classroom, the creation of a community of learners. Could this be extended to the school as a whole?

Providing few answers, the administrators told me that I had good questions, but explained patiently that I really didn't have ownership in my classroom because I was expected to teach the prescribed fifth-grade curriculum. This came as a surprise to me. I had always thought that I had ownership within the confines of the school's and state's curriculum. I felt defeated. Again, like Alex and Mike, my philosophy (like their ideas, which were so important) was being restricted. I felt all year as the boys were taught different approaches in one-to-one settings that I had no idea what they were learning, what strategies were used, or how I could build on that learning in the classroom.

In the confusion of the conflicts that seemed to surround me for most of the year, I didn't realize until the end that both boys were able to become part of the class community of learners—Alex to a greater extent than Mike, who seemed at times on the fringe except for writing. The ownership they discovered over time through the response they received in writing workshop gradually spread to reading and other areas of the curriculum. They realized that their ideas were valued and respected. Beginning to take themselves and their learning seriously, they started to take risks with their own ideas by participating in discussions and simulations The personal investment they made in learning led to greater independence. Alex no longer had to be the class clown. He realized that his baby voice could be substituted by a more mature voice. As I struggled to provide a supportive environment—one that responded to them with respect and gave them time to grow at their own rate—I realized that they were able to develop some sense of control or authority over their learning despite the disruptions caused by their IEP schedules. Through this ownership these special learners discovered that they had a voice.

Alex and Mike taught me about my own need for ownership, something I had taken for granted in the past. In other years I did not feel as hampered or trapped by IEP regulations, the problems of scheduling, and communication between teachers. My year of frustration was not due to pull-out/put-in programs; it had more to do with my philosophy and the setting—the environment I wanted for my special learners. If the environment with the skills teachers was consistant with the environment in the classroom, if there was congruency, if there was collaboration, if we had all worked together for the benefit of the boys, perhaps ownership would not have been an issue for me personally. As the school year ended and I had time to reflect, I was left with two nagging questions: Do children own their own minds? and How do teachers maintain ownership of their philosophy within the classroom and the system? Both of these questions will, no doubt, provide the seeds of reflection in years to come.

References

Babbitt, N. 1975. *Tuck everlasting.* New York: Farrar, Straus & Giroux.

Blume, J. 1972. *Tales of a fourth grade nothing.* New York: Dutton.

Glacobbe, M.E. 1976. Learning to write and writing to learn in the elementary school. Pp. 131–47 in *The teaching of writing: 85th yearbook of the National Society for the Study of Education,* edited by Anthony R. Petrosky and David Bartholomae. Chicago: University of Chicago Press.

Weaver, C. 1994a. *Reading process and practice from socio-psycholinguistics to whole language, 2d ed.* pp. 544–550. Portsmouth, N.H.: Heinemann.

———. 1994b. *Success at last: Helping students with AD(H)D achieve their potential.* pp. 196–220. Portsmouth, N.H.: Heinemann.

9

The Power of Influence: Effecting Change by Developing Ownership

Margaret Stevenson
Edmonton Public Schools

> You only know the fish are alive when you see them swimming upstream.
>
> Elliot Eisner (1990).

This story covers the last ten years of my career, during which time I was supervisor of language arts (K–12) in Edmonton, Alberta, a school district with 70,000–80,000 students and 4,000 teachers and administrators. Over those ten years I worked with several consultants whom I was able to select on the basis of their beliefs about the nature of language and the role of language in learning, their experience as teachers, and their leadership qualities. Together, we became a team. Our role was to provide leadership, advice, and assistance for students' language learning and related programs.

It was important that we maintain a close working relationship with those with similar interests and responsibilities at the local university, at the provincial department of education, and with colleagues in neighboring school districts. We also established and maintained a network of friends and colleagues across Canada, the United States, and England. All our colleagues and contacts contributed to our efforts to influence the teachers, administrators, and parents in our school district.

I use the term *influence* deliberately because curriculum supervisors and consultants had no power to require teachers or administrators to change anything that they were doing. Our influence had to come from their understanding that our beliefs were based on sound theory, were consistent, were well articulated, and were translatable into action at the classroom level. The view of language that we espoused could be called holistic. This applied whether language was being expressed through writing and speaking or being received by reading and listening. It also applied whether English was being learned as a native or "other" language and to languages other than English. The term *holistic* implies that language is considered in "chunks" large enough to convey meaning. In fact, meaning is central to the holistic approach, "which is also known as 'real books' in Britain and occasionally literature-based learning, language experience or emergent literacy" (Smith 1992, p. 440). A holistic approach assumes that the skills of language (listening, speaking, reading, and writing) support one another and apply across all subject areas. The basis of this philosophy is respect—"respect for language (which should be natural and authentic, not contrived) and respect for learners (who should be engaged in meaningful and productive activities, not in pointless drills and rote memorization)." (Willinsky 1990, cited in Smith 1992, p. 440).

The Change Process

James Britton (1982a) told us time and again that "change is contagious; teachers catch it from each other." Fullan calls this phenomenon "shared meaning," describing it as "a group of teachers using the innovation with some degree of consistency" (1991/1992, p. 8).

That significant teacher change is a very slow, deep process and that teachers learn best from each other is reinforced time and again in the literature and research on teacher change (Fullan 1991, 1982; Stephens 1987; Lambert 1988). Teachers emulate one another, either on an informal or formal basis, adopting and/or adapting the practices of peers that they consider successful and effective. Reflection time and support are needed. Many complex and interrelated ideas must first come together in the minds of teachers before the change can become part of the program for the students.

It is also important to note that those who introduce change (policy makers, university professors, administrators) often treat teachers in exactly the same way as they criticize teachers for treating the students. New curricula emphasize the importance of being sensitive to where students are, what they think, and why; yet, the same curricula are introduced to teachers in ways that ignore what *they* think and why. Teachers undergoing change need to be helped to see change as part of a learning process and themselves as learners.

Change always carries a certain amount of ambiguity and uncertainty. Cognitive dissonance is common, as teachers have the feeling that they are confronting more information than they can handle. This is the case whether others impose the change, whether teachers volunteer to participate, or whether they initiate the change. In each case the meaning of change is often not clear at the outset, and uncertainty and discouragement are bound to accompany the change.

The change that we were advocating meant influencing teacher's philosophical beliefs so as to be open to the theory behind a curriculum change. Teachers needed to become acquainted with the practical aspects of change in the classroom and to relate that to their beliefs, that is, their philosophical position. It was also important for them to discuss their beliefs and classroom activities with one another. This is a far more difficult approach to change than asking teachers to use new material or to try a different strategy (Fullan 1982).

Ownership

One overriding theme emerges from the story of our work with teachers and administrators—and indeed from all that we did to facilitate change during those ten years. We were involved in helping teachers and administrators take ownership of the literacy lessons in their classrooms/schools. To do this, they needed to have an understanding of the language learning of children, a philosophical position based on that understanding, and literacy programs consistent with their philosophical position.

Frank Smith (1989) has always been a strong promoter of teacher ownership.

> The basic question is, who is to be in charge of classrooms—teachers or outsiders? All the prescribed programs, all the pre-specified and detailed objectives, and all the mandated assessments are impositions from outside. They interfere not only with the autonomy of teachers but with the ability of teachers and students to act together in pursuit of learning. . . . Teachers must become more professional, they must regain control of classrooms. (p. 358)

Patrick Shannon (1989) has a similar observation.

> Publishers attempt to make all the important decisions concerning goals, content, sequence and even the language of literacy lessons, leaving teachers with control over only the pace with which they follow directions as they lead their students through the materials. (p. 627)

Shannon suggests, as an alternative, a holistic language philosophy that "offers teachers and students more control over their lessons," starting from "the premise that literacy lessons are . . . negotiations between and among students and teachers." (p. 627)

Providing Leadership and Support

Key vehicles to help teachers to take ownership of change were our teacher support groups. The origin of these groups demonstrates how leadership can take advantage of teachers' initiatives. Our first language arts summer session was organized because we followed a teacher's suggestion. Michael, who had attended the annual International Reading Association conference that May, spoke to me upon his return about an exciting session presented by Ethel Buchanan from Winnipeg. He was so impressed he asked if I could possibly arrange for her to give a workshop for our teachers. I knew that her strategies and theory would support our position on language learning and would speak directly to teachers. I was happy to arrange the workshop, which became the two-week summer session attended by twenty-five teachers.

On the last day of the summer session the teachers, although excited, were sober and apprehensive when they realized they were going to be on their own and that they would need support. Mostly from different schools, they had to have some way to stay in touch for sharing their successes and failures and for moving ahead. As a result, they organized a support group, a concept eagerly adopted by other teachers. The consultants and I attended their meetings, provided liaison with language arts activities at the district level, and facilitated the exchange of ideas and projects across all groups; still, the responsibility for meeting and programming remained with each group. In all, eight groups of elementary teachers met regularly; then, junior high teachers organized a support group. Eventually, 200–250 teachers were involved.

Some of these groups undertook major projects. One group planned and carried out the first student writing conference in the school district. It involved a full Saturday of workshops for two hundred children, grades 2–6, a mammoth undertaking for a group of fifteen to twenty teachers with full-time teaching commitments.

Another group spent a full year planning and taking part in the production of a videotape explaining their language arts programs. Since this project was undertaken cooperatively with the local university, the videotape is used both with teachers and parents in the school district and with teachers-in-training at the university.

The teachers expended much creative talent and energy in these meaningful programs, striving to convince and demonstrate to parents and principals that what they were doing was in the best interest of children.

Networking

To build support for the changes we desired, the language arts consultants and I worked through a series of networks, both within and outside the school district.

Within the District

Since we believed that language played a critical role in learning in all subjects, we initiated and encouraged close cooperation with other subject supervisors and consultants. We sponsored joint presentations at district workshops, sessions for administrators, and school professional development days. Most important of all, we included teachers as presenters, because they speak with authority and credibility about the classroom. Supervisors and consultants can provide only the theoretical background and talk about ''the way things should be'' in the classroom. Teachers demonstrate ''the way things are'' in the classroom.

We also realized how important it was that key members of senior staff understand what we were about so that we could count on their support. We gave information to the directors of curriculum and student assessment and to the associate superintendents who worked with principals. As administrators in our board often passed on articles to advance particular views, I responded to each article I received with two others that considered the issue from my theoretical position. I also attempted to arrange time for senior administrators to meet the visiting scholars we brought in. There seems little point in providing professional development for teachers if their supervisors are not educated as well.

Special information-sharing sessions and workshops were planned for principals. I also wrote a monthly paper for principals, sharing my point of view on issues that they previously identified, including the (over)use of workbooks and duplicated exercises and the teaching of thinking skills in isolation.

Current articles on language arts research and practice were regularly distributed to the reading specialists in the district, and a yearly session was held to update them on our work. Several of the reading specialists and principals were also members of teacher support groups, thus extending and reinforcing the network and the concept of ''ownership.''

Undoubtedly, our most significant networking success within the district was with student assessment. This networking began when two consultants were assigned halftime with language arts and halftime with student assessment to develop, pilot, and implement districtwide writing assessment at grades 5 and 11. The two consultants believed, along with the rest of our team, that the assessment of language must be consistent with our beliefs about the way that language is learned.

The value of this network became evident when we received word from the superintendent that we were to develop statements of outcomes in language arts that applied across elementary, junior, and senior high schools. We were also responsible for developing written achievement tests based on those outcomes for students in the third, sixth, and ninth year in school that were to be piloted, revised, and ready to administer in eight months. The alternative was that experts external to the district would develop the tests for our students (not a scenario we would consider).

The guidelines agreed on for the developing of the outcomes statements were that they must reflect the integrated nature of language, they must be applicable from grades 1 to 12, and they must not be great in number. As well, they must be specific enough to form the basis of the achievement tests. A tall order, but not impossible.

Our eight language outcomes were soon developed. The greatest challenge was trying to develop questions that would reflect, as much as a test situation can, the language arts program that we supported in the schools. We wanted to be able to demonstrate what we expected teachers to do in their own classrooms. For example, we expected teachers consciously to assist students to develop language skills in all subject areas, to require students to express thoughts and feelings fluently and precisely in writing, and to provide opportunities for personal response to literature and for supported opinions. We expected teachers to ensure that their students had opportunities to write in different forms for varied purposes and audiences. Our tests needed to reflect this kind of program, not only to support the teachers but also because we knew that the test, once applied, would affect programs, since, for good or bad, this is the nature of testing (Searle and Stevenson 1987). Through the tests we hoped to give more power to those teachers whose programs were based on what we felt were sound principles of language learning.

With the understanding and support of the student assessment department, we were able to develop tests that met all the requirements. In the years since, various forms of the tests have been developed, but the constant is that students are always required to demonstrate what they can do with language. The only way that teachers can prepare students for these tests is to teach them throughout the year how to read, understand, and appreciate various forms of fiction and nonfiction.

There is no doubt that the tests are having a positive influence on the language programs in the district. Besides making writing a priority, many school staffs have also broadened their approach to teaching literature. Teachers have a better understanding of the role of language in learning and of the need for consistency between philosophy, program, and assessment. Our influence on student assessment staff has maintained for thirteen years, through three directors of student assessment and other staff changes.

During his many visits Britton constantly focused our attention on the key role of the principal in effecting change. He recommended an intensive program of professional study for principals, starting with language, as a step in securing their understanding and commitment. He also made specific suggestions to principals about professional development in their schools. Their long-range aim, he felt, should be to have each school become a professional development unit for its own teaching staff.

Attention to the in-service needs of school administrators gathered even more momentum after an incident in an elementary school. After several parents complained about the language arts program in one classroom, the assistant principal spent some time observing the program, and reported to the principal that the complaint was not justified. As the parents were still complaining, the principal asked me to review the program. My analysis was that there was no program; the children went from one workbook to another and from there to a worksheet. The parents had every reason to complain.

I approached the associate superintendent of that area with my concern that decisions were being made about children's language learning by administrators with inadequate backgrounds. I sought his cooperation in providing a series of workshops on the language learning of children for principals and assistant principals in his area. We worked it out together. The series of five or six workshops was then requested by the associate superintendents of other areas. Thus began the first curriculum in-service in the district planned just for school administrators.

We also established a pattern of having each external consultant give at least one session just for school administrators. We wanted very much to provide them with enough background that they would feel comfortable discussing language-related issues with external consultants, other principals, teachers, and parents.

We were aware, too, that principals learn best from other principals, just as teachers learn best from other teachers. Having outstanding principals from other school districts as guest speakers and providing time for discussion promoted an exchange of ideas and often resulted in intervisitations. Because principals are definitely the key to change in the schools, and we wanted them on-side.

Outside the District

Besides our network within the district, our language arts team maintained a professional association with those who worked in language learning at the local university, the provincial department of education, and other school districts. We also called upon the expertise and assistance of external consultants.

Staff Exchanges with the Local University

For three consecutive years we were fortunate to be part of staff exchanges with the education faculty of the University of Alberta. Three professors worked with the language arts consulting staff, while three consultants taught courses for the education faculty. There were benefits on both sides. Consultants could draw upon their school district experience and contacts while working with teachers-in-training at the university. Working directly with teachers and administrators, the professors could experience firsthand their problems and successes.

External Consultants

Over ten years I was able to invite many experts in language learning to talk to our teachers, consultants, and school and central services administrators. Often, members of the board of trustees attended as well. The visitors' sessions varied from one-hour presentations to two-day miniconferences. We shared speakers with other school districts and with the university; we shared expenses to secure speakers that were already coming for teachers' conventions or conferences. Our visitors all had one thing in common—their beliefs about the nature of language learning and the role of language in all learning were consistent with ours. Our visitors came from universities and school districts in England, the United States, Australia, and across Canada. They were often professors, but they also were school administrators and teachers themselves. Of all our external consultants, there is one, James Britton, who stands out as having the most significant long term influence on teacher change in our district. Britton first came to our school district in March 1980 and stayed for five weeks. In 1981 and again in 1982 he returned for three weeks. Subsequently, he made yearly visits of two or three days until 1988, spending time in schools at all levels working with teachers. He also met with groups of teachers, administrators, consultants, department heads, and parents. Britton spent several half-days consulting with the student assessment department. At the conclusion of the 1980, 1981, and 1982 visits Britton (1980, 1981, 1982b) sent to the board of trustees a report documenting his concerns. Noting the changes he had observed since his last visit, he suggested direction for the next year. Britton's reports provided strong support for teachers, as well as an understanding of the change process that came from years of working with teachers in many countries. In his 1980 report to trustees, Britton summarized his views on change as follows,

> Change in the system will come about primarily, in my view, by contagion from teacher to teacher. This requires time, and immediate rewards cannot be expected. It requires, above all, consultation time for teachers themselves. I believe serious consideration should be given to any measures that would devote resources to reducing teaching loads and increasing opportunities for staff consultation within schools and between schools.

Change would come about, then, as teachers internalized the new ideas and tried alternate strategies while constantly checking with one another. In time, teachers would "own" the ideas and would continue to help one another. Change would spread slowly throughout the district. This actually happened through meetings of teachers and administrators, both formal and informal. Teachers also facilitated change by visiting others' classrooms, by writing about their teaching experiences, and by sharing their writing. As Fullan (1982) has noted, change is a process, not an event. It takes time and commitment.

Helping Schools Develop Their Programs

As a group of consultants trying to effect change, we faced a dilemma. Though we had a real sense of direction for language arts education, our aim was always for teachers to develop their own programs based on their beliefs about the nature of language and the role of language in learning. We wanted teachers to "own" their programs, not just adjust them according to the prevailing board policies and assessment.

We needed, therefore, to develop and provide resources that would enable teachers and principals to develop consistent programs within each school. To do this, we first needed to develop a written statement of our own beliefs.

After spending three weeks in the district in 1982, Britton expressed a concern: "There seems to be an increasing anxiety among teachers that the system they work in may be becoming less supportive of what they are trying to achieve, and even, at certain points on certain occasions, hostile to it." He concluded, however, on a more positive note (Britton 1982b):

> But I do believe the proposal to draw up a language arts policy document and seek ratification for it at Trustee level would be an effective way of restoring confidence among teachers in the system. The Board's own statement of objectives and Alberta Government (Department of Education) statements on Language Arts provide, I believe, a suitable framework within which such an instrument of language arts policy might be constructed. (p. 12)

Britton's guidelines, extended discussions with the language arts team (supervisor and consultants), and Dennis Searle's work with our teachers were the basis for our position paper, written in 1982 by Searle during his exchange from the University of Alberta. This ten-page document briefly describes our point of view about the nature of language and about the role of language in learning. It deals with the relationship between language and thought and more extensively with the implications for learning and using language in the school, concluding with the responsibility of schools.

Our language position paper was examined not by the board of trustees, as Britton suggested, but by the superintendent of schools and his senior administrative staff. After discussion, it was renamed "A Language Working Paper," and we were authorized to make it the basis for our continuing work with teachers, administrators, and parents.

Subsequently, Searle conducted a series of workshops for principals, who discussed the contents of the document as well as the implications for program, assessment, and reports to parents. Also developing brochures outlining the document, Searle distributed them to parents at both the elementary and secondary level.

"A Language Working Paper" and the brochures performed several functions. They presented in tangible form our point of view about language—a consistent message available to all elementary and secondary school principals and teachers. They established a starting point for individuals' reflections on their beliefs about the role of language in learning. Britton (1982a) always stressed "the importance to teachers of a rationale, a theory that is consistent with and supportive of their practices. It provides us with a running code of operational principles, a way of monitoring our own practice, a way of effectively influencing other people and defending our own position" (p. 187). In this way teachers immersing themselves in change were finding support for their teaching.

"A Language Working Paper" and the brochures also urge school staffs to develop a school position on language learning and to begin to look at the consistency of their philosophical position with school programs, assessment, and reporting. A teacher or administrator who knows the school position on language learning and how it relates to school programs can discuss it reasonably with parents and the community—whether the question is about curriculum, material, assessment, or the report card.

Developing a school language policy requires that the teachers and principals examine their own beliefs about the nature of language and the role of language in learning, that they discuss these beliefs, and that they put together a position statement acceptable to all. As difficult and time-consuming as this process is, it is only the beginning. The next step is to ensure that a school's programs (including curriculum, teaching strategies, and materials), assessment, and procedures for reporting to parents are consistent with the policy. This step is critical because in some cases schools have developed a policy that is then placed on the shelf.

Sometimes, schools don't start with a policy; but, in the process of examining what they are doing and why they are doing it, they may end up with one. After developing "A Language Working Paper," Searle spent much of his time with us working with school staffs as they came to grips with the need for this consistency. He spent considerable time with one staff who said that they wanted to revise their procedure for reporting to parents. After one frustrating half-day session, the teachers decided that they could not do anything about report cards until they first examined their assessment procedures. Searle returned for a second session, which was no more successful than the first. The teachers then decided that they could not do justice to assessment until they had looked carefully at their programs. Eventually, the teachers and principal realized that they needed to start with a school language policy, which they developed with Searle's help. From there they worked back through school programs and assessment until, several months later, they came up with a reporting procedure consistent with *their* policy. Printed on their reporting form, the school language policy became a model for other schools. Only through taking ownership and working through the process themselves did teachers understand the importance of a point of view about language to all aspects of their teaching.

A breakthrough in developing and implementing school language policies came in 1983–1984, when five new elementary schools opened. Their principals were able to select teachers whose beliefs about the nature of learning were consistent with their own. Several principals chose to focus on the role of language (listening, speaking, reading, writing) in learning and on children's active use of language in all its forms. I hope that this decision reflected our early commitment to the professional development of administrators. As a result of the principals' focus, many of our teachers' support group members were able to teach in schools where the library was indeed the "heart" of the school and where a room was planned and furnished as a publishing house for children's written work.

Evidently, all the work we had done over several years with teachers and administrators was paying off. We were convinced of this when, in 1985, two of our elementary schools were the only ones in western Canada selected as Schools of Excellence in Language Arts from across North America by the National Council of Teachers of English. In 1987 three more of our schools were selected.

In 1986 the principal of one of the prizewinning schools was named an associate superintendent in charge of about thirty-five elementary, junior high, and senior high schools. Because this principal believed so strongly in the importance of building a school program on a sound philosophy of students' language learning, he made the following requirements of all his principals:

> During 1986–1987 school principals and staff would develop their philosophical position with respect to the role of language in learning.

> During 1987–1988 principals and school staff would make plans to implement their language policy.

> During 1988–1989 principals and school staff would begin the process of implementing their language policy.

Until that associate superintendent left his position four years later, the priority in those thirty-five schools was language, supported by in-service sessions and workshops for principals.

What we had begun through influence (because we had no power) was continued through the mandate of an associate superintendent. And the network of those knowledgeable about language learning continues to expand as the principals and teachers from those thirty-five schools move to other schools and positions in the district.

Professional Development of Consultants

Language arts consultants were carefully chosen, based on their background in language and its role in learning, their successful teaching experience, and their ability to work well with others, both in proactive and reactive roles. Learning how to be a consultant, though, is done mainly through on-the-job experience.

My expectation was that the consultants would continue to grow in their knowledge of language learning and that they would constantly apply this knowledge to their work with teachers, administrators, and parents. To facilitate this, the consultants received their own copies of relevant published material, which stayed with them when they left to study or to take another position.

The concept of the consultants' being valued "members of the club" was enhanced by having each external consultant spend a couple of hours just with the consultants. Our consultants entered into discussions with, and asked questions of, James Britton, Margaret Meek Spencer, Frank Smith, Dorothy Watson, Jerome Harste, Arthur Applebee, Ken and Yetta Goodman, Don Rutledge, Ethel Buchanan, John Dixon, Donald Graves, Jane Hansen, Moira McKenzie, Elliot Eisner, and others. These were valuable contacts for the consultants, who were also encouraged to attend conferences, workshops, and summer sessions outside the district. They turned to the people that they had met in our district for further instruction. As one consultant commented: "Everything was intended to reinforce what we believed about children and their learning. There was consistency in the people we brought in—it wasn't just anybody."

The record of our language arts consultants over the last ten years speaks for itself. Three have completed a Ph.D. degree. Two of those are now on staff at the local university—one in elementary and one in secondary education. Five consultants have completed M.Ed. degrees in the last ten years. School administration claimed six consultants; of those, two are now associate superintendents, each responsible for about thirty-five schools. Two of our former consultants now provide language expertise to the student assessment department. One is performing a valuable role in personnel. Some have returned to their first love, teaching, and refuse to consider an administrative role, preferring to work with children. From this variety of positions they continue to influence language arts education in our schools. The closeness and the feeling of being "members of the club" have continued. Four years after my retirement we still meet over dinner once a month—to share. The network is strong.

This story of the last ten years of my career as a language arts supervisor is now complete. I worked through a position of influence with a team of consultants to effect change by helping teachers and school administrators develop a philosophical position on the nature of language and the role of language in learning. What can be learned from this experience?

Without doubt, our experience indicates that this kind of change takes a long time. Seven to ten years are the numbers usually cited for making significant change. This certainly has implications for those who make appointments and who outline expectations in school districts. We based our efforts on the belief that teachers and principals (as well as supervisors and consultants) need to work from a carefully considered philosophical position and that it takes time for people to develop this position for themselves.

The processes that we used in effecting change are consistent with contemporary change theory (with an important exception that I discuss later). The concept of networking is well established, supported, and very effective. Britton talks about change as being contagious and that teachers catch it from one another. In the same vein Frank Smith (1992) comments: "Effective teachers demonstrate what can be done (and their own attitude toward what can be done) and they help others to do it. They make newcomers members of clubs to which they themselves already belong" (p. 435). Inviting principals to membership in the club is just as important. In this way they, too, will take on ownership of the ideas and facilitate the change.

The principal as key to change in the school is well documented in the literature (Fullan 1982, 1988, 1991). In acknowledging this, we spent time and effort increasing principals' knowledge base and assisting them to apply their knowledge in their schools.

An important part of our work, and one which I see as an exception to current change theory, is the active role of teachers who see themselves as professionals. These professionals work from a philosophical position, a point of view about language. They make decisions about what they will do in their classrooms and what materials they will use. Teachers will "become their own experts" when, as Britton recommended, each school becomes a professional development unit for its own teaching staff. Gambell (1988) describes such teachers as "the new professionals." Seeing teachers as "taking increased responsibility for their own inservice needs," he maintains that "self development is a hallmark of the new professionalism" (p. 24). We were able to encourage this new professionalism.

Such "new professionals" have banded together in groups, as in the teacher support groups described earlier. The power of these groups was illustrated at a conference of the International Reading Association in Edmonton in April 1992. Addressing teachers, Adrian Peetoom of Scholastic, Canada, commented that the content of publishers' displays at conferences across North America had changed noticeably over the last few years, from sets of basic readers to trade books in children's literature and professional books for teachers. This happened in response to teachers, who had decided that the use of basal readers was not consistent with their beliefs about children's language learning.

These teachers are part of a "grass roots" movement whose members are now holding their own conferences all over North America, attracting as many as four thousand registrants. Only publishers whose publications meet the teachers' standards are invited to display their materials. There is a need for more information on the power that these teachers have been able to generate through their support groups and in their role for initiating change.

Our district no longer has a leadership position in language arts (or any other curriculum area); however, I believe that the work we started ten years ago will continue. It will thrive because we concentrated our efforts on having teachers and principals take ownership. In the meantime, "I pin my hopes on the small circles and quiet processes in which genuine and reforming change takes place." (Rufus Jones, quoted in Britton 1982, p. 214)

References

Britton, J.N. 1980. *Report to the board of trustees*. Edmonton Public Schools, Edmonton, Alberta.

———. 1981. *Report to the board of trustees*. Edmonton Public Schools, Edmonton, Alberta.

———. 1982a. *Prospect and retrospect: selected essays of James Britton*. Edited by G.M. Pradl. Montclair, N.J.: Boynton/Cook.

———. 1982b. *Report to the board of trustees*. Edmonton Public Schools, Edmonton, Alberta.

Eisner, E.W. 1990. Keynote address presented at the 80th annual conference of the National Council of Teachers of English, Atlanta, Georgia, November 18.

Fullan, M. 1982. *The meaning of educational change*. Toronto: OISE.

———. 1988 *What's worth fighting for in the principalship: Strategies for taking charge of the elementary school principalship*. Toronto: Ontario Public School Teachers' Federation.

———. 1991. *The new meaning of educational change*. 2d ed.. New York: Teachers College Press.

———. 1991/1992. Understanding the change process: An interview with Michael Fullan. Part One. *The Developer*, December/January, 1–8.

Gambell, T.J. 1988. The new professionalism: Critical questions for teaching literacy. *Elements* 19(2): 23–25.

Lambert, L. 1988. Staff development redesigned. *Phi Delta Kappan* 69(4): 665-68.

Peetoom, A. 1992. Address to International Reading Association, Edmonton, Alberta.

Searle, D. 1981. "A language working paper." Edmonton Public Schools, Edmonton, Alberta

Searle, D., and Stevenson, M.T. 1987. An alternate assessment program in language arts. *Language Arts* 64(3): 278–84.

Shannon, P. 1989. The struggle for control of literacy lessons. *Language Arts* 66(6): 625–634.

Smith, F. 1989. Overselling literacy. *Phi Delta Kappan*, 70(5): 353–59.

———. 1992. Learning to read: The never-ending debate. *Phi Delta Kappan* 73(6): 432–41.

Stephens, D. 1987. Empowering learning: Research as practical theory. *English Education* 9(4): 220–28.

10

Dialectics of Ownership: Language as Property

Patrick Shannon

Pennsylvania State University

Our daughter, Laura, attends the State College Friends School as a first-grade student. Once a week her mother, Kathleen, and I (and sometimes her four-year-old brother, Tim-Pat), teach in Laura's classroom, supporting students' writing, reading, and mathematics. Laura's teacher, Teacher Eileen (TE), allows us time and choice to pursue our own projects while teaching: Kathleen literally built the school library (shelves, collection, and card catalog), confers with students during writing workshop, and started a K–1 newspaper. I attempt Share Book Experience, listen to students during reading workshop, and teach some mathematics. Tim-Pat enjoys the headphones and blocks.

During the reading and writing workshops at Friends School, all students own their literate behavior, the location of that engagement, and the schedule through which they will share the products of literacy. Students select books from tubs to read according to their interests and abilities; these tubs offer many more stories than nonfiction (something we're working on) and range from caption to chapter books. Their choices of what and how to present the books they read suggest independent judgment about what they value in books and in life. When writing, students select topics, genre, and style in order to write what they mean and to give expression to their experience. Their published writings vary from posters to patterned language books to collected reports to chapter stories. These instances of ownership seem to drive the Friends School literacy program and individual students' concepts of literacy as the development of personal understanding of the world.

In a fit of enthusiasm Kathleen and I once proposed to Laura's class that we rewrite some folk tales, perform them before video cameras, and sell them as a fund raiser. After TE and the school administrator supported our initiative, we began by reading a wide variety of folk tales aloud on three successive Tuesdays. After each reading we discussed the tales' plots and similarities to other versions. During these discussions students were hesitant to comment on the books unless they had seen a Disney or Fairy Tale Theater version of the folk tale, and then they were convinced that the book author's interpretation was incorrect. Although multiple versions of the same tale helped a little, real progress on interpretation began only after we read Jon *The True Story of the 3 Little Pigs by A. Woolf* (Scieszka 1989). Reading this book aloud both facilitated and constrained the discussion. Students were more willing to talk and "play" with the ideas of the folk tales, but thereafter they limited their discussions to the three animal tales: "The Three Little Pigs," "The Three Bears," and "The Three Billy Goats Gruff."

Students selected a tale they wished to rewrite, and Kathleen, TE, Teacher Cynthia (a halftime classroom aide), and I began to work with four groups of four students each by reading several versions of their selections and discussing possible plot structures. We attempted to chart the salient features of each version to determine what it was that students considered essential to their rewritings. During these discussions students were quick to declare their favorite versions and to point out which versions were nonsensical (for example, Ruth Hillert's retellings were panned because she simplified the stories too much and left out vital information).

Each group rewrote a folk tale—sometimes with pictures, sometimes with teachers acting as scribes, and sometimes with "we'll work it out during the play." They declared a title and decided who would play which part. These steps overlapped considerably, for example, in one retelling of "The Three Bears," three students chose to be Goldilocks. The play was written accordingly; however, when the one Bear disclosed her plans to wear a bearskin during the play, two Goldilocks switched to Bear parts and again the play had to be rewritten.

After two Tuesdays, students settled upon four titles and plots: "The Three Billy Goats Gruff" (an exact copy of the traditional tale, starring Joe, Kaila, Andy, and me); "Two Pigs and a Wolf" (a story about a wolf visiting two sleeping pigs, starring Sasha, Sarah, and Walter; Jamie chose not to participate); "Goldilocks and Thunderbolt" (a traditional retelling except that Goldilocks rode everywhere on horseback, starring Scott, Jesse, Paul, and Anja); "Goldilocks and the Three Bears: The Day After" (starring Laura, Walton, Abby, and Zahra).

"Goldilocks and the Three Bears: The Day After" reversed the plot of the traditional folk tale, added a detail from Cinderella, and twisted the climax. You see, Goldilocks left her shoes at the Bears' residence when she jumped out the window; and the Bears, who as children's author, Paul Galdone, suggests "never did anyone any harm," decided to return them to Goldilocks. Luckily, Goldilocks having attended camp that summer, her name and address were written inside her shoes; thus, it was easy for the

Bears to find Goldilocks's house. Just before the Bears arrived, Goldilocks had cooked spaghetti and had gone for a walk while it cooled. Finding the house open, the Bears entered ("friends open the door and yell 'anybody home?'"); they ate the spaghetti ("not to be mean, but it smelled so good"); they sat down to rest in the only chair available ("they were tired after a long walk and a good meal") and broke it; then they lay on her bed upstairs ("there was no place else to sit").

Upon her return Goldilocks was not pleased to find the spaghetti eaten, her chair broken, and three Bears in her bed. When she demanded an explanation, the Bears replied that they were only trying to return her shoes from the day before. Goldilocks then apologized for "messing up" their house the day before. The Bears acknowledged that they "see how easy it is to mess up someone else's house. You haven't eaten yet. Let's go out and have some spaghetti." Goldilocks and the Bears shake hands and go off arm in arm in search of spaghetti.

Who Owns This Activity?

Although this may not be the first question that comes to mind, in the context of this book, it is the only question that counts. Ownership is considered a cornerstone of the New Literacy (Willinsky 1990).

> With the best topic, the child exercises strongest control, establishes ownership and with ownership, pride in the piece. (Graves 1983, p. 22)

> What should never be forgotten, however, is that the *force* of revision, the energy of ownership, is rooted in the child's voice, the urge to express. (Graves 1983, p. 168)

> If we want our adolescent students to grow to appreciate literature, another first step is allowing them to exert ownership and choose the literature they will read. (Atwell 1987, p. 64)

> Authenticity is essential. Kids need to feel that what they are doing through language, they have chosen to do because it is useful or interesting or fun for them. They need to own the processes they use: to feel that the activities are their own; not just school work or stuff to please the teacher. What they do ought to matter to them personally. (Goodman 1985, p. 31)

> By having ownership in what they do, by following their own questions about topics, they are able to create new concepts and make new connections in their schemata. They select and take on projects; they make them their own, thereby making their knowledge their own. It is this ownership that fosters intellectual autonomy. "Owning" an activity or project leads to knowing how, why, and what to do. (Pappas, Kiefer, and Levstik 1990, p. 39)

To own or to take or get possession of a topic, a book, an activity, or process appears to be fundamental to learning to use language purposefully to achieve one's interests. According to New Literacy advocates, teachers should acknowledge this fact. They need to develop classroom conditions that will not only permit but also facilitate students' taking possessions of their language and language use. Ownership can make easier other aspects of language learning: control, voice, choice, authenticity, and intellectual autonomy.

Although it can be argued that Kathleen and I owned the project (because we initiated it) and that TE owned the context in which the project took place (because she allowed all of us to begin), Friends School students owned the content, structure, characters, and action of the videotapes. The students negotiated among themselves which folk tales to rewrite. They decided what the new plots would be and how to tell those plots, who would play which part, and why the characters would behave and talk in certain ways. This control enabled students to find themselves within the project, and it set the project apart from other activities in which students are expected to fill roles that adults define for them (for example, Tim-Pat is now taking Suzuki violin). That teachers were involved did not diminish the students' pride in their work, but it did provide a realistic experience of control.

Ownership provided these students opportunities to develop their voice through talking, writing, artwork, and acting. While discussing books, rewriting folk tales, and directing plays, students found opportunities to express themselves creatively and to have others consider their thoughts and actions seriously. The rewritten folk tale and its reiteration in video form are material expressions of students' voices to which they can return. They can examine how these artifacts represent just who they are at the moment and, perhaps, who they wish to become. Ownership affords all students an extended opportunity to experiment in ongoing process of the developing and refining their own voices.

Students made many choices during these events, but they were not free to choose to write a different story. They chose which group they would work with, which part to take within the play, and which props would be necessary. On one occasion, a group chose to start all over again rather than to continue with a rewritten tale that no longer fit their interests. Jamie chose not to participate in the plays but decided that she could be involved directly in "rolling the credits" at the beginning of each videotape. Students could exercise the right of choice (not just pick among teacher offered options) only during those aspects of the projects over which they had ownership. And, of course, each was responsible for the choices he or she made.

Ownership and authenticity are closely related. Is ownership made possible because language use is authentic, or is it ownership that makes language use authentic? Of course, students do not own all the possible authentic language uses in which they participate. For example, I've put students through a few holiday pageants that had real audiences but that had little to be owned by students. Friends School students seemed to find the folk tale project useful, interesting, and fun, and the audience for the videos was real (customers who would buy the tapes as a fund raiser for other school projects).

The videos were the students' creations. They developed or decided to reproduce the stories, characters, and sets for staging. Beyond these artifacts they made some discoveries that should help them to examine critically other stories told, written, or performed. To prepare to rewrite the stories, students engaged at several levels in analyzing folk tales by a variety of authors. In short, students created new knowledge for themselves and new processes of critique that may enable them to demonstrate an independence of mind if they continue to develop and practice them in other settings. Because analysis was not the objective of the project but a spontaneous reality of the discussions, this was not an attempt to transfer fully formed analytic strategies from teacher to students. Rather, it was a demonstration of students' intellectual autonomy in operation during aspects of the project over which students took ownership.

Ownership, then, is a useful concept for educators who seek to understand how students learn particular content and processes under particular conditions, either individually in the reading and writing workshops or in group projects. It enables educators to acknowledge the importance of control, voice, choice, authenticity, and intellectual autonomy in learning for both students and teachers, who must work together to develop conditions in literacy programs that permit and facilitate language users' ownership. In this sense teachers and students must own their classrooms, their language and learning, and their entire educative experience.

Ownership as a Complex Issue

So considered, the concept of ownership seems positive, simple, and straightforward, but nothing in life is completely positive, simple, or straightforward in all circumstances. While providing opportunities for learners, ownership also constrains that learning in particular ways. Looked at from a different perspective, the concept of ownership gives learners a false sense of individuality, offers an overly personal view of literate life, and may prevent students from engagement in a critical public life. In short, New Literacy educators must look past current views of ownership as an individual right if they hope to empower students in classrooms and schools through literacy education.

Individuals do not own their language. Although each one of us can speak personally, none of us has a truly personal voice. Individuals don't speak to each other but rather "historically and socially defined discourses speak to each other through individuals" (Gee 1992, p. 5). Discourse is an identity kit that comes complete with the appropriate costume and instructions on how to act and talk so as to be recognized for membership in a socially meaningful group. Any socially meaningful group has an identifying discourse that members use to make themselves understood to other group members and to exclude nonmembers from the conversation. Nationality, gender, race, social class, and ethnicity serve as general discourse categories, but occupations, geographic residence, and avocations are also categories of discourse. And, of course, these discourses overlap as gender, race, and social class affect our job opportunities, places we live, and what we enjoy doing. Accordingly, any individual, regardless of age and experience, is the meeting point of many—sometimes conflicting—socially and historically defined discourses.

During the video project the importance of discourse becomes most clear in the climactic twist in "Goldilocks and The Three Bears: The Day After." Goldilocks and the Bears negotiated a settlement for their disagreement instead of running from their problems (responsibilities) as in the traditional (and other Friends School) versions or in fighting over the disagreement as in "The Three Billy Goats Gruff" or "Two Pigs and a Wolf." This group of five- and six-year-olds radically departed from the violence of traditional folk tales. The participants in "Goldilocks and the Three Bears: The Day After" (Laura, Walton, Abby, and Zahra) can be distinguished from their classmates primarily by the length of their enrollment in the Friends School. Other groups had mixtures of gender, race, age, and ethnic background similar to this group, but most in the other groups were not Quakers nor had they attended Friends School for more than two months at the time of the project. Laura, Walton, and Abby had attended Friends School for two years and had participated in its explicit social curriculum of conflict resolution, they evoked a mediated solution to their conflict. Even in this artificial context, they introduced a Quaker voice; as a result, the Quaker meeting can lay claim to partial ownership of that particular video (although they cannot lay legitimate claim to the others).

At the same time, we cannot suggest that Friends School students owned individual choices they made during the folk tale project. Their choices were influenced by opportunities and constraints that their lives have offered them; that is, they are social and historical beings, just like the rest of us. Perhaps this fact is best explained through references to the influence of the Walt Disney Corporation within the process of interpreting and choosing folk tales. Despite the diverse backgrounds (racial, economic, religious, national, and intellectual) the Friends School class shared the experience of watching and sometimes reading Disney versions of many folk tales; understandably, they interpreted their world accordingly. Without explicit intent, perhaps, the values and implicit social relations of the Disney Corporation are embedded in the social practice, ideas, and choices of most North American children in the latter half of the twentieth century, maybe well into the twenty-first. Does Disney have partial ownership of the folk tale project and our profits?

Ownership, then, appears to be a social event in which the discourses and other historical forces operate—sometimes explicitly, but more often implicitly—providing the illusion of individualism and masking the origins of values, attitudes, and opinions. If students are to find themselves through language use, then it seems that they must push past the illusion of singular personal voice to acknowledge the others who speak through them. In this way they can locate themselves within immediate social practice and in history. At the same time, acknowledging multiple voices does not necessarily mean that students must accept all values and practices within individuals' voices. Once the discourses and values are identified, individuals can examine, interrogate, and decide what it is they hope to stand for and what it is that they once were but no longer want to be. Only when educators and students explore this multiple ownership can students develop intellectual autonomy through the sorting out of contradicting discourses within their voices.

This view of ownership expands the concept of intellectual autonomy that Pappas, Kiefer, and Levstik (1990) raise in their statement about "making their knowledge their own." Beyond an individual's construction of knowledge and rules for understanding, intellectual autonomy includes the ability and intention to hold that knowledge and those rules problematic. Probing who benefits and why they benefit from these constructions is as necessary as "knowing how, why, and what to do." In developing intellectual autonomy, Friends School students (and teachers) need to reflect upon the processes and messages of the folk tale project, not just to participate in the project. What does it mean that Quaker and popular (for example, Disney) discourses compete within the projects? How does the profit motive within the authentic language use influence the project process and outcome? What social lessons are learned from the negotiation of story and action with four adults? with peers? How does the inclusion of artistic and dramatic, as well as literary, expression influence which and how students participate and what they take from the folk tale project and its social context. Each of these explorations of multiple ownership, as well as many more, can help both teachers and students to develop intellectual autonomy concerning the relationship between school activities and social and political life outside schools. And the five- and six-year-olds at Friends School started to ask such questions when comparing the videos during their premiere; in fact, they noticed and commented upon the Quaker ending and how it differed from the others.

If language users acknowledge that multiple discourses operate within each individual's thoughts, language, and actions and that historical forces influence their choices, then they must understand intellectual autonomy as a political process. They will examine whose ideas, values, and interests will be validated within individual consciousness and within the social circumstances in which individuals participate. It is not that politics must be brought to intellectual autonomy, to discourses, to literacy, to historical forces, or to ownership. These phenomena are profoundly and fundamentally political. Students (and teachers) cannot escape being politically imposed upon by various groups and forces within their daily lives—each with its own agenda for social organization and benefit. Intellectual autonomy increases when students and teachers challenge the false sense of individuality; when learners examine these political interests; and when teachers introduce different forms and modes of organization, values, ideas, and interests to be weighed for their social advantages against the status quo.

A Poor Social Metaphor

The psychology of ownership is often personal, private, and exclusionary. The objects (and only objectified phenomena and things can be owned) become personally associated with their owners. Often, we act as if these things, these possessions, define the individual. We are what we own, eat, read, and so on. Of course, this psychology drives the advertising industry as things—cars, houses, appliances, clothes, hairstyles, and even languages— are offered to us as our primary means of expressing and reflecting our true selves. They become our representation to those with whom we do and do not speak directly. The psychology of ownership is at the center of our materialism; If it's not our own, then it's a source of envy.

Anything we own becomes our property, and as such, we have certain rights over the objects protected by law. For example, the U.S. Constitution offers us the right to feel secure with our possessions and to use them as we please, as long as we do not directly harm others or their property. Security means that our property is not connected or encumbered by others—it is not public; that is, our property is not open to public inspection, unless owners wish to make it so, and it need not be adjusted or altered at the suggestions or needs of others. It is ours to do with as we wish. Property alienates us from others.

Although ownership and property do not necessarily mean privilege, certainly some among us own more than others do, and accumulation of property is an expression of social and political power that can be and has been acknowledged and used as privilege. This power and privilege offer some individuals and groups advantage over poorer individuals and groups in the accumulation of more things. So considered, it is easy to recognize North American nations as class societies with differential power and privileges accorded to each social rank.

The psychology of ownership is based on a sense of scarcity. In this sense, ownership means conflict. Individuals compete for ownership of particular things; once something is owned, it cannot be owned by others. Although mass production of goods has decreased this competition to an extent, it has also increased the desire to own. Within industrial societies (or even postindustrial societies) owners must acquire more and more things in order to satisfy the needs created through advertising (and to keep the economy afloat, as we are once again learning in the 1990s). Efforts to own more goods leave us less and less time for, and interest in, the well-being of others, who may or may not own the means to food, shelter, clothing, and medical care in order to participate fully and actively in public life.

Granted, advocates of New Literacy challenge teachers' and curriculum publishers' ownership of language and literacy education in schools. They critique the canon in literature, the skills orientation in reading and writing instruction, and the exclusively academic focus of elementary and secondary school language arts programs as expressions of teacher and curricular monopolies of purpose, processes, and products of language use in schools. They seek to transfer this authority to students to enable them to direct, inform, participate in, and evaluate their language education. Through this authority students can become subjects, not objects, within their classrooms and will be liberated from the current tyranny of teachers, textbooks, and tests. What is not, however, altogether clear in New Literacy advocates' writing is if or how they hope to avoid perpetuating the psychology of ownership within students' literacy development.

As my quotation of New Literacy advocates implies, the theories that underlie New Literacy portray reading and writing as personal, private, and exclusionary. Although advocates argue that reading and writing are social activities, they typically mean that individual readers and writers follow social conventions (in a primary or secondary discourse) during literacy events or that literate events often take place in public. At the same time, though, their conceptions of control, voice, choice, authenticity, and intellectual autonomy often suggest that an individual's consciousness controls the making of meaning according to personal interests (see Baker and Luke 1991 for further discussion of New Literacy and individualism); that is, individuals own the meaning of texts they read and write; it is their property with the rights of privacy and exclusion. This is the logic through which the phrase ''everyone has the right to his or her opinion'' gains authority.

As property in a New Literacy classroom, reading and writing become the way in which individuals invent themselves and are accorded value by peers and teachers. In order to act authentically and to develop a true voice, students must acquire reading and writing, which brings power and privileges (even within this context). Although ability grouping may be absent from New Literacy classrooms, individuals who demonstrate literacy are valued differently from those who appear illiterate or aliterate. Through these displays individuals express and reflect themselves through accumulation of the things called reading and writing. A free market of ownership does not exist even in New Literacy classrooms. The different valuation and the power and privilege that accompany it offer advantages for acquiring more academic property.

Once owned, meaning and the act of reading and writing become personal private property and, as such are not encumbered by others—that is, dependent on their definitions or opinions. There is no set of standards against which to match individual readers' and writers' meaning or process to determine the correctness of that understanding or practice. The products of reading and writing, as well as the processes, are not necessarily subject to public scrutiny or adjustment, unless the owners see them as not reflective of owners' intent, voice, or self. Acquiring reading and writing as property is a private matter that takes place in a social context. According to New Literacy theory, making reading and writing one's own requires an introversion of concerns to explore personal interests, practices, and meanings. It is a contemplative matter that necessarily stands apart from both the social reality and social action that surround it and the individuals who are to own their literacy development.

The Dialectic of Ownership

New Literacy advocates' writings about the theory and practice of ownership tell students and teachers to look within themselves to find the questions and answers to direct their literate lives. This introspection will help them use reading and writing to find themselves, to learn to be truthful and authentic, and to become fulfilled and complete. In this sense, ownership can be a personally liberating phenomenon. Yet, as I have tried to explain, this is but one side of ownership. So considered, ownership necessitates turning our backs on others in order to preserve the myth of individualism, a myth that serves social classes differently by forcing us to ignore the social, economic, and political realities of ownership. To see this dialectic, the competing positive and negative forces within ownership, educators must expand the current conceptualization of ownership within New Literacy.

Kathleen and I hope that New Literacy educators will demonstrate and convey this dialectic of ownership to all the Lauras and Tim-Pats in schools. Perhaps a first step is to make explicit the heretofore hidden curriculum of ownership in New Literacy classrooms. To this point, students acquire a sense of ownership through the organization of New Literacy program and practice around individual interests, but with little explicit talk about ownership. To explore the benefits and the limitations of ownership, teachers and students must make individualism in literacy development problematic and acknowledge social and historical influences.

Within this exploration, the fundamental elements of ownership change. Control becomes the negotiation with others (including those with different amounts of power and privilege) to ensure individual and collective participation in classroom and community decisions and in literacy practices. Voice becomes acknowledgment of the multiple social and historical elements of discourse spoken through individuals. Choice becomes the intersection of historical influences, within a particular context, that affect individuals' decisions. Authenticity becomes the realization that control, voice, and choice are social, historical, and political phenomena that condition, and are conditioned by, individual and group action. And intellectual autonomy becomes the evaluation of competing interests that collide within our language and liter-acy. Together these expanded elements of ownership fashion a social moral-ity that helps us not only to affirm ourselves but also to face each other, to investigate our differences, and to decide collectively how we wish to live together in and out of schools.

References

Atwell, N. 1987. *In the middle: Writing, reading, and learning with adolescents.* Portsmouth, N.H.: Boynton/Cook.

Baker, C., and Luke, A. 1991. *Toward a critical sociology of reading pedagogy.* Philadelphia: John Benjamins.

Gee, J. 1992. What is literacy? In *Becoming political: Readings and writings on the politics of literacy education*, edited by P. Shannon. Portsmouth, N.H.: Heine-mann.

Goodman, K. 1985. *What's whole in whole language?* Portsmouth, N.H.: Heinemann.

Graves, D. 1983. *Writing: Teachers and children at work.* Portsmouth, N.H.: Heine-mann.

Pappas, C., Kiefer, B., and Levstik, L. 1990. *An integrated language perspective in the elementary school.* New York: Longman.

Scieszka, J. 1989. *The true story of the 3 little pigs.* New York: Penguin.

Willinsky, J. 1990. *The new literacy.* New York: Routledge.

11

Writing a Difference in the World: Beyond Ownership and Authorship

Catherine DuCharme
California State University, Long Beach

Mary Poplin
The Claremont Graduate School

Sally Thomas
The Claremont Graduate School

Literacy instruction in the United States has changed in many classrooms as teachers embrace the writings of Graves (1973, 1983), Calkins (1983, 1986), Macrorie (1984), and Atwell (1987), to name a few influential writing process educators. We do not wish to devalue the positive approaches that the writing process movement has championed; many practitioners and educationists have commented on the appropriateness of the writing workshop approach for diverse learners (Fournier et al. 1992; Harste, Woodward, and Burke 1984; Flores, Cousin, and Diaz 1991; Hayes, Bahruth, and Kessler 1991; Miramontes and Cummins 1991; Goodman, Goodman, and Flores 1984). We believe, however, that the time has come for us to challenge ourselves to reflect upon authorship and ownership from a multicultural and critical perspective. For example, we certainly would not argue with allowing children to self-select topics for writing and/or encouraging students to compose and illustrate their own books. When these activities are ends in themselves, though, we question whether or not they respect multiple world views and culturally different perspectives on authorship and ownership. Lisa Delpit (1993) speaks of this problem:

The dilemma is not really in the debate over instructional methodology, but rather in communication across cultures and in addressing the more fundamental issues of power, of whose voice gets to be heard in determining what is best for poor children and children of color . . . But both sides need to be able to listen, and I contend that it is those with the most power, those in the majority, who must take the greater responsibility for initiating the process. To do so takes a very special kind of listening, listening that requires not only open eyes and ears, but open hearts and minds. We do not really see through our eyes or hear through our ears but through our beliefs. To put our beliefs on hold is to cease to exist as ourselves for a moment— and that is not easy. It is painful as well, because it means turning yourself inside out, giving up your own sense of who you are, and being willing to see yourself in the unflattering light of another's angry gaze. It is not easy, but it is the only way to learn what it might feel like to be someone else and the only way to start the dialogue. (pp. 138–39).

Authorship and Ownership in the Writing Workshop

Those who advocate the writing workshop approach assume that authorship and the subsequent feeling of ownership of a text leads to one's gaining a sense of responsibility and vitality in the world (Graves 1973; Calkins 1983; Harste, Woodward, and Burke 1984). There are, however, world views that contradict these notions. Those of us inside the dominant culture must face two issues here. First, our notions of the rugged individual—who grows through a process of becoming separate and distinct from others—is not shared by even most of the globe. Second, by valuing individualism above all else, we fail to help students not in the dominant class enter the power arena. Do we believe and act on these beliefs because we are racist? No, because we are unconscious of alternatives to the individual view and unaware of the implicit power we hold by virtue of being Euro-American and nonpoor.

Paula Gunn Allen (1989) articulates the alternative view of nature eloquently in introducing her collection of Native American writings, traditional and contemporary.

Individualism works best for members of the mercantile class, not for their servants or laborers . . . the writers themselves do not necessarily recognize their own sources. Writers of any tradition don't. We tend to think that what is in our minds got there in direct, memorable ways or that we "made it up." In the Western tradition, "creativity" is thought to be a personal talent, arising without respect to the cultural matrix the creator lives in, a concept derived from the concept of private ownership. Ideas are seen as property, and the one who owns them is thought to be the legal beneficiary of whatever payments might accrue to the use of the ideas. . . . The collective unconscious, while culture-specific in most particulars, is the ever-renewing source of all our stories. (pp. 18, 23)

Allen is suggesting here that the myth of ownership of writing is true for all of us. The view of authorship and ownership as individualistic, and thus sacred, in Euro-American tradition, leads to other actions that disempower students of color. Newman (1991) states:

> It's precisely the notion of ownership that's keeping teachers from raising clarity and correctness with students. I understand why a number of researchers have argued for children's ownership of their writing—it was to keep us teachers from doing what we've done a lot of: leaving our bleeding red marks all over students' pages. But the notion of ownership undermines the development of students' writing because it leaves it at the level of fluency without helping children, or older writers, tackle the complex business of bringing clarity and correctness to their texts. (p. 287).

But the more critical story our reluctance to intervene with what is students' own possession comes also from a belief in the natural process of writing. This story of natural development is derived from stories of middle-class and upper-middle-class Euro-American children who have grown up "filled with the stories read to them by parents" (Dyson 1990) and who have implicitly learned the language of "edited English" (Delpit 1988, 1991). Neither we nor Delpit suggest that the writing process not be used; rather, that it be augmented from an explicit knowledge of cultural difference that we as teachers must come to know and share with our students. This extension of process writing should inspire in them (1) a sense of themselves and their rich cultural heritages, (2) an understanding of the power codes of written language in this country so that they may have access to all things, and (3) an understanding and critique of why these differences exist relative to the society in which we live.

These three points extend authorship and ownership in writing in multiple ways. They add a consciousness of multiple world views and a necessity of using writing to help students become more critical in the world. Though he does not go far into the issue of diversity, Willinsky (1990) does propose that we go beyond the writing process (and literature-based reading instruction) to what he calls "the New Literacy":

> The idea [of writing instruction, in our case] is to foster a new level of consciousness in the pervasiveness of language on the street, in the media, in the schools and the family which forms these students' home in the world. . . . In moving between the personal and public poles, New Literacy advocates, myself among them, have tended to speak of literacy principally in terms of its enhancement of personal growth. It now seems closed to the truth of the matter to assume that the personal side of literacy, as the private meeting of self and work, stull partakes of the public sphere. (p. 239)

Paulo Freire (in Berthoff 1990), the best-known liberatory educator, describes becoming literate as a process of coming to some awareness of the world and of one's place in it, one's responsibility not only to read and write but also to act.

> The act of learning to read and write has to start from a very comprehensive understanding of the act of reading the world, something which human beings do before reading words. Even historically, human beings first changed the world, secondly proclaimed the world and then wrote the words. These are moments in history. Human beings did not start naming A! F! N! They started freeing the hand, grasping the world. (in Berthoff 1990, p. 367)

Our intention or purpose for writing, then, must be expanded from individual growth and expression to issues of the world. In a massive qualitative study on the problems of schooling, students from elementary to high school were asked about the problems of school (Poplin and Weeres 1992). One of their major complaints was that their teachers (and other adults) would not talk with them about the important things in life. They felt that schooling was about "old things"; thus, they were left unknowledgeable about a world they were about to enter and act in. One of the lead participant teachers in the project explained that she would like to talk to her students about really serious issues but that no one had taught her how to do this.

What we are proposing is to extend in two ways the writing process that we have all come to know and trust. First, we must become conscious of, and make explicit in our classrooms, cultural differences. Second, we must make our writing workshops places where students and teachers can talk and write about the "important things of life." Thus, what follows is a brief survey of the cultural issues that we must consciously understand as teachers, along with a review of some of the issues raised by critical or liberatory educators. We will tie these issues to the act of teaching writing in the classroom.

Cultural Aspects Affecting Writing Instruction

We can understand cultural issues in the classroom only if we understand the cultural mismatches that youngsters encounter: home and school, linguistic differences, and institutional and personal racism. Nieto (1992) suggests that teachers cannot become multicultural educators until they become multicultural persons. This is difficult because most of us have been educated in monocultural environments, so we must reeducate ourselves. Nieto suggests that to do this we must (1) learn more from books and events about people and events of which we may know little or nothing, (2) confront our own racism and biases, often unconscious ones, and (3) learn to see reality from a variety of perspectives, such as the one offered earlier by Allen on the problem of individualism and ownership of ideas. Unless, for example, we become acutely conscious of differences in discourse styles across cultures, we will fail to notice gifts that students bring to class, and we will miss the special needs that they may have for instruction.

A few of the important differences that we might not understand as writing teachers include written discourse styles, story grammars, text grammars, special cultural knowledge, bicultural gifts, and bilingualism. If we misunderstand these differences, we will have lowered expectations for youth from various cultures (Nieto 1992; Willinsky 1990; Cummins 1989), or we will have unrealistic expectations of implicit knowledge (Delpit 1988, 1991). The complexity of having high and low expectations of students considered "at risk" is discussed in Goldenberg (1989).

Preferred writing or discourse styles vary across cultures (Kaplan 1982; Montano-Harmon 1988). We need to realize that the style we try to teach youngsters is a uniquely American English one. In expository American English, writers are to tell readers what they are going to tell them, tell them, and then tell them what they have just told them. British English is similar, except that writers do not begin by telling the reader what will be told; they do, however, end by summarizing. No other culture shares this writing preference; in fact, most other cultures and languages see it as demeaning. In romance languages, such as Spanish and French, writers use diversions, beginning one story, then seemingly tell a very different one. It is the reader's job to interpret. Also, in romance languages the more eloquent and elaborate the language, the better. In Asian languages writers prefer the eight-legged essay, making eight points, all of which allude to the main point. This meaning is left to readers to determine for themselves.

It is no wonder, then, that Latino students frequently find written on their papers *get to the point, use a sequence, get organized,* and *don't use so many adverbs and adjectives.* Our effort should not be to avoid teaching American English, but rather to do so in an explicit context. Without putting one form or the other down, the teacher can demonstrate differences, teach multiple forms, and explain the reasons they exist and the places they need to be used.

Allen (1989) reveals more about the dominant style in fiction when discussing the difference between Native and European/Euro-American novels:

> The ideal hero [in these dominant novels], a single individual, wrecks his will upon one or more hapless groups (who, one way or another, are generally perceived as in opposition to individualistic goals). He does so by means of engaging in conflict, bringing it to crisis, and resolving that crisis in such a way that individualistic values are affirmed. The classic fictional structure informs most American culture, not only in its refined and popular aesthetic forms, but in most of its institutions, as well.... But the Indian ethos is neither individualistic nor conflict-centered, and the unifying structures that make the oral tradition coherent are less a matter of character, time and

setting than the coherence of common understanding derived from the ritual traditional that members of a tribal unit share. The horrors that visit an Indian who attempts to isolate individuality have been movingly depicted [in Native American literary work]. . . . The Native literary tradition is dynamic; it changes as our circumstances change. It pertains to the daily life of the people, as that life reflects, refracts the light of the spiritual traditions within which we have our collective life and significance. (pp. 5–7)

Allen also speaks of the cycles of stories, "a number of stories that cluster around a more or less central theme and often feature particular characters and events" and raises issues with dominant definitions of novel, short story, and our need for endings. There is an integral relationship between the Native oral tradition and contemporary Native literature. Allen refers to these as "told-to-people stories" and "told-to-page stories."

Philips (1983) documented many discrepancies in *oral discourse features* in her classic ethnography of Native children entering school. Scollon and Scollon (1981) also demonstrated differences in story narratives of Native children, including the conflict between the dominant story style that has a beginning, middle (conflict), and end (resolution) and the Athabaskan style of four parts. They further demonstrated how upon hearing a story from one point of view, listeners from the other view reinterpret these stories into their own preferred style.

Other differences in oral discourse styles that affect the classroom include the oral styles of teachers when giving directions and setting up activities. Ballenger (1992) gives a moving account of her learning a new style of communicating with Haitian children. Delpit (1988) also raises issue of the differences between Euro-American and African American teachers' styles of oral discourse and the responses they elicit from students.

Montano-Harmon (1988) found other interesting aspects of Mexican American students' writing besides the discourse features. She discovered that many of these students did not differentiate in their writing between *informal and formal registers*. Many students wrote as they talked. This may also be true of many students who come to school not having much experience hearing written text or of students who have not become fully literate in their first languages.

This brings us to a discussion of *"cultural capital,"* the knowledge a students does bring to the class. Without an awareness of cultural capital we might not notice, thus reject or overlook, students' knowledge, as we did the case of discourse features. Also, we should ask ourselves, What implicit experiences and rules are we expecting our students to develop naturally for which they do not have the necessary prerequisite experience? Delpit (1988, 1991) is the most incisive on this point.

Delpit (1991) points out that some youngsters, such as many African American students, do not grow up around "edited English" (her phrase for what we have been taught to call standard English); *the explicit rules of the grammar* used as part of the culture of power do not come naturally and must be taught explicitly. She is not advocating a return to grammar instruction separate from process:

> I am definitely not against writing process or writing process theory. My focus is constantly on starting where kids are. Classrooms should unquestionably promote reading and writing for real purposes. Within the context of those real purposes, it might be necessary to have more or less explicit attention to certain conversations or strategies, depending on the needs of children. We have to find the appropriate ways of translating that to the group of children we happen to be working with. What often gets left out of the theory, however, is the issue of culture. People do come from different cultures and from different linguistic and conceptual backgrounds. I get a sense that many of the people writing about writing process. . . . assume that everyone follows a relatively similar path. (p. 543).

Dyson (1990), Epps (1985), and Cazden (1987) are quoted in Delpit (1988) as having made similar points regarding the dangers of not providing some explicit instruction or letting youngsters with similar cultural capital be solely responsible for editing one another's work. Cazden suggested that young writers participate in the talkers/writers community with periodic focus on the cultural conventions of form.

A second problem in our failing to understand students' cultural capital is our *not being able to use the knowledge of these children effectively.* To activate students' own knowledge in the classroom, we must first be aware that it exists. San Miguel (1991) suggests that part of our responsibility as educators and writers is to preserve any culture that is at risk. He likens the Latino child's experience in the classroom to that of the legendary figure La LLorona who represents:

> the sense of limbo—a disconnectedness with the past as well as the future. . . . The Hispanic children in our schools have strong views about life and family, as well as awareness of their own cultural identity, but at first they need a little help trusting themselves enough to express that awareness. This is where we writing teachers come in. We cannot expect these young minds to initiate an open, creative exploration of themselves without an atmosphere of complete acceptance. We need to do more than just accept diverse or alien ideas; we need to cultivate the students' own expressions of these diversities. (pp. 9–10)

San Miguel asks Hispanic students to teach him, the teacher, such things as *mal de ojo, el cu-cuy, la echuza,* and *la llorona* or to describe *quinceanos.* Then he asks them to go beyond simple description and write a tale about these that includes themselves.

Similarly, the students in a qualitative study of schooling (Poplin and Weeres 1992) begged for teaching of African American history, African history, and Mexican history and for reading of books from their cultures.

Obviously, teachers must learn these things explicitly if they are to respect and expand students' cultural capital. Unless we can activate students' own cultural knowledge, we will have difficulty obtaining authentic writing. Instead of authentic self-expression we will receive what students think we want; these may be mere imitations, not true personal reflections informed by their own experiences and culture.

Alongside our own expanding knowledge, we must make our students aware of what it means to be *bicultural and biliterate*. We must ourselves learn of the advantages and hardships imposed in growing up biculturally. We must, in the words of Giroux (1992), "Cross borders" ourselves. Raising issues of the bicultural experience helps students understand and perhaps write about the pain and pleasure that they have experienced as bicultural citizens. It validates the feelings that children often have of being different; it recognizes and deals openly with the feelings of isolation, silence, resistance, and rage. These are the issues that make possible explicit instruction that values all forms of knowledge and discourse; teaches all forms to all students; and, as we shall see later, critiques the reasons for these forms. We thus give students options and expand their chances that their writing can also be a mechanism for personal growth. Texts that intentionally mix styles and languages are models for students of what they can attain in their own writing (for example, Sandra Cisneros's *The House on Mango Street* or Gary Soto's books and poems).

Bilingualism is also a process that few of us who teach really understand. Considerable research suggests that literacy instruction should be first developed in a child's primary language for cognitive, linguistic, psychological, social, and economic issues (Cummins 1981, 1989; Nieto 1992; Ogbu 1986, 1987). Fillmore (1991) has documented the ease with which young children, even upper-class children of well-educated parents, lose their languages as they enter English-only environments. It is important that progressive literacy teachers form alliances with bilingual educators in order that children receive the best possible chances in life. Too many children who are potentially bilingual and biliterate lose these abilities, which could well serve them and the world throughout their lives.

Critical Aspects Affecting Writing Instruction

In 1987 critical theorist Henry Giroux spoke of Graves's writing process and expanded on the discussion. He praised the writing process approach for its "critical insight into the learning process by linking the nature of learning itself with the dreams, experiences, histories, and languages that students bring to schools" (p. 176). He calls on us to be more cognizant of the issues of culture and power inherent, often implicitly, in our curriculum and instructional processes that silence those whom we seek to render writers. Critical pedagogy goes beyond the writing process and beyond learning and apply-ing notions of cultural difference. It calls on us to attend to, and act against, oppressive institutional values and practices and to teach our students to do the same. This extends the conversation about culture, schooling, and writ-ing to include issues of institutionalized racism.

Giroux (1987) suggests four basic elements of a critical pedagogy: "First, in addition to legitimating student experiences and treating curriculum as narrative whose interests must be uncovered and critically interrogated [teach-ing students to recognize these biases, some of which were mentioned above], progressive teachers must develop conditions in their classroom that allow different student voices to be heard and legitimated" (p. 178). In terms of questioning the curriculum, Delpit (1991) furthers the argument:

> I think that whenever you have people who are not a part of whatever cul-ture that you're trying to teach from, it's easiest if you make the rules more explicit. But there's also another piece to it. You don't just learn the culture of power; you also learn about and explore your own culture. Teachers not only have to make conventions and strategies explicit; they also have to make explicit what it is they are making explicit. In other words, they also need to talk about the notions that these conventions are the conventions of edited English, a political entity, one that the political nature of this society demands that people be able to control if they are to be successful. (p. 542)

Fortunately, students' voices are heard and legitimated in a number of examples of critical practice. Shor (1980, 1988, 1992) has perhaps done the most extensive descriptions of a process: after listening to students' voices, he formulates a topic from their voices; they write their individual opinions (an essay) regarding the topic; then they form groups to hear what others have to say. (Here students come to understand that their voice is one among many.) Next, Shor brings to the class textual material, often popular press at first so that students may revise their essays after reading material that has been written on the topic. He brings increasingly complex textual material (such as research), and students continue to revise their own work and to lis-ten to one another. Eventually, he shares his own work on the topic. Topics range from where hamburgers come from to an environmental landfill issue in the local community. Shor works largely with students who are entering community colleges but have not completed their high school diploma.

Solorzano (1989) describes a college class that took up media portrayals of Latino people for their research and writing. This led them to social action, too, as frequently happens in Shor's classes. In an elementary school setting Ada (1988) demonstrates a writing process that deliberately places families of migrant children at its center. Children write, and learn to read from, stories in which their families are the protagonists. Squires and Inlander (1990) and Poplin and Weeres (1992) give examples from high school, and Willinsky (1990) tells of critical literacy projects across ages.

Second, Giroux suggests that "teachers should provide students with the opportunity to interrogate different languages or ideological discourse as they are developed in an assortment of texts and curriculum materials" (p. 179). As students brainstorm and prewrite, teachers must encourage them to go beyond what they know and, as they research, to look beyond the obvious. Students need to ask new questions, not just answer old ones. To aid them, teachers must have knowledge of, and access to, alternative texts. In several history classes in Montclair, California, students write about topics after they have read about a historical event from multiple perspectives. Their teachers provide official and unofficial history texts so that students' thinking and writing expands through multiple perspectives. Here the call by students for their teachers to know history, literature, or any other subject from multiple perspectives is extremely relevant.

Third, Giroux call on us to introduce students to "a language of morality that allows them to think about how community life should be constructed" (p. 179). Students can examine such questions as "what is it this society has made of me that I no longer want to be?" (p. 178). Many researchers have found that even young children as well as adults are preoccupied by the meaning of life—spiritual and moral issues that are rarely raised explicitly in the classroom (Poplin and Weeres 1992; Minns 1988; Keenan, Willett, and Solsken 1993). If we expect students are to recognize the important aspects of life and to act as responsible members of a democratic society, we must raise these issues in our writing workshops.

Fourth, Giroux asks that our classrooms help convince students that they can make a difference in the world. In critical pedagogy, students do not write only for the sake of writing or literacy. They write to find their place in the world and to define their role in its continued transformation.

Writing for Liberation

Stromquist (1991) has suggested that community literacy projects differ from those in school. Schools want to create readers and writers, but communities use literacy to encourage social awareness and transformation. Eugene (1989) also points out that a person of color becomes literate in order to help lift everyone in the community. This kind of literacy is not only transformative, it is liberating as well.

We have suggested that authorship and ownership are not enough reason to teach process writing. Self-expression is a necessary but insufficient reason to teach writing. At first, when we began to write this chapter we conceptualized our argument *for* students of color; soon though, we realized that these matters of cultural inclusion and critical reflection are as relevant and crucial to teaching students in the dominant culture as for anyone else. In fact, if we cannot all learn these things, little will change. We will continue to perpetuate the effects of institutionalized racism that made it difficult for many of us who are white and monolingual to teach in the first place.

We are suggesting. that we dampen our enthusiasm for individuality and ownership in the writing process and infuse our writing process with a kind of critical reflection that can be accomplished only in a culturally inclusive and sensitive environment. This environment must explicitly teach and demonstrate multiple points of view. This critical reflection must allow all of us to talk and write about the important things in life. This reflection in our writing process must help students to critique the society in which we live, to find their voices, and to discover their own destinies. We are advocating literacy instruction, particularly a writing process that is deeply tied not only to the world but also to the communities in which we teach—a process that has the community as the protagonist of our narratives.

We are advocating that there are four intents of writing instruction: self-expression and growth; an understanding of others' self-expression and growth; an understanding of multiple world views; and a critical attitude toward the world. We are advocating not only authorship that is ownership, but an authorship that also liberates us all from oppression and from single world views.

References

Ada, A.F. 1988. The Pajaro Valley experience: Working with Spanish-speaking parents to develop children's reading and writing skills through the use of children's literature. Pp. 225–38 in *Minority education: From shame to struggle*, edited by T. Skutnabb-Kangas, and J. Cummins. Clevedon, England: Multilingual Matters.

Allen, P.G. 1989. *Spider Woman's granddaughters*. New York: Fawcett Columbine.

Atwell, N. 1987. *In the middle: Writing, reading, and learning with adolescents.* Portsmouth, N.H.: Boynton/Cook.

Ballenger, C. 1992. Because you like us: The language of control. *Harvard Educational Review* 62 (2): 199–208.

Berthoff, A.E. 1990. Paulo Freire's liberation theology. *Language Arts* 67 (4): 362–69.

Calkins, L.M. 1983. *Lessons from a child*. Portsmouth, N.H.: Heinemann.

———. 1986. *The art of teaching writing*. Portsmouth, N.H.: Heinemann.

Cazden, C. 1987. *The myth of autonomus text.* Paper presented at the Third International Conference on Thinking, Honolulu, Hawaii.

Cisneros, S. 1984. *The house on Mango Street.* New York: Alfred Knopf.

Cummins, J. 1981. The role of primary language development in promoting educational success for language minority students. In California State Department of Education. *Schooling and language minority students: A theoretical framework.* Los Angeles: California State University, Evaluation, Dissemination and Assessment Center.

———. 1989. *Empowering minority students.* Sacramento: California Association for Bilingual Education.

Delpit, L. 1988. The silenced dialogue: Power and pedagogy in educating other people's children. *Harvard Educational Review* 58 (3): 280–98.

———. 1991. A conversation with Lisa Delpit. *Language Arts* 68: 541–47.

———. 1993. The silenced dialogue: Power and pedagogy in educating other people's children. Pp. 119–39 in *Beyond silenced voices: Class, race, and gender in United States schools*, edited by L. Weis and M. Fine. Albany: State University of New York Press.

Dyson, A.H. 1990. Research currents: Diversity, social responsibility, and the story of literacy development. *Language Arts* 67 (2): 199–205.

Epps, J. 1985. Killing them softly: Why Willie can't write. Pp. 154–59 in *Tapping potential: English and language arts for the black learner*, edited by C. Brooks. Urbana, Ill.: National Council of Teachers of English.

Eugene, T. 1989. Sometimes I feel like a motherless child: the call and response for a liberational ethic of care by black feminists. Pp. 46–62 in *Who cares? Theory, research, and educational implications of the ethic of care*, edited by M. M. Brabeek. New York: Praeger.

Fillmore, L.W. 1991. Language and cultural issues in the early education of language minority children. Pp. 30–49 in *The care and education of America's young children*, Ninetieth Yearbook of the National Society for the Study of Education, edited by S. Kagan. Chicago: University of Chicago Press.

Flores, B., Cousin, P.T., and Diaz, E. 1991. Transforming deficit myths about learning, language, and culture. *Language Arts* 68: 369–79.

Fournier, J., Landsdowne, B., Pastenes, Z., Steen, P., and Huselson, S. 1992. Learning with, about, and from children: Life in a bilingual second grade. Pp. 126–62 in *Ways of assessing children and curriculum: Stories of early childhood practice*, edited by C. Genishi. New York: Teachers College Press.

Giroux, H. 1987. Critical literacy and student experience: Donald Graves' approach to literacy. *Language Arts* 64 (2): 175–81.

———. 1992. *Border crossings: Cultural workers and the politics of education.* New York: Routledge.

Goldenberg, C.N. 1989. Making success a more common occurrence for children at risk for failure: Lessons from Hispanic first-graders learning to read. Pp. 48–79 in *Risk makers, risk takers, risk breakers: Reducing the risks for young literacy learners*, edited by J. Allen and J. Mason. Portsmouth, N.H.: Heinemann.

Goodman, K., Goodman, Y., and Flores, B. 1984. *Reading in the bilingual classroom: Literacy and biliteracy.* Washington, D.C.: National Clearinghouse for Bilingual Education.

Graves, D.H. 1973. *Children's writing: Research directions and hypotheses based upon an examination of the writing processes of seven-year-old children.* Unpublished doctoral dissertation, State University of New York at Buffalo.

———. 1983. *Writing: Teachers and children at work.* Portsmouth, N.H.: Heinemann.

Harste, J., Woodward, V.A. and Burke, C.L. 1984. *Language stories and literacy lessons.* Portsmouth, N.H.: Heinemann.

Hayes, C.W., Bahruth, R., and Kessler, C. 1991. *Literacy con carino*. Portsmouth, N.H.: Heinemann.

Kaplan, R. 1982. An introduction to the study of written texts: The discourse compact. Pp. 138–51 in *Annual Review of Applied Linguistics—1982*, Rowley, Mass.: Newbury House.

Keenan, J.A.W., Willett, J., and Solsken, J. 1993. Focus on research: Constructing an urban village: School/home collaboration in a multicultural classroom. *Language Arts 70 (3): 204–14*.

Macrorie, K. 1984. *Telling writing*. Upper Montclair, N.J.: Boynton/Cook.

Minns, H. 1988. Jaspal's Story: Learning to read at home and at school. *English in Education 22 (3): 40–47*.

Miramontes, O.B., and Cummins, N.L. 1991. Redefining literacy and literacy contexts: Discovering a community of learners. In *Literacy for a diverse society: Perspectives, practices, and policies*, edited by E.H. Hiebert. New York: Teachers College Press.

Montano-Harmon, M. 1988. Discourse features in the compositions of Mexican, English as a second language, Mexican-American, Chicano, and Anglo high school students: Considerations for the formulation of educational policies. Unpublished dissertation, University of Southern California, Los Angeles.

Newman, J.M. 1991. *Interwoven conversations. Learning and teaching through critical reflection*. Portsmouth, N.H.: Heinemann.

Nieto, S. 1992. *Affirming diversity: The sociopolitical context of multicultural education*. New York: Longman.

Ogbu, J.U. 1986. Understanding sociocultural factors: Knowledge, identity, and school adjustment. Pp. 73–142 in *Beyond language: Social and cultural factors in schooling language minority students*. Los Angeles: California State University, Evaluation, Dissemination and Assessment Center.

———. 1987. Variability in minority school performance: A problem in search of an explanation. *Anthropology and Education Quarterly* 18: 312–34.

Philips, S.U. 1983. *The invisible culture: Communication in classroom and community on the Warm Springs Indian reservation*. New York: Longman.

Poplin, M.S., and Weeres, J. 1992. *Voices from the inside: A report on schooling from inside the classroom*. Claremont, Calif.: The Institute for Education in Transformation at the Claremont Graduate School.

San Miguel, C. 1991. La Llorona: Why does she weep? A question of identity for the Hispanic child. *Teachers & Writers* 22 (3): 9–12.

Scollon, R., and Scollon, S. 1981. *Narrative, literacy and face in interethnic communication*. Norwood, N.J.: Ablex.

Shor, I. 1980. *Critical teaching and everyday life*. Chicago: University of Chicago Press.

———. 1988. Working hands and critical minds: A Paulo Freire model for job training. *Journal of Education* 170 (2): 102–21.

————. 1992. *Empowering education: Critical teaching for social change.* Chicago: University of Chicago Press.

Solorzano, D.G. 1989. Teaching and social change: Reflections on a Freirean approach in a college classroom. *Teaching Sociology* 17: 218–25.

Squires, N., and Inlander, R. 1990. A Freirian-inspired video curriculum for at-risk high school students. *English Journal* 79 (2): 49–56.

Stromquist, N. 1991. Adult literacy: Views from the ivory tower. Paper presented at the annual CIES meeting, Pittsburgh, March 14–17.

Willinksy, J. 1990. *The new literacy. Redefining reading and writing in the schools.* New York: Routledge.

12

Liberating Student Intention and Association: Toward What Ends?

Timothy J. Lensmire
Washington University

Traditional writing instruction locks the student into a teacher-controlled discourse in which the teacher assigns writing, the student writes in response, and the teacher evaluates. There is little opportunity for revision, and the purpose of such school writing is often to display academic mastery in evaluative contexts. In such situations students' technical competence to write, as well as their motivation to use writing in ways that enrich and transform their lives, suffer (Applebee 1981; Doyle 1986; Florio-Ruane and Dunn 1985). Traditional writing instruction functions, then, much like other traditional forms of pedagogy to silence students, to deny student experiences and meanings, and to alienate students from the teaching and learning they encounter in schools (Freire 1970, 1985; Giroux 1988; Waller 1932).

In contrast, writing workshop approaches to writing instruction, made popular by educators and researchers such as Calkins (1986), Graves (1983), and Murray (1968), emphasize providing opportunities for children to engage in and practice the craft of writing. A central theme within such approaches is increased student control over writing processes and texts—students have wide powers to determine the topics, audiences, purposes, and forms of their writing. Such control is in the service of student voice. With the support of the teacher and numerous opportunities to collaborate and share texts with peers, children are supposed to gradually become more and more able to realize their intentions in text. This is the primary goal of such approaches.

Writing workshop approaches attempt to disrupt typical classroom discourse, then, in at least two ways. Having some control over topics and purposes for writing, the student makes the first move in an interaction sequence that places the teacher, ideally, in the position of response. But workshop approaches also break a teacher-dominated pattern by allowing and encouraging children to turn away from the teacher, front and center, to one another. In place of a traditionally unauthentic, fault-finding teacher-audience, workshops promote an authentic, meaning-finding one; and peers are a significant part of that audience.

Other chapters in this book demonstrate, convincingly, the promise of liberating student intention and association in our literacy work with children. I point to some perils, some problems that have not been taken up in any serious way by workshop advocates. Specifically, I call into question the notion that we can, as teachers and researchers of children's writing, uncritically support all the intentions that children might bring to their work with text and one another in writing workshops. I do this by examining several of the ways that a stratified peer culture shaped the production and sharing of texts in a third-grade writing class.

In what follows, I first provide some background and context for this work. Then, I tell a brief story about Mary and Suzanne[1] and their play, "The Mysterious Stranger." I use the story to point to disturbing patterns in children's writing and sharing in this workshop and to pose several challenges confronting those of us who are sympathetic to writing workshop approaches and who see them as contributing, in some small way, to the creation of more humane and just forms of life in school and society. I close with another story, this one about Jessie. Jessie, and children like her, seem always to be absent from the stories of writing workshop advocates.

Throughout the 1989–1990 school year, I taught writing five days a week in Grace Parker's third-grade classroom, using a writing workshop approach; I also researched teaching and learning in the workshop as a participant-observer. As a teacher I wanted my students to "come to voice," both in the sense of a private exploration and ordering of experience in the expression of a unique self, and in the sense of greater public participation in the cultural work of naming and renaming the world and their places within it (hooks 1989; Willinsky 1990). As a teacher-researcher, I wanted to study what happened when my students and I went about teaching and learning writing in ways that transformed typical classroom social relations and work. I brought interpretive research assumptions and methods (Bogdan and Biklen 1982; Erickson 1986; Hammersly and Atkinson 1983) to this work, and collected the following types of data:

1. Pseudonyms have been used for all children, staff, and parents who appear in my text. Pseudonyms have also been used *within* children's texts when those texts name other children or staff from the school.

Field notes. Included general narratives of the day's teaching, as well as reflections on specific pedagogical and methodological problems and issues.

Teacher and classroom documents. Included lesson plans; notes to students, parents, other staff; lists of rules and procedures for workshop, forms, sign-out book used in writing workshop library.

Audiotapes. Starting in October, taped class sessions and writing conferences with children in order to do close analyses of discourse in various workshop situations.

Student interviews. Conducted at the end of the school year by colleagues—hour-long interviews focused on the sense students were making of the writing workshop and the difficulties they encountered there.

Student writing. Students' written work was photocopied throughout the year.

I taught in a school that served a largely middle-class, suburban community. Children who lived in a nearby trailer park, inhabited primarily by working-class families, also attended the school. As I worked with these children across the year (and watched them play on the playground, vote for student council representatives, and decide whom to sit by in the cafeteria) I began noticing patterns of association among children that divided along gender and social class lines (if we take the ten-foot fence separating the children living in the trailer park from those living in the surrounding community as a rough social class line). In the workshop, when given a choice, girls worked with girls, and boys with boys. And the boys and girls who lived in the trailer park were at the bottom of informal peer hierarchies of status and power in the classroom.

As I shifted control over aspects of the work of literacy to the students, their relations with one another became extremely important influences on their experiences and writing in the workshop. Peers, as audiences for student writing, brought with them friendship, trust, a "social energy" (Dyson 1989) that could empower young writers. But peers also brought with them teasing, risk, and conflict; they pushed back on the writing students produced—and this despite considerable efforts by Grace and me to help children support and respect one another. In the larger study from which this chapter is drawn, I focused on this underside of our workshop community, and examined how a peer culture with gender divisions and informal hierarchies of status and power influenced children's experiences and writing (Lensmire 1994).[2] I explored how certain *children silenced other children* in

2. I gratefully acknowledge Teachers College Press for permission to reprint parts of my book, *When Children Write: Critical Re-Visions of the Writing Workshop,* in this chapter.

a classroom situation explicitly created to assure that all children's voices would sound and be heard.

I drew on the literary theories of Bakhtin (1981, 1986) and Kristeva (1986) to analyze child-authored texts in relation to the social contexts of their production. For Bakhtin, texts respond to preceding and anticipated texts and are sensitive to audience and social context. Texts are "dialogic," in that they are responsive to others and to their texts. In my analyses I did interpretations of children's texts where peers (not only teachers) were important audiences, and in which children drew not only on their conversations with teachers and their readings of books, but also on the words, meanings, and values of their peer culture to construct their texts. In other words, I placed young writers in a social context in which peers were important audiences and sources of material, in order to investigate how a gendered, stratified peer culture intersected with the official work of the writing workshop.

I turn now to some of that official work—work that Mary and Suzanne were pursuing with me out in the hall one morning. Both were popular children in the classroom. Suzanne enjoyed writing poetry and reading it to classmates during sharing time. She moved with ease and confidence among peers and teachers alike. Mary was less visible than Suzanne in the public life of the workshop and often collaborated with friends in her writing. In this case she wrote a play with Suzanne that would teach me much about the varied intentions children can pursue with their writing.

A local theater company sponsored a playwriting competition that Mary and Suzanne wanted to enter. They gave me a rough draft of their play, "The Mysterious Stranger," to read and to type for the competition (see Figure 12–1 for the first page of their draft).

I finally read their play late one Thursday night. I noticed the list of characters, which included a witch/queen, princess, stranger, prince, and mouse. I also noticed what I thought was an appropriation and transformation (à la Bakhtin 1986) of adult talk that they had come in contact with. Toward the bottom of their first page Mary and Suzanne have the witch recite the following lines after she locks the princess in the tower:

> Click-Clack,
> Snip, Snap, Snout.
> I've swallowed the key,
> She can't get out.

As the reading specialist in the school concluded all her readings of books to children with the rhyme "Snip, snap, snout, my tale is out," I guessed that Mary and Suzanne had appropriated this rhyme for their play.

I also wrote in my notes that night that the play

> was quite good. I especially liked how consistent the characters were—the
> prince was incompetent throughout. There was a good sense of humor in it

Figure 12–1 The first draft of "The Mysterious Stranger"

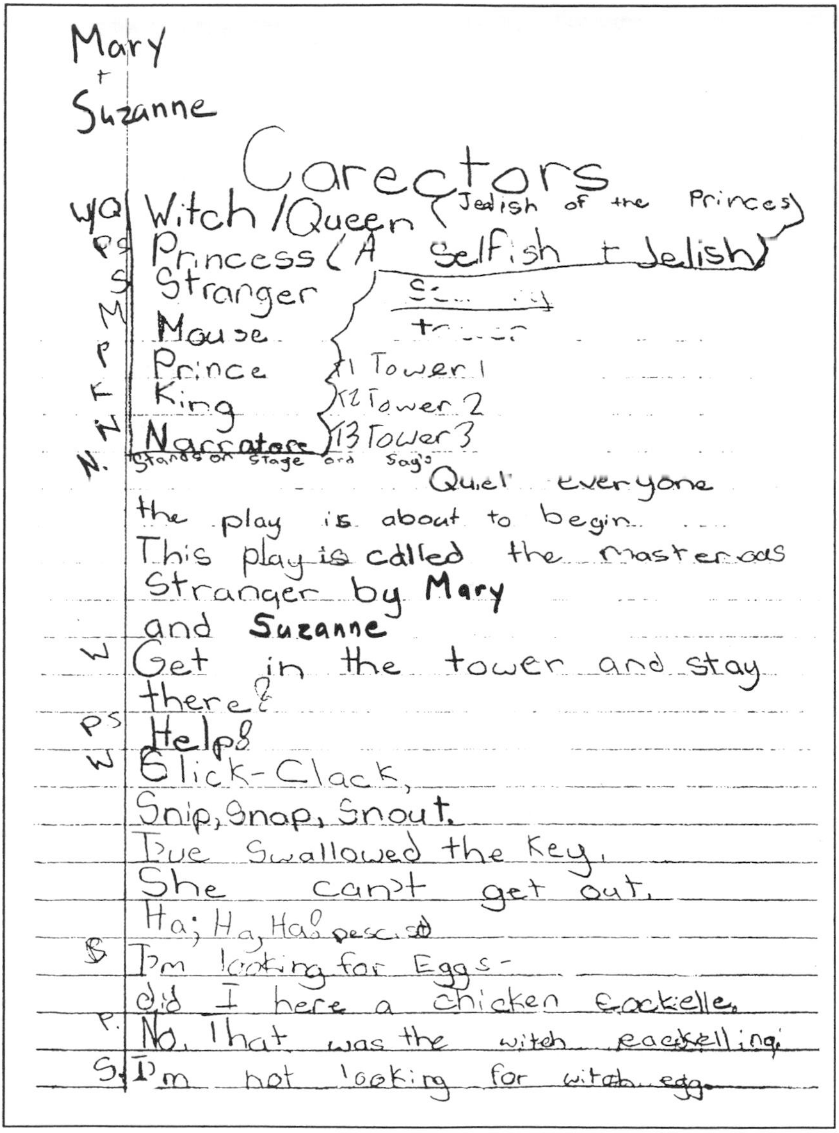

Mary
+
Suzanne

Carectors

WQ Witch / Queen (Jelish of the Princes)
PS Princess (A Selfish + Jelish)
S Stranger
M Mouse
P Prince { 1 Tower 1
K King { 2 Tower 2
N Narrator { 3 Tower 3

N. Stands on stage and say's Quiet everyone
the play is about to begin.
This play is called the masterous
Stranger by Mary
and Suzanne
W Get in the tower and stay
there!
PS Help!
W Click-Clack,
Snip, Snap, Snout.
I've Swallowed the Key.
She can't get out.
Ha; Ha, Ha!
S I'm looking for Eggs-
did I here a chicken cackelle.
P. No. That was the witch cackelling.
S. I'm not looking for witch egg.

(I liked the "I'm not looking for witch eggs" line). The dialogue moves along. I was a little puzzled by the mysterious stranger—why name the play that? and he was never explained. (Field notes, 3–22–90)

When I met with Suzanne and Mary the next day, my first response to their play—a response that sought to support their intentions and purposes for the piece (what Graves 1983, calls "following the child," p. 103)—was that I thought it was funny and coherent. I pointed to humorous lines and character consistency as reasons that the play worked as well as it did. A second response, born of my hopes to live out an antisexist pedagogy, was to pay special attention to the fact that the *hero* of the play—the mouse, who eventually chews away the foundations of the tower in order to free the princess—was *female*. I told them that I thought this was great, given that female characters in books and plays often get saved by male characters, a suggestion that women can do little for themselves. I liked the fact that their play was different.

So far, so good. We were sitting out in the hall, editing their draft so that I could type it for them, and filling out the official entry form for the competition. My signature was needed as a guarantee that the play was Mary and Suzanne's original work.

In the middle of our discussion of the mouse, Suzanne, with some hesitation, told me that they had "copied" the play from a book. I later found the book in the school library: *Picture Book Theater* by Beatrice Schenk de Regniers. Regniers's book featured two plays written for children, one of which was entitled "The Mysterious Stranger."

A long discussion ensued, since the meaning and moral content of the word "copied," for my third graders, was not at all stable across situations and children. Sometimes children would condemn as *copying* one of the very things I hoped would happen—that texts written by adults or children would inspire young authors to write their own versions of a borrowed setting, plot, character, or theme. Other times, children happily copied published stories word-for-word and called them their own. I realized, as I talked with Suzanne and Mary, that I really did not know how to talk about plagiarism very well and that I was far from being articulate in ways that would make sense for young children. In my notes that night I described our discussion as

> ... a difficult rhetorical situation. I'm trying to explain about plagiarism, which isn't easy anyway, to third graders, which makes it even harder. And lurking behind my talk is thoughts of Bakhtin and post-structuralists—all writing is a sort of copying. I finally hooked into the idea of the author working hard to make things sound the way they do, so she deserves credit. Suzanne's response was, 'Wouldn't she be happy that we wanted to put on her show?' (Field notes, 3–23–90)

Later, when I had a chance to look at Regniers's version, I realized that Mary and Suzanne had done a rather skillful job of condensing the original— I even decided that I liked Suzanne and Mary's version better than hers. I also realized that Mary and Suzanne were most interested in *performing* a play, not writing one. In fact, they had already drawn up a list of children from the class who were to play the various characters. And later, much later, when I was writing up the larger story of this writing workshop, I found out what strange and awful things children can accomplish with their little stories and plays.

Figure 12–2 shows Mary and Suzanne's list of characters and players. In the column at the left margin are the characters' names in the play. In parentheses next to this column of names are the names of children that Mary and Suzanne thought should play those parts. (I did not ask Mary and Suzanne what the Ys next to some of the children's names meant. My guess is that the Ys were used to record which children had agreed—said "Yes"—to perform in a future production of the play.) Except for Joshua, who was Suzanne's fifth-grade neighbor, all the children listed were from the classroom.

Not all characters in plays are created equal. Three characters who had speaking parts in Regniers's original version had *no* lines in Mary and

Figure 12–2   Mary and Suzanne's casting

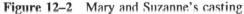

Mary

Mouse (Maya) Y
Princess (Maria)Y
Stranger (Ken)
King (Paul) Y
Prince (Troy)Y
Witch (Lori)
Queen (Carol)Y
Tower 1 (John)
Tower 2 (Leon)
Tower 3 (Robert)
Dancers (Suzanne + Joshua) Y
Narriattor (Bruce)

Suzanne's adaptation: Tower 1, Tower 2, and Tower 3. These characters were to stand on the stage from the beginning to the end of the play, *present* throughout, *but mute*. These roles were assigned, by Mary and Suzanne, to John, Leon, and Robert, three boys at the bottom of the classroom's informal pecking order. Two of these boys—Leon and Robert—lived in the trailer park. The third child, John, was probably the most talented writer in the room. He was also one of the children most teased and picked on by children. All the other children in the play (except for Joshua) were popular boys and girls in the class.

In its valuing of certain children over others, Mary and Suzanne's list points to an interesting and ultimately disturbing larger pattern in the texts that children produced and shared across the year in this writing workshop. In general, children with little status in the room tended not to write themselves or their friends into their stories as characters. Children with more status did. The result was that *only certain children* appeared regularly as characters in the stories read by children during sharing time and housed in our workshop library of student-authored texts: *children with the most status and power* in the room. Less popular children usually did not appear in children's stories; when they did, their inclusion did not necessarily suggest positive regard.

Thus, certain children were privileged in the content of the texts of the workshop, just as certain children were privileged in Mary and Suzanne's list of characters. The contrast can be sharply represented with the opening pages from books written by children toward the bottom and the top of the peer pecking order. The first two pages of William's book *The Junkie House* (*junkie* from *junk,* not a reference, at least not a direct one, to drug users), are reproduced in Figure 12–3. The opening page of Carol's book, *Spies*, appears in Figure 12–4.

In his story, William does not name the main character after himself or anyone else in the room. In fact, in this instance William's main character is referred to only as "a person," "the person," and "he" throughout the story. In Carol's story, however, the main characters are named for children in the room; specifically, a group of four girls of relatively high status, including Carol herself. Three of the children's names are shortened and stylized, with the effect, for me, of suggesting characters who are tougher or more sophisticated than characters named by the full names: Car (from Carol), 'Zanne (from Suzanne), and Lis (from Lisa). Several children in interviews mentioned that high-status boys and girls in the room had better clothes than other children did. The attention to clothes and hair in Carol's illustration is striking, especially in contrast to William's illustration.

Why did children such as William not publish fictional narratives like Carol's, with characters named for himself and his friends? I am not sure. If they had reasons that they could articulate, I did not ask for them—I discovered this aspect of children's texts long after I was done with my work with these children. I do know, from working with them across the year and from

Figure 12–3   The first two pages of William's book, *The Junkie House*

There were two black dogs and two black cats. They lived in a junkie house.

One day a person opened the door and stepped into the house. And the cat jumped on him. The person threw the cat.

Figure 12–4   The opening page of Carol's book, *Spies*

It was time for the club.
"Come on," said 'Zanne. So they
went to the door that led them to
the laboratory under the ground.

their interviews, that less popular children often considered peers risky, threatening audiences for their work (a few even refused to share with peers, and felt safe only if sharing texts with me and other adults). I also know that these children, as well as most of the other children in the room, preferred writing fictional narratives to more autobiographical, personal narratives, and that they preferred fiction, in part, because it avoided direct exposure of their experiences, values, and feelings to the scrutiny of others (Lensmire 1992; see also Barnes and Barnes 1984, who report on secondary students with similar concerns).

My best guess, then, is that less popular children felt uncomfortable naming themselves as characters in the public stories of the workshop because this would place them—even if only as characters in fictional narratives—at the center of attention and under the scrutiny of peers. This would not explain all their decisions. Sometimes, perhaps many times, they simply were interested in writing about other characters in other stories. Children with more status and influence, in this interpretation, felt less vulnerable. When they wrote, they felt comfortable placing themselves in their stories as characters.

Or, perhaps, the children at the top were also uncomfortable in the workshop, but for different reasons. Sharing time and the workshop library offered children of low status and influence in the room numerous public opportunities to influence opinion or to impress peers and teachers with their humor and insight. And with few exceptions, these children *did* take advantage of opportunities to share their work with peers during sharing time and in our classroom library. Unlike the playground or the cafeteria, or before and after school, these public spaces were watched over closely by teachers who would not allow unpopular children to be shouted down or pushed around. Perhaps the pecking order was a little more up for grabs than I have suggested, and the workshop was an open but structured place in which (Britton 1978) there was

> an exchange of evaluations between authors and their readers, an exchange in which reputations are made and lost, influences wax and wane, values gain and lose currency, and the cultural pattern of a social group is sustained and evolved. (p. 17)

Children at the top wrote themselves into their texts as an assertion (and reassertion) of their importance, their rightful place at the front of the room and the focus of attention. From this perspective, they named themselves in their texts in the name of order, in defense of hierarchies that were continually threatened by upstart classmates who did not know their place.

Still, in their inclusions and exclusions, in their evaluations, these public texts valued certain children more than others. And the children receiving valorization on the page were children who did not live in the trailer park, were children who already enjoyed status and influence within the peer culture, even if they had to work to keep it.

It is disturbing enough to realize that children's texts might reflect, in some way, differences in status and power among children. But we must also consider the active role that texts might play in producing and maintaining these relationships. Texts are rhetorical, have effects in the world. They can influence others' conceptions of themselves and their worlds, make them laugh, hurt them, make them feel connected to others, safe or unsafe, encourage them to speak and write or remain silent. Such was some of the work children's texts did in our writing workshop.

The micropolitics of peer relations played itself out not only on the playground and behind my back but also in the writing that children chose to make public in the spaces created and authorized by me, the teacher.

When I loosened the lid on student intention and association in the room, peers became extremely important influences on student experiences and writing in the workshop. These influences were not all positive. Children evaluated and excluded one another in ways that echoed some of our society's worst sorts of divisions and denigrations. Children divided themselves up (sometimes in less disturbing, more temporary ways) in ways that allowed for changing evaluations, new friends and enemies. But they did, at any given moment and with more or less permanency, differentiate among their peers in terms of who was and who was not a friend, a desirable collaborator, a trusted audience in conferences and sharing time.

For educators who are, like me, sympathetic to workshop and other progressive approaches to the teaching of writing, my work poses at least two challenges.

First, we must transform our conceptions of children as writers, and allow ourselves, in our work as teachers and researchers, a less romantic conception of children. For workshop advocates such as Graves, Calkins, and Murray, the writer's struggle is the effective expression of something that is inside (Berlin 1988). As Willinsky (1990) has noted, these advocates have "happily taken the personal and public aspects of literacy to consist of a one-way street: the individual finds a vehicle in writing for those deep and hidden thoughts at the core of the self and goes increasingly public with them" (p. 208). Lost in such a conception of written literacy is a sense of the embeddedness of writers in the social contexts within which they work (Bakhtin 1981, 1984; Volosinov 1973).

Thus, instead of simple, straightforward, transparent, innocent children, we must allow ourselves to see children as often sophisticated, strategic, complex, with sometimes questionable intentions. Part of this transformation will include paying more attention to the immediate peer culture, to social relations among children and the meanings and values that they assign to each other, texts, and teachers. The peer culture is an important backdrop upon which children's texts are written and given their local, particular meanings.

Workshop approaches do encourage teachers to know children, but this is usually thought of as knowing individual children (see, for example, Graves 1983, on individual children's "unique territories of information," pp. 22–28). I am not denying the need for knowledge of individual children. I am arguing that such a focus can blind us to the ways that children are connected to one another, blind us to the more or less shared meanings and values that children bring to their activities and texts.

The second challenge before us is to articulate goals for our workshops and classrooms that go beyond supporting individual student intentions, and include a vision of the type of classroom community in which we want our children to write and learn. Workshop approaches have aligned their goals with individual children's intentions without considering that the ends some children pursue may not be beneficial for other children, or even for themselves (Gilbert 1989). There are bullies on the playground, and peer cultures maintaining divisions among children by class, race, and gender. We affirm these aspects of children's lives when we commit ourselves to supporting, uncritically, student intentions. As Goodman (1992) has noted,

> ... given our cultural values, putting an emphasis on increasing the personal freedom of students will probably result in anti-social, egotistical posturing among children rather than the free child so often lauded in the radical school literature. Children's true individuality (rather than their self-indulgence) can grow only within a community structure in which there are restrictions and expectations placed upon the individual by that community. (p. 102)

Our goals for children in the workshop, then, must be closely tied to a vision of the sort of communities that we hope to live and work in—in our classrooms and in society. Elsewhere, I argue for what I call an engaged pluralistic classroom community (Lensmire 1994). I draw on Dewey's (1956) vision of classrooms as embryonic democratic societies, as well as on other theorists working critical pragmatic themes (including Bernstein 1988; Cherryholmes 1988, 1990; Habermas 1984, 1987). An engaged, pluralistic classroom community is one that celebrates the heteroglossia of children's voices in the classroom, the multiple social and personal intonations and evaluations that attend children speaking and writing (Bakhtin 1981). Recognizing and affirming differences among children, it encourages them to learn from, be enhanced by, those differences. It is a classroom community

> based upon mutual respect, where we are willing to risk our own prejudgments, are open to listening and learning from others, and we respond to others with responsiveness and responsibility. (Bernstein 1988, p. 18)

These challenges have not been taken up in any serious way by writing workshop advocates and other progressive educators and researchers who call for the increased liberation of student intention and association in classrooms. Such writers have pointed, with good reason, to the traditional teacher and textbook as primary enemies of student voice in schools. And in response to dry, meaningless work with text, they have promoted the admirable goal of honoring and supporting individual student intentions for writing. But increased student control over writing activities and texts, even as it solves problems of student apathy and alienation, creates new problems that need to be addressed if workshops are to help *all* children gain power over print.

I turn, now, to Jessie, and conclude my story with hers. Jessie's story lends urgency to our efforts to take up new conceptions of children as writers, and to envision and work toward engaged, pluralistic classroom communities, in our teaching and research with children.

    Jessie was the classroom's "female pariah"—Thorne's (1986) name for those girls in elementary classrooms and schools who are ostracized by peers "by virtue of gender, but also through some added stigma such as being overweight or poor" (p. 175). Jessie was not small, and she came from the trailer park. Nearly everyone in the class, in their interviews, said that she was the least popular person in the class and the least desirable to work with. Bruce, for example, called her "idiotic, dumb," John said that she stunk, and Mary that she never brushed her teeth. Only a few children said that they had worked with her in the class. The regular classroom teacher and I often intervened in verbal fights between Jessie and other children. Jessie was by no means a passive victim—she fought back (and started a few fights herself) with volume and sarcasm.

    In her interview Jessie said that she had only a few friends in the class—Janis and Karen (both from the trailer park)—and a few others in the other third-grade class. She said that she sometimes conferenced with Janis and Karen and shared her finished pieces with them, but usually she kept her work to herself. When asked, "Whom do you write for?" she said, "Um, myself. I just write for myself. Or sometimes I'd write a story to somebody, and let them read it" (Interview, 5–30–90). Although she published four books across the year, she did not share her books during sharing time or in our classroom's writing workshop library. In contrast to most of her classmates, she looked almost exclusively to adults as audiences.

    Jessie had decided that it was too risky to share her stories with peers. After identifying children she did not want to conference with, Jessie described how she would feel if she were forced to conference with them:

Intr: What would they do with your writing? How would you feel if you had to conference with them?

Jessie: I would feel like a jar of slime. Being sat on.

Intr: So maybe they don't treat you very well?

Jessie: Yes. No, like getting cut in half. (Interview, 5–30–90)

Later, she said that she never shared in front of the whole class because they would make her feel the same way in that situation. (She resisted numerous attempts by me to have her share with small groups of classmates, even though she often eagerly shared her work with Grace and me.) Her description of how her peers would accomplish making her feel "cut in half" during a sharing session surprised me. I had expected her to predict verbal attacks on her work when she finished sharing a story. Instead:

Because, 'cause, for some people, it, nobody would, would um, *answer*, or *ask them questions*. I know that. [my emphasis]

Jessie feared silence, a rejection expressed not with words but with no words, when there were supposed to be words; an active silence. Jessie's comments assumed aspects of the sharing session that Grace and I had worked hard to put in place. If an author asked her classmates for specific help in relation to the piece she was reading, then we expected children to respond to the author's request in their response before going on to other topics—"nobody would answer." If the author did not set up the sharing session this way, we expected children to first talk with the author about what they liked and then move to questions that they had about the work— "or ask them questions."

From the beginning I worked hard to make the writing workshop, and its conferences and sharing times, a safe place for children to write and share their work. We did many activities to help children respond to one another's writing in helpful ways. Grace and I were quite active at times in sharing sessions, reminding children before we started that we needed to respect and support our fellow writers, as well as intervening during sharing sessions when children seemed unsupportive. Perhaps Jessie's fear of silence reflected her knowledge of the active role that we took during sharing. She may have known that we would address hurtful student comments, but she was less sure (as I am) that we could address *no* comments, no answers or questions.

Obviously, these teacher efforts were not enough to make the classroom a safe place for Jessie to share her texts with peers. Jessie's peers were a significant part of her not feeling safe. When asked why other people felt comfortable sharing their stories in front of class, Jessie said, "Because they have lots of friends."

One of the consequences of Jessie's relations with her peers was that her writing was never shared in the public spaces of the writing workshop. Thus, most children never encountered Jessie's retelling of "Sleeping Beauty."

Once upon a time there was a beautiful princess, and her name was Jessie. One day, she was sleeping, and she heard a noise so she got up and went upstairs to the room upstairs. When she opened the door she saw a spinning wheel.

When she was spinning at the spinning wheel, she poked her finger. Suddenly she fell asleep, and everyone fell asleep too. Just then a prince came.

He snuck into the castle and found the princess and kissed her. And suddenly everybody awoke and the prince became an empire.

Bruner (1990) believes that the stories we tell and write "mediate between the canonical world of culture and the more idiosyncratic world of beliefs, desires, and hopes'' (p. 52). Our stories represent a sort of compromise between how we think the world is (given to us in the "canonical world of culture") and how we, as individuals, would like the world to be. When we tell stories, we both draw on given, cultural narratives about the world and our place in it, and manipulate and twist them in ways that express our idiosyncratic worlds.

The twists that Jessie gave to a more canonical version of "Sleeping Beauty" (from the Grimms, for example) are charming; they suggest self-importance, youth, movement. Her princess is named Jessie instead of Rosamond. Jessie the author (as well as Jessie the princess) avoids altogether the angry witch who casts a death spell on the young princess, and the good witch who transmutes that spell to sleep. Jessie seems impatient with sleep, so instead of one hundred years of it, she has her princess "suddenly" fall asleep, only to be awakened almost immediately by a prince who "just then" arrived. In the Grimm version, the two live happily ever after together. Jessie's princess and prince may do likewise, but she leaves this open. Jessie, however, is not content with some sort of romantic bliss for the two. Her version ends with the rise to power of her prince: He became an "empire."

Jessie's story may also be read against another "canonical world of culture"—the peer culture in which Jessie participated. The rift between canonical peer world and Jessie's "more idiosyncratic" one is wide, and leaves the peer one looking anything but charming, even grim, for Jessie. In that peer culture, Jessie was not beautiful in the stories that others told about her. She labored to avoid those who would cast spells to "cut her in half" or turn her into a "jar of slime." The school year was long, and she had little chance of association (nor did she say she wanted it) with the powerful.

Jessie wrote herself and a vision of the world on the page, but others seldom heard her voice or saw her vision, at least not in the public spaces the workshop provided. The absence of Jessie and her "Sleeping Beauty" from the public spaces of the writing workshop reminds us that the liberation of children's intentions and associations in the classroom represents both promise and problem in our progressive pedagogies, and that peers—for better and for worse—have something to say about who speaks and is heard in our classrooms.

References

Applebee, A.N. 1981. *Writing in the secondary school: English and the content areas*. Urbana, Ill.: National Council of Teachers of English.

Bakhtin, M.M. 1981. *The dialogic imagination*. Austin: University of Texas.

———. 1984. *Rabelais and his world*. Bloomington: Indiana University.

———. 1986. *Speech genres and other late essays*. Austin: University of Texas.

Barnes, D., and Barnes, D. 1984. *Versions of English*. London: Heinemann.

Berlin, J. 1988. Rhetoric and ideology in the writing class. *College English* 50(5): 477–94.

Bernstein, R.J. 1988. Pragmatism, pluralism, and the healing of wounds. *American Philosophical Association Proceedings* 63(3): 5–18.

Bogdan, R.C., and Biklen, S.K. 1982. *Qualitative research for education: An introduction to theory and methods.* Boston: Allyn and Bacon.

Britton, J. 1978. The composing processes and the functions of writing. In *Research on composing: Points of departure,* edited by C.R. Cooper and L. Odell. Urbana, Ill.: National Council of Teachers of English.

Bruner, J. 1990. *Acts of meaning.* Cambridge, Mass.: Harvard University Press.

Calkins, L.M. 1986. *The art of teaching writing.* Portsmouth, N.H.: Heinemann.

Cherryholmes, C. 1988. *Power and criticism: Poststructural investigations in education.* New York: Teachers College.

———. 1990. Reading research. Unpublished manuscript.

Dewey, J. 1956. *The child and the curriculum* and *The school and society.* Chicago: University of Chicago.

Doyle, W. 1986. Content representation in teachers' definitions of academic work. *Journal of Curriculum Studies* 18(4): 365–79.

Dyson, A. H. 1989. *Multiple worlds of child writers: Friends learning to write.* New York: Teachers College Press.

Erickson, F. 1986. Qualitative methods in research on teaching. In *Handbook on research on teaching.* 3d ed. Edited by M.C. Wittrock. New York: Macmillan.

Florio-Ruane, S., and Dunn, S. 1985. Teaching writing: Some perennial questions and some possible answers. Occasional Paper No. 85. East Lansing, Mich.: Institute for Research on Teaching, Michigan State University.

Freire, P. 1970. *Pedagogy of the oppressed.* New York: Continuum.

———. 1985. *The politics of education: Culture, power and liberation.* South Hadley, Mass.: Bergin and Garvey.

Gilbert, P. 1989. Student text as pedagogical text. In *Language, authority and criticism: Readings on the school textbook,* edited by S. deCastell, A. Luke, and C. Luke. London: Falmer.

Giroux, H. 1988. Literacy and the pedagogy of voice and political empowerment. *Educational Theory* 38(1): 61–75.

Goodman, J. 1992. *Elementary schooling for critical democracy.* Albany: State University of New York.

Graves, D. 1983. *Writing: Teachers and children at work.* Portsmouth, N.H.: Heinemann.

Habermas, J. 1984. *The theory of communicative action: Reason and the rationality of society.* Vol. 1. Translated by T. McCarthy. Boston: Beacon Press.

———. 1987. *The theory of communicative action: Lifeworld and system: A critique of functionalist reason.* (Vol. 2). Translated by T. McCarthy. Boston: Beacon Press.

Hammersly, M., and Atkinson, P. 1983. *Ethnography: Principles in practice.* London: Tavistock.

hooks, b. 1989. *Talking back: Thinking feminist—thinking black.* Boston: South End Press.

Kristeva, J. 1986. *The Kristeva reader*, edited by T. Moi. New York: Columbia University.

Lensmire, T. 1992. Peers, risk and writing. Paper presented at the annual meeting of the National Reading Conference, San Antonio.

———. (1994). *When children write: Critical re-visions of the writing workshop.* New York: Teachers College Press.

Murray, D. 1968. *A writer teaches writing: A practical method of teaching composition.* Boston: Houghton Mifflin.

Thorne, B. 1986. Girls and boys together . . . but mostly apart: Gender arrangements in elementary schools. Pp. 167–82. in *Relationships and development*, edited by W. Hargup and Z. Rubin. Hillsdale, N.J.: Lawrence Erlbaum Associates.

Volosinov, V. 1973. *Marxism and the philosophy of language.* Translated by L. Matejka and I.R. Titumink. Cambridge, Mass.: Harvard University Press.

Waller, W. 1932. *The sociology of teaching.* New York: Wiley.

Willinsky, J. 1990. *The new literacy: Redefining reading and writing in the schools.* New York: Routledge.

13

Scaffolding: Who's Building Whose Building?

Dennis Searle
York University

What has made the teaching of language arts exciting for me since I began in 1966 had been the continuing growth in our understanding of what language is and how it is learned. There has been a constant interaction between research into language and the teaching of language that has brought researchers into the classroom and turned teachers into researchers. The interaction is crucial but demands constant, critical evaluation. Recently, language teaching has picked up from research the concept of "scaffolding," and this concept has begun to be discussed in journals as a teaching strategy. I am concerned about how scaffolding is interpreted and about what happens when teachers and consultants apply this notion to classroom teaching. At the base of my concern is the fundamental question of who is in control of the language.

Understanding Scaffolding

To understand how scaffolding can be misapplied, we need first to see what the concept was intended to describe. Bruner (1975) explains one form of interaction between a young child and its mother like this: "In such instances mothers most often see their role as supporting the child in achieving an intended outcome, entering only to assist or reciprocate or 'scaffold' the action" (p.12). Bruner and Ratner (1978) expand on the concept, identifying some features that contribute to effective scaffolding. These include a familiar semantic domain, predictable structures, role reversibility, variability, and playfulness. Bruner's view seems to make sense—that scaffolds support children to interact and learn from their use of language. This was certainly picked up by other researchers, including Scollon (1976) and Cazden (1979). Graves (1983) interpreted his approach to conferencing from a scaffolding point of view.

As a concept, then, scaffolding has an extremely respectable pedigree, and it does help us understand some child-adult interactions. One key to remember is Bruner's original statement that when scaffolding, the adult works to "support the child in achieving an intended outcome." Graves claims that "scaffolding follows the contours of child growth" (p. 271). The active, initiating child stays in control of the language and the experience while the adult operates effectively in response to the child.

Undoubtedly, this kind of responsive scaffolding can, and does, occur in school. Kreeft (1984) gives a good example in a written dialogue between teacher and student. The student is writing about a recent holiday is San Diego; the teacher uses the personal experience of a similar holiday to support the student's extended writing on the topic. By asking simple question such as "Do they still have the dancing waters?" the teacher triggers extended description and personal evaluation in the student's journal entries. Kreeft likens this dialogue to Wells's (1981) notion of the teacher as "leader from behind."

Ignoring Students' Intentions

Schools, however, are rarely effective in allowing children either to initiate topics or to shape the experience for themselves. As a result, scaffolding can more often become the imposition of a structure on the student. Kreeft's article shows such an example: In response to a statement by the student about wishing to be a rock star, the teacher offers a set of career guidance information such as "Do you play any musical instrument? Rock stars need to study music so they can interpret it and write their own." The student responds minimally to this scaffolding because, I think, the teacher has not honored the original intentions.

I have encountered other examples of this approach to scaffolding. In an address to the Canadian Council of Teachers of English, Cazden (1981) suggested and demonstrated intervention in young children's show-and-tell sessions to help the children learn to speak in focused, extended narrative. In Cazden's examples, however, the children's understanding, valuing, and excitement about the personal experiences were negated as they were led to report the experience in an appropriate form. Applebee and Langer (1983), in advocating "instructional scaffolding," give an example in which teachers scaffold students' science experiment reports by providing a sheet of questions outlining the required steps. Undoubtedly, these outlines help the student report the experiment more completely, but do they really help in learning the purposes and nature of scientific writing? Why, for example, are the students performing and reporting the experiment? Whose intentions are being honored in the report?

It appears, in fact, that the term *scaffolding* is being used to justify some longstanding and, in my view, questionable classroom interaction patterns. The following excerpt from a show-and-tell session observed in other research (Searle and Dillon 1981) shows a teacher's "supporting" a grade 1 student. Notice that the child's experience is taken from him and is molded according to the teacher's view of what is relevant and interesting.

T: Oh, boy! What's that?

Ch: [pause]

T: Maybe you'll explain to us about what this is. [addressing other children] If you know, don't tell. Would you turn right around so we can all hear?

Ch: A walkie-talkie.

T: Do you just have one of them? How many do you have?

Ch: One.

T: How many do you need to listen?

Ch: Two. My brother has one.

T: I see. Can you show us how it works? You turn it on first. Is this where you turn it on?

Ch: Um, that is where I talk to my brother.

T: I see. That's called the [inaudible]. That's where you can talk to your brother. I don't imagine you can talk to him now. Did he bring his to school?

Ch: [shakes head]

T: And how do you talk? Let's pretend that Jason is talking. No? You are not going to show us? How many have used a walkie-talkie?

Ch$_1$: I lost my walkie-talkie. [Class starts to chatter]

T: Just a moment, please. If you have anything to ask, you put your hand up. Yes?

Ch$_2$: How long did you get it?

Ch: Christmas.

T: At Christmas.

Ch: Yeah.

T: We usually say, "How long *ago* did you get that?" Have you had a lot of fun with it? Well, who would like to talk next?

This teacher described the teacher's role in such sessions as taking pressure off shy students and modeling questions and comments. In fact, the situation was changed into one in which the child was left to figure out the teacher's understanding and intentions. This feature of classroom life has been noted by other researchers, notably Barnes (1976) and Edwards and Furlong (1978). In understanding how scaffolding works outside the classroom setting, we should remember that "the routines of action and the rules behind them are accepted because of a co-operative motive, but they do not create the motive." (Trevarthen 1980).

Scaffolding and Control

The adequacy of the metaphor implied by scaffolding hinges on the question of who is constructing the edifice. Too often, the teacher is the builder; the child is expected to accept and occupy the predetermined structure. Scaffolding, in this sense, provides a rationale for those who feel that children's language is deficient and that, therefore, children need to be taught the "necessary" language. The notion of scaffolding, however, should not be used to justify making children restructure their experience to fit their teacher's structures. What we should be doing, instead, is working with children, encouraging them to adapt their own language resources to achieve new purposes that they see as important.

Wells (1981) has shown that schools differ from homes as environments for language learning in that there are fewer opportunities in school for children to initiate language activities and that there is less response to these initiatives when they occur. This indicates that schools are a poor environment for Bruner's original concept of scaffolding: "supporting the child in achieving an intended outcome." Students have had little to say in determining what counts as knowledge and how knowledge should be shaped in schools. Only when teachers are ready to turn over more control to students can scaffolding be an effective classroom strategy for language development.

References

Applebee, A.N., and Langer, J.A. 1983. Instructional scaffolding: Reading and writing as natural language activities. *Language Arts* 60: 176–83.

Barnes, D. 1976. *From communication to curriculum.* Harmondsworth, England: Penguin Books.

Bruner, J. 1975. The ontogenesis of speech acts. *Journal of Child Language* 2: 1–40.

Bruner, J., and Ratner, N. 1978. Games, social exchange and the acquisition of language. *Journal of Child Language* 5: 391–401.

Cazden, C. 1979. Peekaboo as an instructional model: Discourse development at home and at school. *Papers and Reporter on Child Language Development.*

————. 1981. Keynote address to Canadian Council of Teachers of English, Vancouver, B.C.

Edwards, A.D., and Furlong, J.V. 1978. *The language of teaching: Meaning in classroom interaction.* London: Heinemann.

Graves, D. 1983. Writing: Teachers and children at work. London: Heinemann.

Kreeft, J. 1984. Dialogue writing—Bridge from talk to essay writing. *Language Arts* 61: 141–50.

Scollon, R. 1976. *Conversations with a one-year old: A case study of the developmental foundations of syntax.* Honolulu: University Press of Hawaii.

Searle, D., and Dillon, D. 1981. The role of language in the classroom. Paper presented at the annual meeting of the American Educational Research Association, Los Angeles.

Trevarthen, C. 1980. The foundation of intersubjectivity. In *The social foundations of language and thought,* edited by D. Olson. New York: W.W. Norton.

Wells, G., ed. 1981. *Learning through interaction: The study of language development.* Cambridge, England: Cambridge University Press.

14

Teaching and Learning Together in Teacher Education: "Making Easter"

David Dillon with Linda Anderson, Joyce Angio,
Nancy Kahan, Anna Rumin, and Ron Sherman
McGill University

If we hope that elementary and secondary teachers will foster their students' ownership of their own learning, then teachers need to experience owning their learning in their teacher education programs—at least, that is, if the general assumption holds true that teachers teach as they have been taught. As a teacher educator, I will explore in this chapter the notion of ownership of learning in teacher education programs, specifically by reflecting upon my experience in a course I taught several years ago in which I tried to foster students' ownership of their learning. Then, several students from the course will reflect on the experience of coming to own their learning. We finish by reflecting together on issues and insights related to teaching and learning in this way. With a great responsibility in this regard, teacher education faces a particularly difficult challenge in achieving this goal in a university environment that has traditionally not fostered this kind of learning.

Ownership Through Learning and Teaching: Two Sides of One Coin

The notion of ownership of one's learning derives from a constellation of learning theories that are generally called "constructivist" theories. The classic example is still perhaps the lifelong work of Piaget, who theorized that learners basically *construct* their own intelligence through generating and testing hypotheses to make sense of the world they encounter. While much of the "data" for learners' hypothesizing come from the feedback of others around them, the ultimate work and responsibility for what is learned is the learner's. This kind of "homemade" learning assures internalized, or long-term, learning. If learners have basically made their new understanding through their own constructivist efforts, then—so the thinking goes—their learning "belongs" to them. Hence, the notion of learners' *ownership* of their learning.

This view of learning is diametrically opposed to behaviorist theories of learning, which explain learning as shaped by the initiatives of those around learners who "teach" them. In such a view of learning, the understanding "belongs" to those who pass it on and shape it in learners.

A major addition to constructivist learning theory developed in the 1970s, particularly through the work of Britton (1970), was the recognition that a learner's *language*, both talk and writing, could be a powerful tool in constructing one's new understanding. In other words, human beings learn by structuring, and they structure to a large extent by "saying," orally or in writing. Thus, educators came to realize that one's language use could not only reflect one's learning but also cause it—and help a learner "own" his or her own learning.

To extend this theory more specifically to school learning in classrooms, learners come to a domain of public knowledge and try to make sense of it, that is, learn it. Public knowledge is usually structured and "languaged" in a general, abstract, impersonal, logical, and neutral fashion. Learners come to it with their personal knowledge—specific, concrete, personal, narrative, and often evaluative. To learn the new, public knowledge, they must reconstruct it for themselves. Their only starting point, their base of strength, is their personal knowledge. Their major tool for reconstructing—and making their own—the new information is their personal language. Thus, to learn new information effectively and well, learners must actively play with, and hypothesize about, the new information, particularly through exploratory and heuristic use of their language. They must find aspects of their personal knowledge and experience that link with the new information as points of breakthrough to new understanding. In summary, through their own efforts, they rebuild for themselves what many others have already learned; thus, they come to "own" it for themselves.

Note that my explanation thus far has focused on a view of *learning*. Indeed, "ownership" has traditionally referred to learning. What has been less well developed and articulated has been the other side of the coin, an approach to *teaching* that fosters students' ownership of their learning. The essence of this approach to teaching is for the teacher to share with learners what has traditionally been the teacher's role and to take on partly the traditional role of the student. Thus, rather than teachers' and students' playing mutually exclusive roles in the classroom (the teacher asks questions and students answer them; the teacher determines tasks to be done and students complete them, and so on), this approach to teaching implies teacher and student roles that are largely mutually inclusive and shared (both teachers and students pose questions and try to answer them; both teachers and students set tasks and complete them, and so on). For this reason Freire (1972) coined new terms for teacher and pupils—teacher-pupil and pupil-teachers—to reflect these shared roles better. The rationale for this shift is that the traditional role of a teacher (active, "languaging," reconstructing public knowledge) is a strong example of an "ownership" view of *learning*; in fact, that view of learning explains the old saying, "If you want to learn something well, teach it." If, therefore, traditional teaching has been such an effective means of *learning*, it is only logical to share that role with learners in order to enhance their ownership of their learning.

This approach to teaching designed to foster constructivist learning in the classroom is generally the opposite of more traditional and prevalent approaches to teaching, which seek to pass on already-existing public knowledge to passive learners who are supposed to take it on—and to give it back at evaluation time to demonstrate their learning. Barnes (1976) referred to such an approach as transmission teaching; that is, the teacher *transmits* already-existing knowledge to learners who receive it. Freire (1972) referred to it metaphorically as a banking approach: the teacher tries to make deposits of knowledge in the students' heads, to be withdrawn at exam time. Such approaches leave little room for learners to reconstruct new knowledge, and eventually to "own" their learning. Indeed, the ownership of the knowledge clearly remains with the teacher, who "rents" it to the learners.

My exploration of the notion of "ownership" of learning—which forms much of my background as a teacher—has thus far been rather general and abstract. Now we can explore the notion in more concrete and practical detail. I will do that by recounting and reflecting upon my experience in one teacher education course I taught recently in which I tried to live these ideas about teaching and learning.

My Attempt to Foster Ownership of Learning

The course I am focusing on, Language and Learning Across the Curriculum, is interesting since a key aspect of its content is teaching in such a way as to foster students' ownership of their learning. The teaching approach I describe below could, nevertheless, apply to any course. This particular one, a required graduate-level course that met one evening per week over a semester, was composed of mostly elementary and secondary teachers representing a range of subject area specializations with both mother tongue and second-language orientations. With an enrollment of thirty-five, though, the course logistics were more like those of an undergraduate course.

In structuring its content, I established several key, foundational principles, or conceptual pillars, upon which the course rested.

1. Learners construct their own knowledge by structuring their experience, and their own (exploratory) language use is a major means by which they structure, or place a shape upon, their experience.

2. The two major shapes that language appears to place on experience (that is, the two major worlds of knowing created through discourse) are (a) explanation and (b) story.

3. The above principle is true, but in different ways, across a range of sociocultural differences: gender, social class, culture, language group, and so on; thus, it is a *plural* principle.

4. The purpose of this learning process within school can be personal and social transformation (rather than cultural reproduction and assimilation).

I determined a key text or two for students to read for each major point. To support and expand the ideas in the key texts, I chose a number of articles from professional journals describing particular teachers' efforts to live these principles—in a wide variety of ways—in their own elementary and secondary classrooms. We were able to spend approximately three-to-four weeks on each key point. (See Figure 14–1.)

This broad and general framework (my own construction of knowledge) is the only structure of knowledge I tried to provide for the class. Within this framework, I deliberately left a great deal of "space" within which I expected all students to "construct," or fill in, their own more specific details of knowledge. (Of course, even my broad framework of knowledge— the four key points above—had to be reconstructed by each student if not already understood.) The next major issue is the support that I tried to offer through my teaching for their construction, or ownership, of knowledge.

My general directions to students for their learning process were essentially simple, yet complex and challenging for them at the same time.

1. *Try to "say" what you think you are learning about the course content.* This "saying" could be oral during the small-group discussions during each class or written in the learning journal that I asked students to keep outside of class. The grist for this "saying" mill was obviously the readings I provided (or others that students encountered), the brief explanations or questions I provided in class, and what classmates had said. It also needed, however, to contain students' prior experiences in classrooms or beyond, and I deliberately tried to direct their attention to that personal experience. Their ultimate task, though, was to try to construct, through one's own "saying," one's own knowledge and understanding, using ideas from many sources but synthesizing and transforming them within oneself.

Figure 14–1   Key texts for major points

COURSE OUTLINE

Topic	Readings
I. Introduction: And Now For Something Completely Different!—Or Is It?	Carlos Castaneda. *The Teachings of Don Juan: A Yaqui Way of Knowledge.* (optional)
II. Theoretical Overview	James Britton. *Language and Learning.*
III. Application: Explanation	Douglas Barnes. *From Communication to Curriculum.*
IV. Application: Story	Louise Rosenblatt. *The Reader, the Text, and the "Poem."* Betty Jane Wagner. *Dorothy Heathcote: Drama as a Learning Medium.*
V. Sociocultural Framework A. Gender B. Culture C. Class	*Choose one*: Marilyn Belenky et al. *Women's Ways of Knowing.* Shirley Brice Heath. *Ways with Words.* Carolyn Steedman. *The Tidy House.*
VI. Purposes, Whys	Paulo Freire. *Pedagogy of the Oppressed.*
VII. Pulling It Back Together Again	Amy Tan. *The Joy Luck Club.*

N.B.: Copies of articles distributed during the term will supplement the texts.

---

2. *"Go on—don't stop."* Students could follow the first direction easily enough, but they always tended to stop their "saying" when approaching what they felt was the edge of their knowledge. Indeed, I often encouraged them to start posing questions, as they felt they approached their own personal frontiers, in order to mark a sense of direction into the unknown territory. I urged them, however, to push on, to try to answer these new questions they had just posed. At first puzzled, students were often subsequently surprised to discover how much "farther" they could go. For most of them, it was their first experience within a formal course structure of bringing to conscious, explicit awareness the knowledge that was implicit *within* them by "saying" it. Even as they moved ahead farther than they

originally thought they could, they hit another frontier and another set of seemingly unanswerable questions. The task, of course, was the same as before—go on.

3. Since most of this group of students were concurrently teaching in their own classrooms, I was able to add another direction for them: *Try to "live" in your classrooms what you think you are learning about the course content.* When students were able to pursue this means of "action knowledge" (Barnes 1976), the results were often particularly powerful as a source of new insight or new questions. These experiences often formed a major topic in small-group discussions and journal entries. Even when students did not concurrently have their own classrooms to teach in, I encouraged them to imagine, to visualize what their attempts to live ideas from the course would look like in a classroom and to try to "say" them.

When this learning process works ideally, it becomes a self-directed, self-maintaining process driven by the learners' own efforts. It is like the process of riding a bicycle in which the rider continually loses balance and regains it (through a change in steering, and the like), loses balance and regains it, and so on. In the learning process it is a matter of losing one's conceptual "balance" through new questions at the edge of one's knowing, regaining it through "answering" these questions, losing it again through further questions, and so on. Another metaphorical way of thinking of the process is, not *following* one's path—as if the path already existed—but *creating* one's own path. Regardless of the metaphor, the process is hard work for a learner. (One student said that struggling to construct new knowledge, especially by trying to "say" it, made her feel as if her "brain was sweating" with exertion.) Yet, when the process works well, students clearly feel that they have "authored" their knowledge and therefore "own" it; they have the "authority" that comes from the effort. Instead of painting by numbers, they feel as if they were making "real" painting.

My interventions as teacher were largely to cause and to support this process of learning. Thus, I tried to explain it, to "coach" students in it, to step in for offering possible next questions, to ask them which of their experiences fit with these ideas or not, and so on. Occasionally, I contributed information directly—apart from my selection of texts and articles—but only very selectively. I tended to focus only on the few keys points that I had established for the course and to look sensitively for opportune "openings" in which to introduce them, either to individual learners or to the whole class. Indeed, one of my major roles in this process was generally *not* to provide students with my own "right" answers. To do so would have severely short-circuited the constructive process I had tried so carefully to foster. This stance of mine often caused frustration for an individual learner, but I held firm and returned to individual support of that student's learning process and efforts. I often reflected back to students—like a mirror—what I thought I saw them doing, where I thought they were at, especially what I thought they were not seeing themselves. I was careful to provide only my assessment of their learning, not to say that they were right or wrong, nor to suggest what they should do with it. The next step was up to them. Another major intervention I made was to try to cause the bicycle riding metaphor for learning that I mentioned above. If students were truly lost and "off balance," I tried to support them in finding balance again. Still, I found it far more typical that students tended to keep their safe, predictable balance—even in the face of new information—so I often tried to upset (as gently, but firmly as possible) their comfortable balance, either with new information and questions or with an unusual learning activity (such as, reading esoteric material, writing poetry to music, or seeing a film). Losing their comfortable grounding was usually scary for students, but only when that happens can major learning and change occur. My metaphor for myself as teacher is *midwife*. I can help students in the process of giving birth to their own learning, but ultimately I cannot do it for them.

A few brief words on *evaluation*. I proposed to the class that evaluation be *holistic* and *shared* equally. This meant that *all* their work (journals, class discussions, readings, individual conferences, and so on) became the basis for evaluating their learning because I wanted them to feel free to put their efforts into the means of learning that they felt would be effective for them. It also meant that we shared equal responsibility for evaluating their learning, including the final grade. This sharing of evaluation was simply a logical extension of my (teacher-pupil) sharing with them (pupil-teachers) the responsibility for questions posed, answers tried, materials and experiences used, and the like. It was also a necessary step, I believe, to help them feel safer in creating their own path.

A typical evening's class would start with my returning the previous week's journal entries to the class and mirroring back to them as a group what I saw as key questions they were tackling, topics they were not yet engaging, conclusions they were tentatively coming to, contradictions they were entertaining, and so on. I often did some "coaching" of their journal work, sometimes using examples of particular students' entries (with permission) to illustrate the many ways in which journaling could work. I would then summarize where we were in working our way through the four major principles of the course. At key transition points into a new principle, I would provide a brief explanation of the principle and its relation to our past work. In lieu of explanation, however, I often asked them to go through an experience embodying this major principle and to reflect on what it was like. For example, in the story section of the course I asked the class to read a short story together and compare their wide range of responses to it. On another occasion within this topic, we tried creating poetry and discussed what that was like. And so on. I always asked them to spend a good bit of the class time in small groups discussing the previous week's readings and their week's classroom experience (and sometimes beyond)—particularly trying to discover what conclusions they reached from the reading, what new questions it prompted for them, and what new light it shed for them on their teaching. Each small group would then report back to the whole class, who could respond to them; and I would try to reflect back to them where the whole group seemed to be in their inquiry. In the sociocultural framework part of the course, smaller groups who had read different material on different topics (gender, culture, or class) reported on those readings to the rest of the class and led a class discussion on those topics. Each class session would finish with my distributing several shorter readings that seemed appropriate for the coming week and with my suggesting a key question or two for them to consider as they moved ahead into the next stage of their learning. (My conferences with individual students—at either my initiative or theirs—were usually a microcosm of my key strategies used in class but tailored to what I knew more specifically about the individual.)

You have just seen this course from "behind the teacher's head" (to use Britton's famous phrase). Yet that is only one version of the story that occurred on Wednesday evenings in room 433 and in our homes, communities, and classrooms throughout the rest of the week. Since "ownership" has traditionally referred to *students'* learning, this chapter would violate notions of ownership if the course were not also presented "from behind the learner's head." Thus far, you've heard only the teaching half of the story; therefore, several representative members of that class will tell their stories of how they experienced the course, particularly around the issue of the *ownership* of the learning.

The Other Side of the Coin: Students' Learning Experiences

The graduate course we took was both interesting and confusing. For me, it was a brand new experience; my first graduate course at McGill (gasp!) all the way across the country in a strange culture and a strange city. I suppose I also had expectations of what it meant to be a graduate student: a lot of reading, hard work, studying, knowing a lot. Part of this came from my undergraduate degree in science, where excellence in your studies meant to ventriloquize on demand with a high degree of fidelity. So this was some of the baggage I brought to the course.

At first, I did not know what to read of David. He was a wonderful, sharing, open individual who was encouraging us to do something, leading us down a path somewhere; but for the longest time I couldn't make out where he was leading us or why. And when was the course going to really begin after this introductory fluffy stuff? When was he going to start pouring into us the things that were really important to know?

By week 4 I began to sense that something strange was up. Other students in the course—and I, too, I must admit—were becoming a little frustrated. This was unlike anything we'd ever encountered as students. The teacher was not telling us what was right, what things were important to know, what we had to memorize. Over coffee we shared our frustrations, our sense of when things were going to get up to speed. None of us had any question about the competency of the instructor or believed that he was slacking off and not coming to class prepared.

My impression of the course changed in this fourth week when I got my journal back and listened to what David had to say about the journals. He said that beginning soon he was going to withdraw/step back from the journals and begin merely to encourage us and motivate us to pursue the things that we were interested in. What was it that made me click? I'm not sure. But my training as a student made me the kind of student that *had* to find order in a class. I had to find the big picture in a course or the whole thing did not make sense. So I just began, in this fourth week, to pull together disparate pieces of talk, comments in the journal, and comments from other students to come to the conclusion that we were not in the introductory stages of the course. This was the way it would always be. What meant the most was what you did as a student, how you followed your ideas and beliefs and thoughts under the guidance of David. He was not spying through the journals; it was his window in to see in what direction to encourage you, to witness your thoughts. He asked for handwriting, not because it was more work than a computer but because the act of writing by hand was different; he saw us get emotional as our writing got messy. Who knows what he saw? But I knew what the other students were experiencing—angst, tension, unease. I was going to try to avoid those emotions by simply settling in and taking a run with this course as best as I could.

In the end my learning and thinking really blossomed as a result of these experiences in the course. When David brought in ice skates and Leonard Cohen music and asked us to write poetry and word songs to describe them, I went with it and followed my mind. In my journal it was my thoughts and ideas, although I knew he would read them. I began to see that although I could not ventriloquize as well as my undergrad cohorts, I did have a brain that worked very well; and that brain was the tool that would guide me through this life.

I am not sure why this course worked so well for me. At that time I was in a very comfortable relationship; I was very happy and stable in my life and very willing to learn. I was not forced into studies and I was not teaching, so I had my full day to think and ponder ideas. My partner was also a student and we encouraged one another to follow ideas and to enjoy school. We supported one another as students and people, since both of us had left our families to come here to study, and we had few friends here in this strange place. I also think I was quite mature as a student when I arrived, and flexible to new ideas. I knew I was young (and still think that at twenty-nine) and know that there is a lot more to learn in this world before I leave it. Sometimes the shape of the learning is strange, though. It's like the Greyhound; getting there is half the fun.

My experiences led me to a few powerful realizations. First, your thoughts are all-important, and they are what you do with yourself. No one can really dictate what you do with your mind, although university profs like to think they can. There are several roads that this leads down, and I'm sure for the rest of my life I will be following them. When do you opt out of activities because they are not right for you, because they are not what you want to do with yourself? How do you balance your need for good marks with the prof's attitude that you must memorize and spit back? If learning is what you make from a situation, the questions you ask and the meanings you construct, then what have I been doing in university for the last five years? These are some of the ideas that I continue to think about.

Second, I came to the realization that language was not only a tool to reflect your thoughts but also a tool to *construct* your thoughts. Again, this idea has set me off on a lifelong quest; how then do I teach science? If all that really matters for individuals is the knowledge you build for yourself through the tool of language, then how should I go about teaching in courses with a mandated curriculum and standardized exams? Well, I may never answer this one, but at least now this course gave me some ideas of why I was always in opposition to the transmission approach to teaching. The course opened a new road for me.

In the end I think it was the journal that meant the most. Many classmates, I think, came to loathe "journaling," but I never really tagged it like that with a label. Instead, the journal was a place of opportunity and building thought, not just recording it. To this day I keep a journal of my experiences and ideas that I share with no one. I have a very private stream of thoughts that I share with no one, mostly because I feel unsafe that most of my friends will not understand. But at least now I have a place in my mind where my thoughts are my own, and I like it.

Ron Sherman

It's strange and rather intriguing to write about a learning experience one had more than two years ago. On the one hand, it's a bit frustrating because it's hard to remember in great detail; on the other hand, the time gone by and subsequent experiences make the reflections deeper and richer.

Perhaps I feel that way because the main insight I remember from Language and Learning Across the Curriculum in 1991 was one that was *not* pleasant for me to face. However, having faced it, and having tried to change as a result, I feel better and, very importantly, more confident about my teaching. So, reflecting now on what I learned about "ownership" in the course is an easier and more satisfying task than it might have been two years ago, when the course ended.

We responded to the course and the readings (which were excellent) in a journal that we would hand in every week and receive back the next week with David's comments. True to form, I was several weeks late in beginning this journal; "getting started" is the big problem for me in writing of any kind. David expressed concern, and I hurriedly began the journal, not having fully understood what was required. A midterm interview in his office helped get me on track, but I never found writing this journal to be an easy experience. This was due less to the nature of the task than to the nature of the problems I was facing in my teaching.

I was teaching a course I thought I was familiar with: a grade 10 literature course. I was not, however, teaching it to the high school students I had taught for many years; instead, I was teaching a group of adult education students who were going to night school to finish their high school education. While the course may have been familiar to me, the students were not. I found myself very dismayed by their lack of background in reading and by what I perceived as a lack of insight into the literature we were reading.

I was very preoccupied with this group of students and thought about them a great deal. How could I help them understand and enjoy the literature we were reading? How could I help them gain insight? What kind of teaching would benefit them most? I struggled to find texts they would enjoy and to prepare lessons that would work well. My preoccupation bordered on obsession sometimes, and my journal for David was filled with my observations and worries.

For example, early in the course we had read Morley Callaghan's "The Snob," a story about a college student who pretends not to see his kindly, unpretentious, but badly dressed father in a crowded book department because he doesn't want his upper-class girlfriend to have a bad impression of him. I wrote of being dismayed when students expressed the view that the girlfriend, or the father, was the snob in the story, when it was crystal clear to me that the title referred to the socially climbing student. I lamented their inability to "see" "what the author was doing". . .

David's comments on this seemed blunt and incisive, especially given his unfailingly charming, polite, and kind classroom persona. He pointed out that I seemed to have a "right-answer approach" to teaching literature (something I had vigorously denied elsewhere in the journal), and ought to be aware of it. I think he wrote something like "It's okay to have this approach, but you should at least realize this is what you're doing."

Well, it was an unpleasant shock to read this, especially since I did *not* think this "right answer" approach was all right at all. In terms of my self-professed philosophy of teaching and of my self-image as a teacher, this was harsh criticism. I remember feeling startled and upset.

I was also, however, strangely and sheepishly grateful. David's words confirmed something I had suspected about myself for some time, but had never had either the time or, perhaps, the courage to confront. While I thought of myself as "open" to everyone's ideas, I realized that this was more a theoretical position than anything else. In practice, ideas that fit into my view of a work of literature made sense and showed "insight"; ideas that seemed farfetched to me made me very uncomfortable, even if I tried not to show this. Which is not to say that my views were narrow—I don't think they were—but rather that, when push came to shove, I was the ultimate "authority" in my classroom.

This was a major, if painful, insight into my teaching. Of course, David's comments in my journal were not the only catalyst for it. Although I don't remember the word *ownership* being used, other ideas that came up in the readings and in class discussions contributed as well. What dawned on me was that, like many people I criticized, I was confusing teaching and learning. My brilliant insights into literature were of absolutely no use to my adult education students. They needed to become confident and independent readers and learners, not people who could see what I could. If I were only comfortable with responses that my own understanding could accommodate, that was my problem, and one I had to overcome. Otherwise, I had ownership not only of the text but also of their learning— ownership that rightfully belonged to them, not to me.

It was a chastening experience, having to face all this about myself. I set about trying to change my ways, trying to make my practice as a teacher reflect my theoretical positions.

I remember writing in my journal about one of these attempts. The students were supposed to read a short story at home, and I deliberately prevented myself from reading it before going to class. The rationale was that if I wasn't very familiar with it, everyone else's ideas would seem perfectly fine. (Looking back, this strategy seems rather silly, but in an odd way it worked. For someone who finds it hard to restrain herself from expressing her opinion, not having an opinion in the first place is an effective constraint!)

I later progressed to the point where I could hold my tongue about texts I knew inside and out; I learned to listen more and speak less, to "teach" much less and to let the students learn from their own responses and from one another. I learned to allow them the freedom I had supposed (wrongly) I had been allowing them: to respond to literature out of their own experience, knowledge, ideas, feelings. I think I have become a better teacher. I know I feel much more comfortable with letting the students be the authorities about what they're reading. Sometimes I think I learn more from them than they do from me.

Of course, there are times I want to say too much and moments when I still feel dismayed by what I perceive to be a student's "glibness" or "lack of attention" to a text; I don't want to give the impression that I have undergone a transformation to saintliness. Far from it. I certainly haven't solved all the problems, nor do I expect to. But my awareness of how essential it is for students to own their own learning helps me to cope with many of the difficulties and frustrations that go with teaching.

Nancy Kahan

Early December '90: Reviewed the course outline and reading list for Language and Learning Across the Curriculum and was at the library the next day, looking up and borrowing the books available. I had been looking forward to taking this course (emphasis on *had been*) until I brought the books home and started to read. No problem with Britton and Barnes—this is the "type" of reading I had expected: the serious, straightforward material one proposes to graduate students. . .

Castaneda, however, was another matter. As I turned the pages of *The Teachings of Don Juan*, chilly little doubts began to creep into the comfortable smugness of the heretofore successful Ph.D. candidate: successful in the sense that previously taken courses had been of the traditional transmission model where the teacher teaches, and the students listen and then give it all back in the final paper. Conclusions could be easily drawn from the assigned reading material by any reasonably literate, intelligent student, and success in writing it all up and handing it all back often led to the sense of comfort and smugness mentioned earlier. The *source* of these chilly little doubts was my inability to draw those conclusions: what the devil did Carlos's peyote problems have to do with Language and Learning Across the Curriculum?

Early January '91: The first class did *not* help matters: If I had thought Carlos was going to be a problem, I knew David was going to be an ever bigger one. Woodstock revisited: what next? peace symbols? love beads? Santana? dialogue journals??? Quoting Flaubert, he invited us to "unravel," to "struggle," to "push back the fog," to "live" the course material and to "question." Well, I had certainly begun to question: I was spending seven hundred dollars in bus fare for this?

My first reaction was mutinous: I had no intention of playing his game. My first journal entries were concise, almost terse. No unnecessary words and plenty of quotations and page numbers to show that I was doing the reading (funny expression "doing the reading"; doesn't sound as if it's the same activity as reading). Typed it, obviously. I was going to show him that graduate courses were meant to be taken seriously. David, however, continued to play by his own rules. His scrawled responses to our learning journals parroted a Dale Carnegie motivation session: "Good work!," "Tell me more," "Thank you very much," "Thank you for sharing this" . . . *(Say thank you one more time and I'll scream!!!)* "This guy can't be real," I'd mutter to myself. "What does he want from us?"

At this point I started getting suspicious; I was convinced he had a "hidden agenda" despite all his lofty talk of the importance of each student's achieving personal learning goals. Not only suspicious, but worried also because *(Don't say this too loudly—someone might hear)*—I wasn't catching on! Lost, as they say; the last one to get the joke. *(Who said school should be a safe bower to explore life?)* Second reaction: grab the handiest defense mechanism around: scorn *(because we think it hides our insecurity? Or gives us a chance to save face while we're searching for the answers?)*

Because I *was* searching. Honestly! I was just having a bit of trouble admitting to myself (and to David, and to all the others) that it was taking longer than expected. So, I tried it his way. Tried unraveling, as he called it. A little at a time, bit by bit. Told myself that I could probably trust him since insincere replies to journal entries would be unethical, and he didn't seem to be the unethical type. And that maybe—just possibly—languaging could lead to learning. . . .

Consequently, the first step towards creating the necessary conditions for learning to take place was becoming aware of my attitude towards David's unconventional approach to teaching, and then adopting an open-mind policy. Secondly, I had to play fair: read the articles attentively, participate in the discussions wholeheartedly, and complete the class activities honestly. Last of all, I had to accept to swallow some pride; in other words, the only person to impress in the course had to be myself.

"Unravel . . ."

I found the request to "unravel" very frustrating at first. I often felt as if I'd said everything that was necessary. It took three or four weeks to realize how much was being unsaid. This was perhaps the first milestone. I began to write more, more out of curiosity to see where the writing would take me. I often got the impression that I was going on a trip without a map (something I never do). At times the written words would take me to places I had already been—this was almost too easy, though, and I often realized it. But at other times my writing would take me somewhere new; that was both enjoyable and confusing, depending on what I'd "seen." And other paths simply led to a dead end—and then I had to write to find the way around it.

I found using the metaphor "unravel" (to help us explore new ideas and to compare them to old ones) to be accurate. Like a big ball of yarn, our ideas are strung along a thread, each one attached somehow to the other; however, we can only appreciate the patterns and the texture of each idea as the skein unwinds. Writing in the journals provided us with the opportunity to stretch this "yarn," to examine the multiple fibers that give it its strength, to discover its source, and to get a glimpse of its destination. I think I learned the most from hitting snags in the yarn: writing forced me to pick patiently at the knot until I succeeded in smoothing it out. An unexpected sense of satisfaction came from handling these snags because, as with any unraveled knot, you end up with more rather than less.

Also unexpected was the sense of excitement: too stimulated to even doze off, I would spend the weekly three-hour bus ride home mulling over the evening's activities. While most of the passengers slept, I'd stare out the window, jotting down ideas on scraps of paper from time to time so I could use them for the next journal entry. Why exciting? Because of the power involved, the power to control your own learning. Because of the realization that this power is accessible. Why unexpected? Simply because "school" has usually opted for the shortcuts in order to provide the fastest, least complicated means to an end—a diploma, a job? Unexpected also because after so many years in the system, I was convinced that there wasn't much hope for change.

"Which brings us to . . ."

Change. My four-month experience in the Language and Learning Across the Curriculum course has shaken that conviction. I've decided that there is hope after all. As a teacher I've already modified my approach as a result of that course. One breakthrough came in front of twenty students, when I interrupted an explanation in midsentence because of the realization that the students would grasp the ideas much, much better if they were given the chance to "language" it during a small-group activity. The result was more than satisfactory—it was exhilarating. I was delighted with the depth of their understanding and its relation to their own experience. And although I'd like to say I'm not the same learner, parent, or person as a result of the course, I have to be honest and say that I'm still working on change in those areas; there are a lot of deeply embedded traditions in me yet. But I believe awareness is often the first step.

Quick summary: I learned. Even learned things that I knew. Knew that the attitude kids come to class with affects their potential for learning, but had to learn for myself how far-reaching the consequences could be. Learned that language is used for a lot more than communicating, and that it was about time that this second-language prof learned it. Learned that learning has a frightening, messy side to it, and that it takes courage to accept the changes that might come about as a result. Probably learned all sorts of other things that I'm not even aware of yet. Will keep in touch . . .

Joyce Angio

David Dillon's course was one that students seemed either to dread or to love. The course was in the second term of my first year as a full-time master's degree student in the area of reading and writing education. Previously, I had taught in Toronto for three years before deciding to return to McGill to continue with my studies in the hopes of becoming a better teacher and more of an "expert" in my field. I was immersed in courses that I loved and that I was able to apply to all the different students I had had, from new Canadians to elementary students. One of the requirements of the master's program is a thesis, and I had decided to examine teachers' responses to students' journals for my thesis. I had always used journals of various types with all my students and found that responding was not as easy as I thought it might be. I was curious to know how other teachers responded to journals, what they responded to, and, more importantly perhaps, what they didn't respond to. Thus, the journal that we were required to keep in David's class was the real meat and potatoes of the course for me.

When David asked me to write up my thoughts on the course for this chapter, I went to my "Master's Box" and pulled out my journal that is the size of an old Eaton's catalogue. Everything started to come back to me as I began to reread my entries and David's responses. I closed my eyes and refocused on the classroom, zooming in on the first ten minutes when we would hungrily await as our journals were returned, the room becoming increasingly silent as we searched for and read the responses to our entries. It used to worry me as a teacher that the relationship I would establish with my students in their journals was totally different from the relationship that I had with them in the entire classroom setting. I wondered if this ever bothered David, whether or not he was concerned that for thirteen weeks we would write to him about everything that we were learning and that at the end of the thirteen weeks there would be no more responses. Halfway into the term he said that he would read my journal but not respond to any more of my questions, that it was up to me to begin answering them for myself. More writing, more struggling, more waiting for that magical "I got it!" . . . he was encouraging me to take responsibility for my own learning, to become the owner of my own ideas as I struggled to answer questions.

One of the most magical things that happened was that we were encouraged to write stories as a way of trying to understand things that might have been confusing for us. When David asked me to read my story in front of the whole class, I had a feeling of pride that I hadn't felt since I was in elementary school. I tingled and felt nervous and scared; I wasn't used to reading my composed thoughts out loud in front of anybody. I began writing story after story; my journal appeared entirely without focus, resembling perhaps a lab book full of experiments and inconclusive results. I began to realize the power of writing, how in fact it was a confirmation of thinking, and what a wonderful tool a journal could be.

The journal, however, was not without its problems. To begin with, it was the only major piece of writing that we were responsible for in the course. Our final grade was mutually decided on, based on our participation in class discussions and on our journal, in which we responded to articles, books, and class discussions. We never shared our journals, and a few weeks into the class, gossiping began about what went on in different journals and why students were getting so upset, some on the verge of tears during the class break. At times I felt that the more I "divulged," the better mark I would receive. As an educator I found it problematic that a grade could be assigned to me based on how much I wanted to explore in a personal narrative that took the form of a journal. I wondered if the ultimate form of "ownership" would not have been to challenge us to shape our ideas and learning into a public piece of writing.

Two weeks before the end of the course I walked into David's office and handed him my last journal. I told him that I felt that I had written enough and that this entry contained a final story and a summary of what I thought I had learned in the course. In retrospect I can't believe that I, a student, was informing my teacher that I had done enough and, as far as I was concerned, he could take it or leave it. David allowed me to make that decision. I knew that a great deal of what I had learned in the course wouldn't begin to make real sense for me until I was away from it. Two years later, I have finished my master's degree, and I know that Language and Learning Across the Curriculum has influenced the way I teach and the way I study. I ultimately focused my thesis on students' writing, which is what I realized really interested me. Journals still fascinate me; I keep three of my own: a dream journal, a daily journal, and a teaching journal. Best of all, I feel no need to have any response from anyone else. I am interested only in answering my own questions.

Anna Rumin

I am Orpheus. I seek the part of me that is underground. And although I am he, I am at the same time lured by the music that is his.

This is one of the metaphors that came to mind when I was asked if I would write about my experience in the course Language and Learning Across the Curriculum. This was a course of metaphors! Nothing was what it seemed. You could become as deeply involved as you chose. A second thought occurred to me: I knew there would be a test in this course! The master teacher would not want me to leave McGill without evaluating the course. Yet the choice to do so would be mine and, once the choice was made, I would be responsible for the decision. A third thought was, "Why did I agree to this exercise?" Although two years have lapsed, it is difficult to say how public I can be about my involvement or my vulnerability. I see myself as an intuitive person who looks for meaning in all things. I believe that things happen for a reason although we may not know why just at the moment. Let me try to explain.

In January 1991 I registered for and attended a compulsory course in the Master of Education program at McGill University. I came unsuspecting that

I would be invited to take a spiritual inner journey by way of reflection and expressive free writing. We were asked to struggle: to risk, should we find ourselves in the fog, taking that extra step. Usually, if you are inclined to participate in encounter groups you choose such a course, but this one was required. Whether it was trust or just being naïve, I decided to risk the journey. In retrospect, the presession suggested reading, *The Teachings of Don Juan,* should have given me a clue to what was in store. A week into the course, there was "The Ancient Coffer of Nuri Bey," a short tale of twenty-eight lines. Everyone who has ever read this story knows what is in the coffer . . . each person places there an object, a secret, a treasure according to his own experience. We all bring our own meaning to a story. I chose to keep the keys to the chest. Or so I thought. My choice, my responsibility.

That a reflective journal would be the major source of evaluation was fine with me. The stress of writing exams and making a presentation vanished. I never enjoyed public speaking and gave very little value to my own knowledge. Why would anyone be interested in what I had to say? I preferred to learn by listening. Professor Dillon, as I was still addressing him at the time, praised my first two journal entries, but after the third one I felt that I had been too personal, so I drew back. Much to my alarm he wrote that "I was flitting too quickly from topic to topic." I was so angry that anyone would dare to tell a woman my age that she was "flitting" that I could scarcely contain myself. He was the authority so I suppressed my anger and, being the good female student, set myself to comply to what I felt were his demands. This time I wrote about some of my grief and instead of the expected sympathy he wrote back that I was responsible. Even the most voiceless of us will speak when pushed. I went to see him, but face-to-face he was still the authority. I remember as I struggled to control my tears of anger in his office he said, "Let me be David" as he handed me a tissue.

During the conversation, I said that I had always been a counsellor. "You don't have to answer this," he said, "but have you ever been the one counselled?" I was unable to give voice to my anger. Yet I realized that this was part of the exercise to stimulate and provoke and encourage. I remember that we were asked to watched "The Kiss of the Spider Woman" during the March break. How did this film tie into the course? I reflected long and deeply. When we returned to class I spoke perhaps for the first time. I asked if we embraced the theory would we receive redemption.

Class time was fun. Stories and music, sharing, camaraderie and yet . . . I always dreaded coming. Always that terrible ambivalence. The days between classes were filled with uneasiness that I had said too much or the wrong thing in my journal. The professor's responses to my journals fed my need to be more reflective. I became totally introspective. My family said it was an obsession. Still I continued to struggle and explore towards a greater self-awareness. Struggling seems to bring out the survival instinct. I wrote reams in my journal. I wondered if the professor was reading my writing. I would hide a question in the most obscure place. I risked his wrath. I vented my anger against authority, patriarchal society, and the men in my life, yet I was never judged except, of course, for the one time I was accused of "flitting."

I am a psychiatric nurse by profession and at the time was employed as a school counsellor. I believe in reflection and talking it out. Writing it out was even better for me. One of my greatest discoveries was that I found out what I really thought through freewriting. One of my best experiences was writing a short story. I always felt I wasn't really a writer. We were asked to write a story if possible. No pressure, just if we could. But again, old habits are difficult to break and, being the good female student I am or try to be, I complied. But how I struggled with myself to find an idea. David had introduced me to Ira Progoff's book *At a Journal Workshop*. I tried Progoff's meditation techniques. I went into my darkened bedroom and lay down on the bed. I put all thoughts out of my mind. I tried just to feel and let whatever would come up, come up. Colours emerged. Golds and greens transforming into fields and straw stacks not unlike paintings by Van Gogh and Cézanne. I saw children running and playing, heard laughter. Springing from my bed and taking paper and pencil I wrote for thirty minutes . . . a short story materialised. Later the professor asked me what it meant to me personally . . . As I examined the motifs and explored them according to what they meant to me, according to my narrative, it is a wonder that story stayed locked away for so long. David, I was calling him by his first name now, allowed, even encouraged, the direction I chose. My writing was my own story. My journey was an inner one, deep and painful. Two years have passed and tonight when I re-read my journal, I wept. It is my lived-through-experience. I wrote about my personal myth, and what I knew to be true was reinforced by the book *Women's Ways of Knowing*. I came to value my personal way of knowing and of learning. I began to read *Man and His Symbols* and my life changed in a spiritual way. People who know me say I have changed. I know it better than anyone. Oh, I am still angry, as women we have a right to be, but I understand my anger better. As I come into my own, I remember the philosophy of Freire and am conscious that the oppressed once liberated can become the oppressor.

It was "as if" I came to this course by design. Today as I prepare to write my thesis I am writing about teachers' exploration of self. The assumption is that the more self-aware one is the better teacher one is. Being in touch with oneself allows for a connectedness with students on a deeper level. The realization of self is a lifelong process and not something that is realized in one university course. Yet the more I write the more I realise my work is based on the principles I gleaned from the course Language and Learning Across the Curriculum.

My reservations about a course such as David directed are that there is no safety net. Of course, there are no guarantees in life and we have all experienced grief and pain. It is better to have talked about it than to have kept it inside. Struggle is part of growth but when we ask someone to take an inner journey, there is a risk of remembering something long repressed, there is a danger of depression. A good deal of support may be required and the termination of a course does not guarantee that the individual can cut off her emotional outpouring and tie up the ends like a term paper due the last day of class. Ideally she will be able to continue a process set in motion. Yet, as in therapy there is the transference which needs to be resolved. Each participant, professor and student, will see the other differently, each bringing her own baggage to the experience. What they expect of each other will not necessarily be realistic. Even for the most reflective and intuitive, these reactions can be difficult to comprehend and work out. In the hands of the unskilled, an encounter like this is very dangerous. Those who would deny this have no personal knowledge of this happening. People have developed defenses so that they can cope. Breaking down those defenses, plus removing the support and disappearing after thirteen weeks, can leave poor Eurydice slipping back underground or, even worse, leave her exposed in the wind turning on her pivotal story.

Linda Anderson

Reflections

Thus far, I have presented a brief overview of the academic, theoretical roots of the notion of ownership of learning. You have heard my largely methodological story of the course, based on my understandings of cognitive learning; and you have heard the students' various stories of the course, full of emotional ups and downs, exciting breakthroughs, and lingering concerns. Within their stories are many predictable and familiar elements; for example, individual learners make sense of new information on the basis of their own personal knowledge and experience. Their stories, moreover, contain many less familiar and less discussed aspects of "ownership of learning." It is these less understood aspects that the students and I discussed and that we will focus on now to probe more deeply into the experience of *ownership* of learning in a teacher education course.

First, we wish to comment on the importance for all of us in reflecting on an experience we had together two years prior to this writing. Rather than being a problem, the long lapse in time served rather as a distinct advantage in several ways. What seemed to be left in our memories were only the key, essential aspects of the experience, while unimportant details had faded. Our experience had become distilled, brought into sharp relief over time—and thus clearer and more powerful. Yet, time had also allowed us to place the intense experience of the course, particularly its emotional side, into perspective, to view it with "cooler" eyes from a temporal distance. Finally, the two-year time period served as a true test of the degree of permanent change in any of us as a result of our experience together in the course, what it was like to continue "owning" our learning independently after the official end of the course.

There were several key stages in the course for most of us. First was a pleasant but brief "grace period" or honeymoon as we were all intrigued by new ideas and possibilities for the course. Second was a gradually more disconcerting and frustrating period as the course stubbornly refused to unfold according to the usual expectations. Third was a key point of breakthrough, which occurred in different ways and at different times for different students, often in painful ways. Finally, following the breakthrough, was a period of productive and constructive work, often exciting and unexpected, and frequently having major implications well beyond the end of the course.

What the students seemed surprised by, and unprepared for, was the difficult, emotional side of dealing with being "thrown off balance" in their learning in major ways. The greatest dissonance for them to deal with was not the new ideas safely nestled intellectually in the content of the course, but the different role and expectations that they had to actually *live* in the course. They were stripped of the smug predictability—and thus control and competence—that had marked the rest of their university work. As they brought their "old" frame of reference to bear on this experience, they could only conclude at first that something must be "wrong," since the course was not operating as it "should"—and they felt lost. Clearly, either I was doing something wrong or they were doing something wrong. The various degrees of frustration and even anger generated by this situation were important aspects of this learning situation, but ones the literature on ownership of learning has rarely dealt with in any way.

If the course was ever going to work for them, students had to break through this blocked situation. While the prompt, the timing, the reasons were different for each one, each breakthrough seemed to be characterized by a letting go of resistance, of some degree of acceptance of the situation (even if grudging), an overcoming of enough fear to surrender to an unfamiliar (or at least unrecognized) process. While students may have had many reasons to break through apart from me ("It's a required course," "I'm determined not to fail at this"), I was apparently a key in helping many of them break through this paralysis. That is, they had to trust me enough—as a professional who seemed to know what he was doing, yes, but also as a person who was honest and sincere in what he was doing and who respected them enough and cared for them enough not to knowingly harm them. I do not understand how students read some degree of those qualities in me, but the fact that they did seems vital to the process. I can have the orthodox methodology—the approved techniques of teaching for ownership of learning—down cold, but that alone would not ensure this breakthrough. It comes down finally to who they decide I am and whether or not they will trust me. Once again, the topic of the teacher's personality and the personal rapport between teacher and students is a widely acknowledged, but largely unstudied, aspect of this approach to teaching and learning.

Once students confronted—and let go of—their resistance, then they began taking major steps, usually in surprising, pleasant, and often exciting ways. Many experienced great satisfaction and became somewhat obsessed with their learning. Some may have even begun to realize what a thin line separates fear and excitement in our learning and living. This whole process seems remarkably like the key stages experienced by so many people in dying—at first anger and denial, followed by resistance, and finally acceptance and an incredible peace and enhanced state of satisfaction. Whether or not this analogy is the appropriate one, we need related theories and research to help us understand and explore further the emotional side of this kind of teaching and learning.

As the individual students were going through this common process in different ways, I was emotionally living this process or story in my own role of teacher. As their frustration and anger grew, I tried to use certain teaching strategies to help nudge them to their breakthrough. For example, I went back over some of my key explanations of the process I was asking them to go through, hoping that several more weeks of the course under their belts would render my explanation more sensible. I tried to link aspects of their personal experience with my explanations to help it all seem familiar and recognizable to them. I tried to break the process down into smaller steps and to coach them in those steps. And so on. But what I had to do most was to trust in myself and in them enough to hold to my course. It was scary, not so much for fear of complaints to the dean about my teaching (as happened once), but because of the responsibility I felt for helping to make this creative and transformative learning process of theirs work. My own fear tested my belief in them and myself.

A major aspect of this trust in myself was making tough, risky, intuitive choices about how to respond to the whole class as the course developed week by week, but especially how to respond to individual students in their journals or face-to-face in a conference. I often missed the mark, but in reflection two years later through these five students' recollections, I am still astounded at the difference one comment from me made for some of them, an impact I never could have judged or predicted at the time. What we do not see as clearly in this chapter is the debris of the literally thousands of comments of mine that had little and sometimes even negative impact. Or the few students in the course who never made the major breakthrough despite my best efforts (another chapter in itself). Once again, we desperately need to understand far more about a teacher's emotions, a teacher's choices, face-to-face with a range of individual human beings in all their diversity, complexity, and possibility.

How can we explain this complex process to ourselves? One possibility is to bring to bear upon it the lens of critical pedagogy, since critical pedagogy seems partly and vaguely implied by ownership of learning, but also because it seems to "fit" the students' stories. Critical pedagogy has apparently two basic elements: a new *awareness* within a learner (usually stemming from being "thrown off balance"), leading to a change or transformation in the learner's *behavior* (often characterized as freer, stronger, more self-actualizing behavior—thus the frequently used word *empowerment*). Paulo Freire (1972), one of the major developers of a critical approach to teaching, speaks of living within a critical pedagogy as "making Easter every day." By this, he means "dying" to our old self (as learner, as thinker, as personality) to be "reborn" anew in insight, understanding, action, over and over in a potentially endless cycle of change. Through this metaphor of Easter, Freire joins our separate metaphors above of dying and birth and perhaps helps us see more clearly the experiences of these five pupil-teachers in one course two years ago. His metaphor may help us to inquire more deeply into the experience of ownership of learning—learners' resistance to, and fear of, "death," the pain and joy of new "birth."

If we teacher-pupils are very brave, it may help us see our teaching role in this process, since "making Easter" must refer to the teacher as well. Even as I look back at my course of two years ago, I realize more clearly that I am now less methodological and more intuitive, focused more on the emotional aspects and less on the intellectual aspects of teaching and learning, and more aware of the need for my role and that of my students to be more mutually inclusive and shared. I need to place myself more boldly and more often in strange territory, where my usual rules do not explain everything, where I must confront my fear and resistance by letting go, in short by dying and being reborn as much as my students if I am to help them more effectively undergo that process of transformation.

Whatever metaphor we use to help us probe more deeply some of these less explored aspects of this kind of teaching and learning, we seem to be in need of a new framework that will take into better account this complex, messy, uncontrollable, and emotional business of teaching to foster students' ownership of their own learning. At least within the context of teacher education programs, we can no longer afford to be glib about this notion of teachers' ownership of their own learning. Yet, if our experience in this course is at all representative, it underlines the importance of teachers' experiencing with us what path we teacher educators hope they may explore as teachers of children in their own classrooms.

References

Barnes, D. 1976. *From communication to curriculum.* Middlesex, Englend: Penguin.

Britton, J. 1970. *Language and learning.* Middlesex, England: Penguin.

Freire, P. 1972. *Pedagogy of the oppressed.* New York: Seabury.

Credits (continued from copyright page)